THE FORGOTTEN SECTOR

To L.C. Jain and John Lewis,
pioneers for the rural non-farm sector in India

The Forgotten Sector

Non-farm employment and enterprises in rural India

THOMAS FISHER and VIJAY MAHAJAN
with ASHOK SINGHA

Practical ACTION PUBLISHING

INTERMEDIATE TECHNOLOGY PUBLICATIONS 1997

Practical Action Publishing Ltd
25 Albert Street, Rugby,
Warwickshire, CV21 2SD, UK
www.practicalactionpublishing.com

First published 1997\Digitised 2013

A catalogue record for this book is available from the British Library & Library of Congress

ISBN 978-1-85339-408-9 Paperback
ISBN 978-1-78044-223-5 Digital book

Citation: Fisher, T. (1997) *Forgotten Sector: Non-farm employment and enterprises in rural India*, Rugby, UK: Practical Action Publishing https://doi.org/10.3362/9781780442235

Since 1974, Practical Action Publishing has published and disseminated books and information in support of international development work throughout the world. All print editions are produced and distributed via ethical and sustainable print on demand global facilities.

Practical Action Publishing is a trading name of Practical Action Publishing Ltd (Company Reg. No. 01159018 | VAT 880 9924 76). All profits are covenanted back to its parent group, Practical Action (Charity Reg. No. 247257).

Contents

HIMACHAL
PRADESH
Amritsar
Shimla
Chandigarh
PUNJAB
Hardwar
HARYANA
Meerut
Delhi
Bikaner
Khurja
Agra
UTTAR
PRADESH
Jodhpur
Jaipur
Ajmer
Balotra
Lucknow
RAJASTHAN
Kanpur
Kutch
Ahmedabad
Bhopal
Morbi
Anand
MADHYA PRADESH
GUJARAT
Surat
Nagpur
MAHARASHTRA
Bombay
Nizamabad
Poona
Hyderabad
ANDHRA
PRADESH
Kurnool
GOA
KARNATAKA
Bangalore
Madras
ARABIAN SEA
Mysore
TAMIL
NADU
Kancheepuram
Pondicherry
KERALA
Tiruppur
Coimbatore
Trichy
Madurai
Cochin
Trivandrum
Sivakasi

Map of India

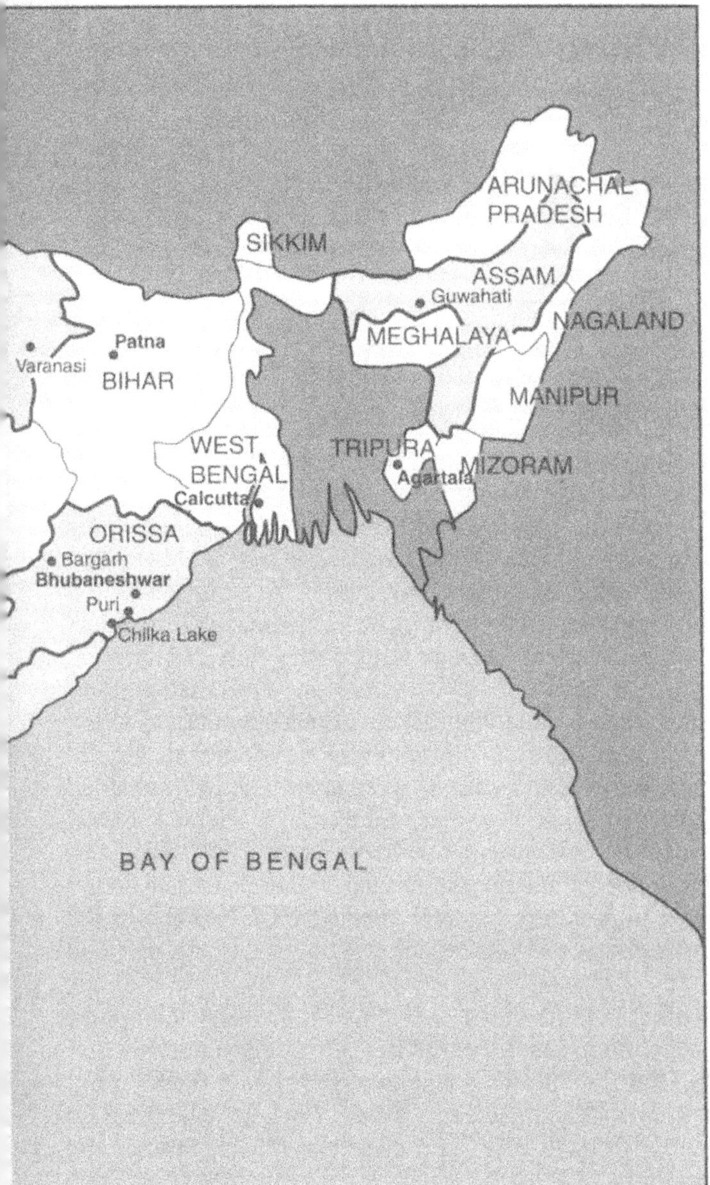
ARUNACHAL
PRADESH
SIKKIM
ASSAM
Guwahati
NAGALAND
MEGHALAYA
Patna
Varanasi
BIHAR
MANIPUR
WEST
BENGAL
TRIPURA
MIZORAM
Agartala
Calcutta
ORISSA
Bargarh
Bhubaneshwar
Puri
Chilka Lake
BAY OF BENGAL

Acknowledgements

This book has a long history going back some five years. While only three authors are named, the book draws on contributions from hundreds of individuals, including many who have assisted in very concrete ways with its contents.

We would like first to acknowledge some one thousand producers in rural India, both men and women, ranging from some of the poorest and most exploited workers to some of the country's largest and most successful entrepreneurs. They have provided us with many insights and, above all, inspiration.

The eleven reports on which this book has drawn extensively are the work of the Study Group on the Rural Non-Farm Sector (RNFS) in which we were involved as Associate Coordinator and National Coordinator respectively. Thus we gratefully acknowledge the significant contributions of the second Associate Coordinator, Savita Mahajan; of the State Coordinators Biswajit Sen (UP and Orissa); B.L. Parthasarathy (Tamil Nadu and AP); Sandeep Dikshit (Rajasthan and Gujarat); Rakesh Kaushik (Rajasthan and Punjab); and Rahul Bhimjiani (Assam), and of the Research Associates, Ashok Singha (Assam, Orissa and UP); Anup Kumar (Tamil Nadu and AP); B.V. Narasimhan (Tamil Nadu and Gujarat) and Dileep Gupta (Punjab). Dayanand Tandon also assisted with fieldwork in UP and Rajasthan, and Raja, Kuldeep Singh and Tashi Tsering were able Administrators and Accountants. Ashok proved invaluable to us, not only as a field researcher, but also as a tireless data processor, writer and supportive friend; he is thus named as the third author of this book. Biswajit provided many early conceptual inputs and frameworks, and his extensive knowledge of the leather sub-sector in UP forms the basis of our account of this sub-sector in Chapter 3.

The Study Group was supported by a distinguished advisory committee comprising Smt Elaben Bhatt, Dr M.V. Gadgil, Prof. Vijay Padaki, Shri S.M. Palia, Dr T.S. Papola, Dr R. Prakasam, Shri Harsh Sethi, Prof. Tushaar Shah, Shri Ram K. Vepa and Prof. Vinod Vyasulu. They assisted in many ways, thinking through ideas and concepts, reading drafts, and contributing to workshops. Research by Dr Papola and Prof. Vyasulu provided some of the initial inspiration for the study, and that by Prof. Shah has greatly strengthened our analysis of cooperatives in Chapter 7.

Prof. Shah was always willing to provide constructive critiques of the numerous drafts we sent him.

The study was jointly funded by the Swiss Agency for Development and Cooperation (SDC) and the National Bank for Agriculture and Rural Development (NABARD). Within SDC we would like to thank Laurent Guye, Christoph Koepfli, Regis Avanthay and Mona Dikshit. Christoph first suggested the idea of the study back in 1991 and provided enormous encouragement as the project developed and was implemented. He provided many conceptual inputs, including the diagrammatic representation of the RNFS given in Chapter 1. His successor, Regis, as well as Mona, continued to back the project, including its vital dissemination phase. Indeed, all at SDC were remarkably supportive and flexible as the study expanded, eventually requiring three separate contracts.

Within NABARD we would like to thank Chairman Shri P. Kotaiah and Managing Director Shri S.K. Kalia for their strong support, as well as Chief General Managers Shri M.C. Bhandari and Shri P.V.A. Ramarao; the NFS group at the Head Office, Bombay, especially Shri Y.C. Nanda, Shri S.S. Bharwani, Shri R. Balakrishnan, Shri G.K. Agarwal and Shri S.R. Aluru; the Deputy General Managers and Managers in charge of the NFS at the NABARD Regional Offices in Ahmedabad, Bhubaneswar, Chandigarh, Guwahati, Hyderabad, Jaipur, Lucknow and Madras, and Shri Suresh Kaushik of the Delhi Regional Office. We thank especially the NABARD District Development Managers we met during the course of fieldwork.

We are deeply grateful for the support of SDC and NABARD which made the study possible. All views expressed in this book are ours, however, and do not purport to represent the official viewpoint of NABARD or SDC in any way.

Many other individuals and organizations contributed to the study. Bharti Ramola at Price Waterhouse, New Delhi was a valuable friend and colleague throughout, and her work on rural credit has contributed significantly to Chapter 5. We also gratefully acknowledge the contributions of Shri A. Sathyamoorthy, former General Manager, NABARD; Shri Brij Mohan, Chief General Manager, SIDBI; and Prof. Malcolm Harper, consultant to SDC. Above all we thank the over 400 officials of regulatory, promotional and credit agencies whom we met in the course of the study, and who provided valuable insights and practical support during fieldwork.

In spite of all these inputs, this book would not have seen the light of day without Thomas Fisher's Visiting Fellowship at the Institute of Development Studies (IDS), Sussex University in the United Kingdom, which provided a good environment and excellent library facilities for expanding and deepening our analysis of the RNFS to make it worthy of a publishable book. We would like to thank Sir Hans Singer at IDS and Mark Holmstrom at the University of East Anglia for reading parts of the manuscript, and Robert Chambers at IDS for his advice. Jenny Skepper provided wonderful administrative support and all the librarians were ever friendly and helpful. The Ford Foundation, New Delhi provided the necessary finance, and we are especially grateful to Jane Rosser, Deputy Representative, for her patient backing as this book progressed. Neal Burton and Mohan Primlani at Intermediate Technology and Oxford & IBH respectively were supportive and friendly publishers.

We would like to thank Dr M.S. Swaminathan, and Shri P.B. Krishnaswamy of the National Foundation of India, for providing encouragement and good opportunities for the dissemination of the study results in India. We also thank, in the UK, Frances Stewart at Queen Elizabeth House, Oxford University, and Mark Holmstrom and, in the USA, Lynn Bennett and Colin Bruce at the World Bank, for arranging valuable seminars at which to present some interim material.

None of us would have survived these years of often intense work without the support of our family and friends, especially Savita to whom we are all deeply indebted. She not only provided enormous encouragement, in spite of bearing the brunt of our bad working habits, but even became deeply involved in the study herself. The study benefited enormously from Savita's suggestion to use Michael Porter's framework of competitive advantage to analyse various sub-sectors. Chirag humoured us as the youngest person to talk enthusiastically of the rural non-farm sector and 'Porter's diamond'; and Humphrey, Helga, Duncan, Clare, Alexander and, above all, Veronica provided essential and warm support in the UK.

Finally, we dedicate this book to two individuals who were not directly involved, but who pioneered the cause of rural non-farm employment in India, and have given us much inspiration. L.C. Jain, former Chair of the All-India Handicraft Board, Member of the Planning Commission, and winner of the Ramon Magsaysay Award, has worked tirelessly to bring policy attention to focus on the problems of the rural non-farm sector. John Lewis, former Director of USAID in India, Chair of the Development Assistance Committee of the OECD, and Dean of the Woodrow Wilson School of Public and International Affairs, Princeton University in the USA, has spanned three decades of scholarly and policy work on the Indian agricultural and rural non-farm economy.

TF, VM

Hyderabad, December 1996

Abbreviations

AP	Andhra Pradesh
ARTEP	Asian Regional Team for Employment Promotion, ILO, Delhi
ASSOCHAM	Associated Chambers of Commerce and Industry
BASIX	Bhartiya Samruddhi Investment and Consulting Services Pvt. Ltd
B.Ed.	Bachelor of Education
BKK	Badan Kredit Kecamatan (Sub-district banks in Indonesia)
BRI	Bank Rakyat Indonesia
CII	Confederation of Indian Industries
CODISSIA	Coimbatore District Small-Scale Industry Association
Cooptex	Tamil Nadu Handloom Weavers' Cooperative Society
CSIR	Council for Scientific and Industrial Research
CSO	Central Statistical Organization
DE	Directory Establishment
DIC	District Industries Centre
DME	Directory Manufacturing Establishment
DUBS	Durham University Business School
EPW	*Economic and Political Weekly* (Indian journal)
FICCI	Federation of Indian Chambers of Commerce and Industry
FPO	Food Products Order
GoI	Government of India
GRIMCO	Gujarat Rural Industries Marketing Corporation
GRUH	Gujarat Rural Housing Finance Corporation
GVA	gross value-added
HORTICO	Uttar Pradesh State Horticulture Produce Marketing and Processing Corporation Limited
IAS	Indian Administrative Service
ICAR	Indian Council for Agricultural Research
IDBI	Industrial Development Bank of India
ILO	International Labour Organisation (see also ARTEP above)
IRDP	Integrated Rural Development Programme
ISB	industry, service and business
ISI	Indian Standards Institute
ITC	(formerly, Indian Tobacco Company)
ITI	Industrial Training Institute

JRY	Jawahar Rozgar Yojana
kg	kilogram
KVIB	Khadi and Village Industries Board
KVIC	Khadi and Village Industries Commission
LAB	Local Area Bank
MIDS	Madras Institute of Development Studies
mm	millimetre
MPEDA	Marine Products Export Development Authority
NABARD	National Bank for Agriculture and Rural Development
NBFC	Non-Banking Financial Company
NCAER	National Council for Applied Economic Research
NDDB	National Dairy Development Board
NDE	Non-Directory Establishment
NFS	non-farm sector
NGO	non-governmental organization
NIC	National Industrial Classification (used by the Census and NSS)
NRDC	National Research Development Corporation
NSDP	Net State Domestic Product
NSS	National Sample Survey
NSSO	National Sample Survey Organisation
NVA	net value-added
OAE	Own Account Enterprise
ODA	Overseas Development Administration (British bilateral donor)
OECD	Organisation for Economic Co-operation and Development
OUP	Oxford University Press
PCB	Pollution Control Board
PCO	public call office
PRADAN	Professional Assistance for Development Action (an NGO)
RBI	Reserve Bank of India
R&D	research and development
RIP	Rural Industries Project
RMW	Rural Main Worker (Census classification)
RNFS	rural non-farm sector
RRB	Regional Rural Bank
Rs	(Indian) rupees
RUDSETI	Rural Development and Self-Employment Training Institute
SDC	Swiss Agency for Development and Cooperation (bilateral donor)
SEEUY	Self-Employment Programme for the Educated Unemployed Youth
SEPUP	Self-Employment Programme for the Urban Poor

SEWA	Self-Employed Women's Association (a trade union in Ahmedabad)
SFC	State Finance Corporation
SHG	self-help group
SIDBI	Small Industries Development Bank of India
SIDC	Small Industries Development Council (industry association in Kerala)
sq.m.	square metre
SSI	small-scale industry
TANSILK	Tamil Nadu Cooperative Silk Marketing Federation
TANSTIA	Tamil Nadu Small and Tiny Industries Association
TDC	Transport Development Council
TME	Technical Monitoring and Evaluation
TRYSEM	Training of Rural Youth for Self-Employment
UNIDO	United Nations Industrial Development Organisation
UP	Uttar Pradesh
UPICA	Uttar Pradesh Industrial Cooperative Association
URMUL	Uttari Rajasthan Milk Union Ltd
USAID	United States Agency for International Development
VAT	value-added tax
WIMCO	(formerly, Western India Match Company)

Glossary

Note: India is a union of states, each with its own government. The government of India is often referred to as the union (or central) government.

bagasse	residual fibre of crushed sugarcane
bidi	an indigenous cigarette rolled with tendu leaf
coir	a fibre made from coconut husks
crore	10 000 000
dhaba	road-side restaurant
dhoti	long cloth worn by men around their waist
ghani	small oil-extraction plant
gur	coarse sweetener made out of sugarcane juice
haat	weekly market in rural areas
Janta cloth	'people's cloth'; scheme of subsidized cloth for the poor
khadi	hand-spun, hand-woven cloth (see Chapter 1, footnote 5)
khandsari	form of unrefined sugar
lakh	100 000
mai-baap	literally, mother and father; patron
mandi	market place, usually for agricultural commodities
mela	a fair or large gathering
mesta	a fibre
octroi	tax charged by municipalities on goods entering their boundaries
panchayat	Village Council
caste panchayat	informal council of elders belonging to one caste
Rozgar Yojna	Employment Scheme
sabai	long fibre grass used to make rope
sari	woman's garment made of one long piece of cloth
Shilpabari	handicraft house-cum-workshop given to rural craftsperson
tendu	a small plant whose leaves are used to roll bidis
unit desa	sub-district levels of Bank Rakyat Indonesia
zamindar	large land owner who until the early 1950s collected land revenue from the peasantry
zilla parishad	District Council

Tables

Appendix 2

Figures

1 Introduction

Employment in India

India has a population of over 900 million people, which is growing at 2.1 per cent a year. Generating productive, sustainable employment for its growing population is thus one of its most urgent concerns. The Approach Document to the 8th Five-Year Plan highlighted the need for India to create *100 million new jobs* in the decade 1991–2000 to ensure full employment in the economy.[1] This is indeed a daunting task.

Where will so many new jobs come from? To achieve the full-employment target, overall employment in India must grow at 2.8 per cent a year. However, employment in agriculture, which accounted for almost two-thirds of total employment in India (Table 1.1), grew at less than 1 per cent between 1977–8 and 1987–8. The growth of urban employment in the formal sector grew at around 2 per cent a year, but most of this was accounted for by public-sector enterprises, which are unlikely to generate such growth rates during the 1990s. Only the urban informal sector has been growing at a faster rate of about 6 per cent a year, and this sector accounts for 15 per cent of total employment. It brings with it, however, social problems of migration, urban growth and the lack of adequate infrastructure.

Achievement of the goal of full employment is therefore crucially dependent on the growth of employment in the rural non-farm sector (RNFS). Between 1977–8 and 1987–8 employment in the RNFS grew at

Table 1.1: Employment shares (%) (1987–8)

	Agriculture	*Non-agriculture*	*Total*
Rural	62	16	78
Urban	2	20	22
Total	64	36	100

Source: computed from NSS, 1987–8 (GoI, 1990).

1. Seventy-eight million jobs for new entrants to the labour force and 22 million jobs for those unemployed in 1990. The final plan document revised the figures downwards slightly to 94 million jobs in total. However, in no year in the first half of the decade did the economy absorb more than 6 million additional workers, and in the early years it was only 3 to 4 million. Thus the backlog of unemployment has only grown.

Table 1.2: Growth rate assumptions for employment (%) (annual, 1992–2000)

	Agriculture	*Non-agriculture*	*Total*
Rural	0.74	8.10	2.25
Urban	0.74	5.00	4.61
Total	0.74	6.38	2.77

Note: The growth rate for agricultural employment assumes the same growth rate as for 1978–88 (Papola, 1992: 239). The growth rate for urban employment is estimated using the growth rates of formal and informal urban employment given above. The calculation of the necessary growth rate in RNFS employment then depends on weighting all growth rates by the employment shares in Table 1.1.

5 per cent a year, and according to the assumptions given in Table 1.2, this growth rate would have to increase to 8 per cent to achieve full employment.

Our concern for employment does not stop, however, at the number of jobs generated. We are no less interested in the quality of jobs in the rural non-farm sector, which can vary enormously, from lucrative entrepreneurial activities to low-paid casual labour in appalling conditions. While the latter is often crucial in providing income to many rural workers in India, we look at ways in which the quality of jobs in this area can be enhanced. Rural non-farm sector jobs are, nevertheless, on average superior to those in agriculture. Workers in the RNFS are better paid, less poor and more educated, and there is also less child labour in the sector. It is in two broad industrial categories only within the RNFS, casual labour in mining and construction, that the average employment conditions may be no better than in agricultural labour, the primary alternative source of employment in rural India.

The quality of jobs is important for the long-term development of rural India, hence our interest in productive and sustainable employment, which can contribute to economic growth. Jobs in the rural non-farm sector build up the skill base of the rural population, are often less capital intensive, use less energy and imported inputs, and make significant contributions to exports, for example of textiles, gems and leather.

Rural non-farm employment has already played a significant role in economic development in states like Gujarat and Punjab. Other states, on the other hand, are in crisis, with stagnant rural economies driving more and more workers to become labourers (especially in agriculture), to take up jobs which are barely productive, to migrate or to become unemployed. In Andrha Pradesh, for example, half the rural workforce is now made up of agricultural labourers. As the proportion of cultivators declines, additional jobs must be generated in the non-farm sector if new entrants are not to swell the ranks of agricultural labourers still further.

The rural non-farm sector can also contribute to poverty reduction. Non-farm employment is particularly important to small and marginal farmers, as well as to the landless, who cannot derive sufficient income from the agricultural sector. In a recent World Bank study comparing the reduction of rural poverty across 15 of the most important states in India between 1957 and 1991, Datt and Ravallion (1996) show that the quantitative impact on rural poverty of above-trend growth in non-farm output is large.

Our concerns also extend to issues of equality and social justice. For example, rural women often become low-paid casual labourers. Likewise, many traditional rural workers have been deprived of their customary livelihoods through powerful interests, often supported by state action. Examples include the denial of the rights of tribals to gather forest produce or of low-caste flayers to flay carcasses, or the extensive corruption in the handloom sub-sector.

And so, the central questions explored in this book are whether, and how, the rural non-farm sector can contribute to the achievement of full employment in India, and to more equitable economic growth.

The rural non-farm sector already provides work to between 40 to 50 million rural workers, or as much as a quarter of all rural employment (Chapter 2), while income from the sector contributes between 25 to 35 per cent of the total income of rural households. Can India develop this sector further by increasing its growth rate of high-quality, productive and sustainable rural employment?

For an illustration of the impact the growth of rural non-farm employment can have on an economy, and of the positive influence of public policy on the RNFS, Box 1.1 provides data on township and village enterprises in China, the only country comparable to India in terms of its population and hence of its need to generate rural employment.

Granted our interest in employment, it is perhaps surprising that we hardly mention rural public works, not even the Maharashtra Employment Guarantee Scheme that has received so much national and international attention (e.g. Acharya, 1990; Dev, 1996). Such programmes will continue to be important for generating rural employment and income until the goals of full employment and poverty reduction have been achieved. They can also contribute to the development of rural infrastructure. However, our interests focus on sustainable employment in the context of long-term economic development, and the issues surrounding public-work schemes, which are entirely dependent on public resources, are very different.

Finally, it is important to note that in the context of rural India words such as 'employment' and 'jobs' can be misleading. Less than 10 per cent of rural workers are employed regularly, and there is much underemployment among the vast majority of those who are self-employed or work as casual labourers. Moreover, many rural households and workers may be

Box 1.1: Township and village enterprises in China

In China the development of rural enterprises has always been regarded as critical to rural modernization, and has therefore received significant policy attention, including ambitious targets set in the national five-year plans. Rural enterprises have been promoted so that surplus agricultural labour can be transferred from agriculture to the rural non-farm sector, rather than migrating to urban centres. It has been reported that China transferred over 100 million rural workers in this way, and the percentage of people dependent on land has been brought down from 70 to 45 per cent.

The township, village and private (TVP) enterprise sector has become the most dynamic part of Chinese industry, where the TVPs are active in all but one of the 14 principal sub-sectors. In 1991 TVP enterprises accounted for 40 per cent of the country's industrial employment, more than a quarter of its output and almost a third of its exports. The dollar value of exports by rural enterprises increased from US$1.2 billion in 1985 to US$13 billion in 1990.

Many township and village enterprises would be considered medium-scale rather than small-scale industries, with 30 workers on average in 1989. Only private enterprises were smaller, with an average of three workers.

What are the causes of China's spectacular success in promoting rural non-farm employment? The 'deregulation of rural China' from 1978 onwards, including opening the rural sector to foreign trade and investment, has probably been the most significant policy change, which unleashed 'a tremendous amount of productive and entrepreneurial energy in rural areas' (Ho). Other factors have been an abundant supply of (cheap) labour, large agricultural surpluses for investments, as well as substantial credit from banks, encouragement of private enterprises, strong performance incentives to workers and managers, export incentives for enterprises, and attention to upgrading technologies and marketing, including through collaboration with foreign partners.

Sources: Byrd and Lin (1990); Fureng (1992); Ho (1994); Islam (1991).

engaged in more than one working activity at any one time. Indeed, their employment patterns change across different seasons of the year, and across different years. The concept of rural non-farm employment may, therefore, incorporate anything from a regular full-time job to off-season work undertaken by agricultural households to supplement their incomes. For these reasons we tend to prefer the term 'livelihoods'. We cannot, however, do without the terms 'employment' and 'jobs', and use them extensively in this book. In particular, for aggregate employment data we have to rely on surveys which often do not capture the true nature and dynamics of much rural employment.

Policies and politics

Because of the concerns outlined above, this book gives extensive coverage both to policies that affect the rural non-farm sector and to recommendations on how these policies could be improved. It is intended for those who design, influence and implement policies, although it raises many issues and challenges even for those more interested in data and statistical analysis.[2]

Unlike in China, the rural non-farm sector has largely been neglected by Indian policy-makers as a residual sub-sector that falls between agriculture and (urban) industrialization. This does not necessarily mean that we advocate a comprehensive policy framework for the sector, which is highly diverse, ranging from primary activities such as mining, through manufacturing and construction, to tertiary services like transport, trading and public services. Enterprises in the sector range from single self-employed workers at home to large factories. Types of jobs vary from well-paid regular employment to low-paid casual labour. In short, the rural non-farm sector cannot be treated as a homogenous sector, but needs to be seen in its component parts or sub-sectors (see pp. 16–18).

Even without this qualification, there are fundamental issues surrounding policy processes. Granted the context of India, where the role of government and the public sector in rural development has been pervasive, we often focus on government policies, especially for regulation, promotion and credit. We look also, however, at the extent to which private producers are organized. We give less attention to the macro context and focus more on the micro economy, where millions of consumers and producers enter into exchange transactions, thousands of firms are born, produce, thrive and die, and hundreds of regulators and officials are active.

Policies as implemented in practice may, however, differ widely from the intention of those policies as originally stated. This is not only an issue of corrupt implementers who distort policies for their own ends, although we shall cite many examples of this. The gap between intention and implementation remains even when policy-makers and practitioners are principled.

On the whole, organizations are responsible for implementing policies, and the relationship between policies and these bodies is a fundamental

2. The data gathered from many different sources, and analysed in Chapters 2 and 6 and Appendices 2 and 3, provide the most comprehensive overview of the RNFS in India currently available.

issue that we address throughout the book. It is not simply a matter of organizations changing given policies in practice. The implementing bodies themselves contribute significantly to the design of policies. In short, we are dealing with a cyclical relationship between the two.

Our concern for how policies are implemented appears self-evident. India, like other countries, however, provides numerous examples of well-intentioned policies being distorted on the ground, and it is remarkable that this issue is not taken more seriously in designing the policies and setting up the implementing organizations; indeed, the tendency since independence has been to create new policies and organizations when the existing ones are deemed to have failed, with little consideration given to the causes of failure, so that the new bodies often founder for the very same reasons as the old. Poor policies and organizations have proliferated in rural India.

Granted that policy and organizational analysis inevitably leads into political considerations, it is as well briefly to outline our own political perspective. In many parts of this book we are highly critical of the current role of government and its agencies in terms of rural development, and often advocate that it be significantly curtailed. In particular, the state has given itself the right to sanction even micro-level economic activities, as well as the organization of producers, and has effectively appropriated control of the basis of millions of traditional livelihoods.

We do not, however, adhere to an ideology that is hostile to every form of government and that believes the solution is merely to reduce the role of government to its minimum. As Killick (1990: 28–9) rightly argues, the question is not so much how big government should be, but rather what kind of government it is, what its comparative advantages are, how it can perform better. We therefore support a shift in the state's role from an often corrupt regulator of the micro-environment and, through public enterprises, an equally corrupt market operator, to the provider of an enabling and more market-friendly environment, of reliable infrastructure and some focused promotional inputs. In particular, we do not believe that all ineffective public agencies should simply be closed down, but analyse how both the environment and the internal practices of these agencies can be changed to enhance their performance. While some agencies which no longer have an appropriate role to play in the new environment will rightly be shut down, the extensive organizational network that India has developed should be regarded as an outstanding resource for rural development, rather than something to be done away with. In some cases privatization may be appropriate, but again 'the degree of competition in an industry is a more important determinant of the economic and social efficiency of an enterprise than the nature of its ownership' (Killick, 1990: 26–7).[3]

3. Bank Rakyat Indonesia, formerly an ineffective and loss-making public bank, whose performance has been transformed, but without being privatized, is an excellent example of this type of organizational transformation (see Chapter 6, pp. 174–6).

We draw support for such an approach from many successful examples of state action in India, notably the Green Revolution, but also more recently the role of technology missions in initiating the transformation of sub-sectors such as telecommunications, and oilseeds and edible oils. There are many international examples to draw on as well, such as the promotion of township and village enterprises in China (Box 1.1), of rural industrialization in Taiwan (Ranis and Stewart, 1993), of rural banking in Indonesia (Chapter 6), or the role of government in the 'economic miracle' of east and south-east Asia in general (see, for instance, Wade, 1990, World Bank, 1993).

India is, of course, different from such Asian countries on account of its remarkable democratic traditions and constitutionalism. Our analysis and recommendations build on these traditions, for example: questioning the right of the state to interfere so extensively in the micro-environment, suggesting greater participation and control by producers in the policy processes and agencies that are supposed to assist them, and strengthening the rights of citizens as consumers. This is in line with recent efforts to strengthen democratic practices in India, such as the creation of new consumer courts, the reform of the Cooperative Act in the first state (Andhra Pradesh) and, above all, the constitutional amendment guaranteeing elections for *panchayats* (village councils).

Nevertheless, while our analysis and proposals fit well into the overall democratic framework within the country, they apply equally well to any context where efforts are being made to strengthen local and public bodies. For example, strong local institutions are found in many countries in east and south-east Asia. The institutional framework we introduce below, therefore, goes well beyond any simplistic belief in a multi-party liberal democracy, however closely or not India might follow such a tradition.

So we believe there remains a significant role for state action to promote the rural non-farm sector, although that role will clearly be very different from the one currently practised in India. Part of it is also to protect the so-called weaker sections of society, such as traditional low-caste workers. Once again, however, we recognize that current policies have largely failed to provide such protection, especially in the economic sphere, and that alternative strategies must be found.

Above we introduced the issues that motivated us to look at the rural non-farm sector, and some of the broad approaches we adopt for doing so. Below we provide the necessary detail and background: a definition of the rural non-farm sector, a brief assessment of some previous research in this area, and an overview of the theoretical frameworks we use to address some of the gaps in that earlier work. For an account of the objectives, scope and methodology of the study see Appendix 1, pp. 233–40.

Definitions: what is the rural non-farm sector?

There is no standard definition of the RNFS, either internationally or within India. The sector is too diverse, in terms of activities, unit sizes and geographic dispersal, to allow a neat classification. This is further emphasized by the fact that the sector is usually defined in negative terms as the rural *non*-farm or *non*-agricultural sector.[4] Positive terms, such as rural enterprises or rural industries, are inadequate: the former may include agricultural activities; the latter tends to exclude rural services, which in most countries generate more employment than does rural manufacturing.

Various countries have their own specific terms: in China discussion centres around township and village enterprises (TVEs), an administrative category by ownership; in India historical causes have often led policy-makers to focus on *khadi*[5] and village industries (KVIs). And yet neither TVEs nor KVIs are coterminous with the rural non-farm or non-agricultural sector, or with rural enterprises or industries. Moreover, the two terms TVEs and KVIs illustrate the very diverse policy perspectives on the RNFS that can exist: in China TVEs are at the forefront of the industrial modernization of the state; in India KVIs belong to a largely traditional and partially stagnant sector.

In order to develop a definition of the RNFS appropriate to the Indian context, Box 1.2 explains the related terms used by various Indian organizations that have a role in the sector. It can be seen that most of the Indian organizations tend towards a narrow perspective of the rural non-farm sector. The traditional policy approach has been to promote cottage-scale units in villages: the individual weaver, the potter, the village shoe-maker. This has been the strategy of the Khadi and Village Industries Commission, which is a major actor in the field. The largest national poverty-alleviation scheme (the IRDP), which targets 40 per cent of its loans on industries, services and businesses (ISB), has also focused on enterprises for the self-employed, and even within the rural small-scale industry (SSI) sector, tiny units have been predominant: in 1987–8 the average fixed investment in a rural SSI was only Rs110 000, with an average of five workers (GoI, 1992c).

The approach of the Indian organizations reflects the political economy surrounding the rural non-farm sector: the traditional rural livelihoods still employ large numbers of rural workers and are thus important as vote banks. Supporting *khadi* is also a vital part of the ritual of political allegiance to

4. Even these terms are not strictly the same: many non-agricultural activities may take place on the farm. However, while we use the term 'non-farm' sector, we include all non-agricultural activities (defined by the industrial categories in the Census; see below), including those which may provide significant additional income to many farm households.
5. Hand-woven cloth made of hand-spun yarn, promoted by Mahatma Gandhi as a symbol of village self-reliance, and in defiance of British commercial interests.

Box 1.2: Official terms in India relating to the RNFS

The Planning Commission of the Government of India uses the term 'village and small industries' (VSI), for which it has a separate division. The portfolio of this division includes *khadi* and village industries, handicrafts, handlooms and powerlooms, coir, sericulture and small-scale industries.

The term 'village industries' is in a sense proprietary to the Khadi and Village Industries Commission (KVIC). *Khadi*, or production of hand-spun, hand-woven cloth, is treated as a separate category, because of its large share of employment and its historical links with the freedom movement. KVIC has a specified list of village industries, which now includes 107 industries.

The Department of Small-Scale Industries of the Government of India uses the term 'small-scale industries' (SSIs) and 'tiny enterprises'. An SSI is defined as an undertaking with an investment in plant and machinery of up to Rs60 lakhs. (This can go up to Rs75 lakhs if the unit is an ancillary unit or is exporting more than 30 per cent of its output.) There is, however, no locational specification, and the majority of SSIs (some 60 per cent) are urban, not rural. The definition of tiny enterprises limits the investment in plant and machinery to Rs5 lakhs. Formerly it excluded enterprises in towns with a population of over 50 000, but this locational restriction has now been removed.

The Department of Rural Development uses the term 'industry, services and business' (ISB) sector in the context of the massive Integrated Rural Development Programme (IRDP), which extends subsidized loans to those below the poverty line. As the commercial banking sector has been very deeply involved in the IRDP, the term is now widely used in banking parlance. Since the Service Area Monitoring and Information System (SAMIS) was introduced in 1990, banks are also supposed to classify and report their advances to the non-farm sector as a separate category. In practice bankers tend to use ISB, NFS and SSI interchangeably, and without any standardization.

The National Bank for Agriculture and Rural Development (NABARD) was the first major public agency in India widely to use the term 'non-farm sector'. It defined the term originally, however, by listing a 'spectrum of small, cottage, tiny and village industries' in 22 major categories of activity (NABARD, 1992). This list has been expanded periodically.

Gandhian ideals. Small-scale industrialists make up a powerful political lobby as well. Even the IRDP, which began as a major attempt at poverty alleviation through self-employment, degenerated quickly into a programme to exercise political patronage rather than to generate sustainable livelihoods.

In seeking to develop a more objective perspective on the rural non-farm sector, it is apparent that the terms used by the various organizations are defined along three dimensions:

- by activity (KVIC or NABARD's list of activities; the IRDP's ISB sector);
- by location in the rural–urban continuum (rural, village, in towns up to 50 000); and
- by the size of the enterprise (small, tiny, cottage).

These three dimensions can be termed sub-sectoral, spatial and scalar, and the RNFS needs to be defined along all of them (see Figure 1.1). Below we look more closely at each one in turn.

Sub-sectoral dimension The Census of India categorizes all workers into one of the following nine 'industrial' categories:

(I) Cultivators
(II) Agricultural labourers
(III) (Workers engaged in) livestock rearing, forestry, fishing, plantations, orchards and allied activities
(IV) Mining and quarrying
(V) Manufacturing, processing, servicing and repairs
  (Va) In household industry
  (Vb) In non-household industry
(VI) Construction
(VII) Trade and commerce
(VIII) Transport, storage and communications
(IX) Other services

There is no consensus among the various organizations about which of these categories should be included within the rural non-farm sector. Approaches range from including only household industry (Va) to incorporating all activities in categories III to IX. For our study we have included all activities in categories IV to IX. In our presentation of RNFS employment data in Chapter 2, we therefore exclude activities in category III; in selecting sub-sectors and conducting fieldwork, however, we were not rigid in this exclusion. While many of them are performed as activities allied to farming, category III activities are increasingly being pursued for commercial rather than subsistence purposes, and in many states we reviewed the processing of the primary products concerned. Thus, for this study, RNFS activities comprise all manufacturing, proces-

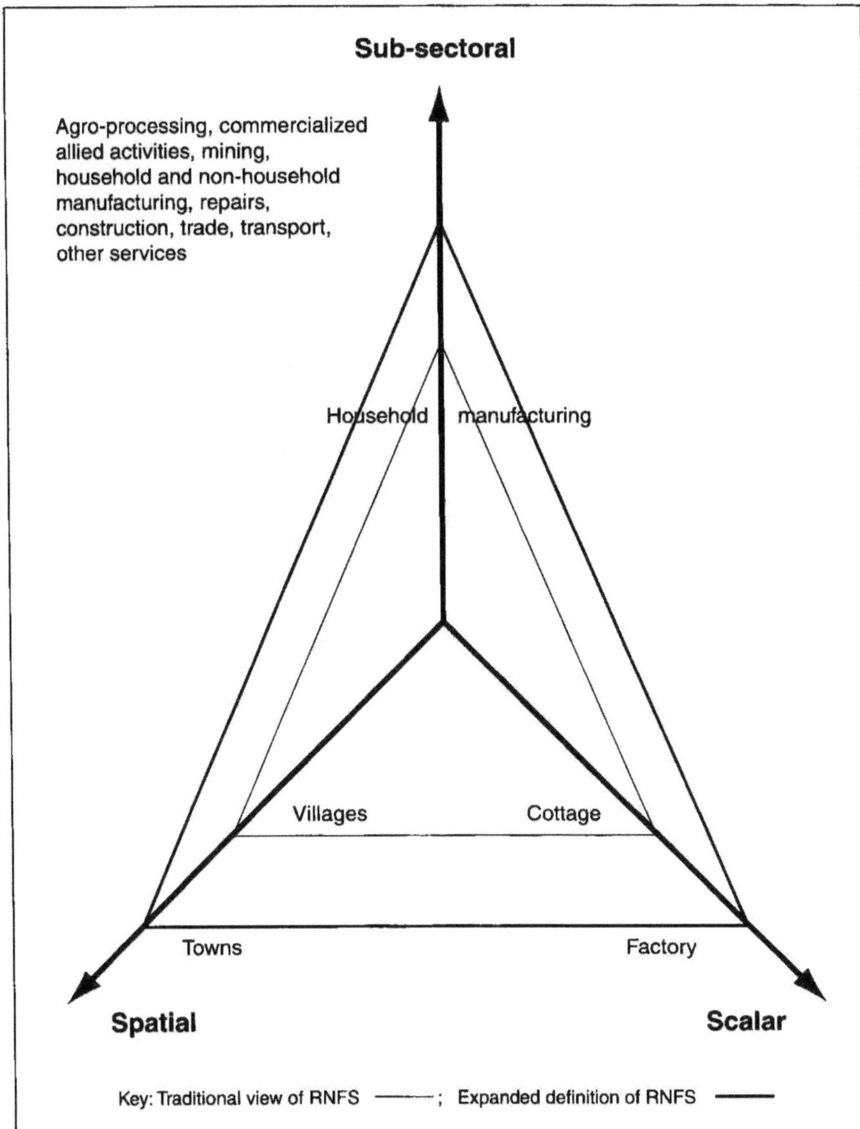

Figure 1.1: *Diagrammatic representation of the RNFS*

sing, construction and mining, as well as all services; in short, a very diverse range of activities.

Spatial dimension The mandates of most agencies with a rural focus are limited to villages or towns below a certain population. Until recently, for example, the Reserve Bank of India allowed NABARD to refinance loans only in towns of up to 10 000 head of population, although this limit has now been increased to towns of up to 50 000 persons. The Khadi and Village Industries Act allows KVIC to support units in locations with a population of up to 10 000 (although KVIC is now focusing its activities on even smaller villages).

There are strong arguments, however, for loosening such restrictions. Rural towns, especially *mandi* or market towns, play a critical role in the rural non-farm economy as places for purchasing inputs and selling products, while economic sub-sectors rarely honour the rural–urban divide any more. For example, for most activities the minimum economic scale of operation is now too large to be supported by local demand from a village, or even a cluster of villages, with the result that changes in urban or even foreign markets may have a significant impact on rural livelihoods. Such markets must therefore be considered in any policies to generate rural employment. Likewise many rural inhabitants commute to towns for work. Seeking to define them as rural or urban workers makes little sense.

In consequence, we covered many rural towns in our fieldwork, and in our definition of the RNFS we include rural towns with populations of up to 50 000. This is, however, a definitional criterion; in contrast, policy which adheres to a sub-sectoral approach may need to extend into even larger towns and urban centres. However, the Census and the National Sample Surveys define rural areas to include only villages with a population of less than 5000.[6] So all the rural employment data from these sources (including those cited in this book) include only workers who reside in such villages (see our analysis in Chapter 2).

Scalar dimension The Central Statistical Organization (CSO) uses the following size categories:

- 'own account enterprises' (OAEs): enterprises employing only the owner-worker or his or her family workers;
- 'non-directory establishments' (NDEs): enterprises with at least one and at most five workers, of whom at least one is a hired worker;
- 'directory establishments' (DEs): enterprises with at least six workers, including at least one who is hired; and,
- 'factories': manufacturing enterprises employing at least 10 workers if they use power, or at least 20 if no power is used. There is no equivalent category for service enterprises.

Traditionally, policy for rural enterprises in India has focused on tiny, or at most small units, in effect OAEs and NDEs. This has been justified on the grounds that such tiny undertakings maximize employment potential. This

6. Population densities and even employment profiles are also taken into account.

claim is far from proven (see Chapter 2), and tends to reinforce the existing perspectives on the sector, drawing attention away from the more dynamic parts, such as directory establishments. In fact there seems to be no good reason to restrict the RNFS, at least in definitional terms, to any particular size of unit, and our definition of the RNFS includes outfits of any size.

Drawing these arguments together, we define the rural non-farm sector as follows:

> The RNFS comprises all non-agricultural activities – mining and quarrying, household and non-household manufacturing, processing, repairs, construction, trade, transport and other services – in villages and rural towns of up to 50 000 population, undertaken by enterprises varying in size from household 'own-account enterprises' all the way to factories.

This definition of the RNFS along three axes (sub-sectoral, spatial and scalar) is summarized in Figure 1.1. The inner triangle represents the traditional understanding of the sector in India and other countries; the outer triangle represents the expanded definition.

Such definitional issues are not simply niceties. The inner triangle effectively limits the RNFS to household manufacturing, the only part of the sector that is declining. With such a definition it is not surprising that Indian policy-makers have tended to regard the RNFS as a traditional area without much potential for growth. The expanded definition, on the other hand, incorporates all the dynamic parts of the sector, such as manufacturing outside of the household, service enterprises and somewhat larger undertakings, including those in rural towns.

A brief review of some research on the rural non-farm sector

A recent World Bank survey of rural non-farm employment (Lanjouw and Lanjouw, 1995) opens with the following statement:

> The rural non-farm sector is a poorly understood component of the rural economy and we know relatively little about its role in the broader development process. This gap in our knowledge is the product of the sector's great heterogeneity . . . coupled with a dearth, until recently, of empirical or theoretical attention.

Indeed, Lanjouw and Lanjouw go on to suggest that policy-makers and planners make policy for the RNFS 'unencumbered by evidence'. This is in spite of the fact that research on rural non-farm employment dates back 20 years or more,[7] and the first model of an agrarian economy to incorporate

7. See, e.g., Mellor and Lele (1973); Johnston and Kilby (1975); Mellor (1976); Vyas and Mathai (1978); World Bank (1978); Chuta and Liedholm (1979). Several volumes of collected articles on the RNFS appeared in the mid-1980s; see, e.g., Chuta and Sethuraman (1984); Ahmad and Chowdhury (1985); Mukhopadhyay and Lim (1985); Choe and Lo (1986); Shand (1986); Islam (1987).

non-agricultural activities was developed by Hymer and Resnick in 1969. Why then is there so little understanding of the RNFS that could guide policy-makers?

Past research has tended to focus on data analysis, especially of employment, income, productivity and inter-sectoral linkages, which has proved important in mapping the sector in different countries. Linkages between the agricultural and non-agricultural sectors have received special attention, especially from those trained as agricultural economists. The following comments from Hazell and Haggblade (1991: 515) are representative:

> The rural non-farm economy is intimately linked to agriculture. A substantial share of rural manufacturing involves agro-processing and the production, repair and supply of farm inputs. Moreover, the dominant sectors in the rural non-farm economy consist of trade and service establishments that cater largely to rural consumer demand. The prospects for growth in the rural non-farm economy will, therefore, hinge on future agricultural performance.

It may then come as a surprise that we deal very little with such linkages in this book. We do not in any way deny their importance, not least in generating demand for non-farm products and services; however, significant research on them has already been conducted, including in India, and the policy recommendations that arise from detailed modelling and estimating of growth multipliers are often uncontroversial: for example, invest in agricultural development and rural infrastructure; focus on small- to medium-sized farms; get relative prices right.

We believe that the RNFS deserves attention on its own account, and not only as a sector dependent on agricultural development (which reinforces the apparent residual nature of rural non-farm employment). Several reasons can be cited to justify this attempt to balance the past emphasis on linkages with the agricultural sector:

- Processing of agricultural produce into food products, commonly assumed to be the primary source of rural non-farm employment, in fact accounts for only 4.1 per cent of RNFS employment (see Table 2.3, p. 30).
- Some dynamic sub-sectors in the RNFS, such as textiles, leather, diamond and gem processing, chemicals and ceramics, rely heavily (some almost exclusively) on urban and export demand, and not just on demand from rural households. Cottage enterprises producing products and services for village consumption[8] are no longer the dominant part of the rural non-farm economy.

8. The traditional 'Z-goods' in Hymer and Resnick's model (see Ranis and Stewart, 1993). While Hymer and Resnick (1969: 493) used this 'purposely vague title to indicate the heterogeneity of the group' of activities, the term captures well the belief in non-farm occupations as residual activities in rural areas.

- There are linkages not only from agriculture to the rural non-farm sector, but also from the RNFS to agriculture. These have 'more often been neglected' and include, for example, improvements in agricultural markets and internal terms of trade, modern inputs and improved technologies, and incentives for increasing productivity and savings among agricultural households (Ranis and Stewart, 1993: 79–80).
- In particular, granted that between a fifth and a quarter of the rural labour force in India is primarily engaged in the non-farm sector, and between a quarter and a third of rural household income comes from non-farm activities, demand from the rural non-farm sector itself is a crucial component of overall demand in rural areas.

Moreover, the focus of research on data analysis and inter-sectoral linkages has rarely captured the imagination of policy-makers, at least in India. Nor does it provide many insights for policy-makers grappling with the diversity of the rural non-farm sector, in which each sub-sector may require very different promotional strategies. Policy recommendations tend to fall into two areas: macro-policies relating to terms of trade, pricing, tariffs and exchange rates; and specific programme or project inputs.[9] As mentioned above, we focus on the micro-economy, and analyse why standard policies, and programme and project inputs, have often not proved effective in a sector as diverse as the RNFS, and in a country as large and varied as India.

Data analysis and inter-sectoral linkages also tend to ignore wider political and social issues which influence strongly the rural non-farm sector. Above all, they ignore the organizational dynamics through which policies are implemented and which form such a central theme of this book.

Thus our hope for this book is twofold: first, that it captures the imagination of policy-makers in India about the potential of the rural non-farm sector to contribute to full employment as well as to rural development and to poverty reduction; second, that it will help to move the agenda of international research on the rural non-farm sector on to new terrain, which will provide a more comprehensive framework of analysis, thus enabling policy-makers to make decisions on the basis of sound evidence not only from economic analysis, but also from an understanding of policy and organizational processes.[10]

To this end we have had to develop suitable conceptual frameworks, not only for our analysis with its broader focus, but also in order to provide policy-makers themselves with the necessary analytical tools to develop

9. See for example, Lanjouw and Lanjouw (1995: 35–43). Ranis and Stewart (1993), in comparing rural non-farm development in Taiwan and the Philippines, adopt a more comprehensive perspective, ranging from macro-policies to the role of decentralized farmers' organizations.
10. The publication of Koppel *et al.* (1994) also draws on a variety of different disciplines in analysing the RNFS.

new approaches towards the RNFS; in particular, we have used both sub-sectoral and institutional analysis, which we describe below.

A brief introduction to conceptual frameworks

Sub-sectoral analysis

Due to the enormous diversity within the rural non-farm sector, ranging from primary activities through manufacturing to tertiary services, it is not possible to design, at least in any detail, policies which are appropriate to all the different undertakings within the sector. The evidence suggests that uniform policies for small-scale, and for *khadi* and village industries have not been particularly helpful; even the Green Revolution focused on specific crops in specific areas.

The rural non-farm sector needs to be seen, therefore, in terms of its component parts, or its sub-sectors. Haggblade and Gamser (1991: 1) define a sub-sector as 'the network of firms that supply raw materials, transform them and distribute finished goods to a particular consumer market'. Normally a sub-sector is delineated by a final product (such as tiles) and includes all firms engaged in raw-material supply, production and distribution of that product, but in some cases the defining characteristic could be a key raw material or a commodity (such as leather), with the sub-sector spanning the alternative transformations and distribution systems stemming from it.

For the purposes of our study, we categorized sub-sectors into three groups (see Chapters 2 and 3):

- *high-share*: those which already generate a high share of employment in the RNFS;
- *high-growth*: those in which RNFS employment is growing at a rapid rate; and
- *emergent*: those which are only just emerging as part of the RNFS, and thus do not feature prominently in past data.

It is not possible, however, to calculate precisely the employment generated by each sub-sector. Both the Census of India and the National Sample Surveys use the National Industrial Classification (NIC), which categorizes economic activities on the basis of their final product or service. In a few cases the NIC major (two-digit) groups, such as repairs (39), correspond roughly to a sub-sector. In most cases the major groups incorporate minor (three-digit) groups which are so diverse that we prefer to use the minor groups to correspond to sub-sectors. For example, major group 32 comprises the manufacture of all 'non-metallic mineral products', including pottery, bricks and ceramics; in the Indian context, however, the minor group 322, 'manufacture of earthenware and earthen pottery', is a significant sub-sector in itself.

Even the NIC minor groups do not make it possible to calculate the total employment within a sub-sector like pottery. For example, there are separate groups for wholesale and retail trading of many products, but not of pottery alone. Thus in Chapter 2, in analysing the employment generated by high-share and high-growth sub-sectors, we are forced to use the employment figures given under the NIC major or minor group encompassing the actual production of the product or provision of the service, without trying to calculate how many jobs are engaged in the backward and forward linkages around the finished product or service.

The methodologies for sub-sectoral analysis developed by Haggblade and Gamser (1991), and others, allow practitioners to determine strategic interventions which have the potential to generate a significant impact on a chosen sub-sector, for example in terms of new jobs for poor people. The methodologies are less satisfactory in determining why a sub-sector has or has not been growing in the past, and whether it will be able to thrive in future. Policy-makers need answers to these questions if they are to choose the most promising sub-sectors to promote. Thus the choice of potential sub-sectors (the first stage of sub-sectoral analysis) comes before the choice of strategic interventions appropriate to the specific sub-sectors chosen (the second stage).

To help policy-makers to choose, we have adapted the framework of 'competitive advantage' developed by Michael Porter (1990). Porter identifies four determinants that promote or impede the creation of such advantage in an industry: factor conditions (underlying the traditional concept of comparative advantage); demand conditions; related and supporting industries; and firm strategy, structure and rivalry. In Chapter 3 we describe the framework in greater detail, and summarize the results of our sub-sectoral analysis using the framework.

The implications of a sub-sectoral approach for policy-making are significant. First, policies designed to assist the rural non-farm sector as a whole are unlikely to be effective. For example, policies that assume that there is only one important constraint, which, if addressed, would allow all the diverse RNFS sub-sectors to grow, are clearly inappropriate. The provision of credit in particular has often been seen in this light.

Second, organizations engaged in the rural non-farm sector in India often have a narrow focus on smaller units in the most rural locations. However, sub-sectors rarely restrict themselves to a particular size of unit or to rural areas only. Almost all sub-sectors in the RNFS depend on activities in urban areas, and often involve units of many different sizes. So analysis of a sub-sector might reveal that a large urban processing unit is critical for generating non-farm employment in rural areas!

Policy-makers clearly need to focus much more carefully on selected sub-sectors, analysing their potential and the constraints they face, and seeking to address these. Examples of such a strategy in India do, of course, exist, such as the promotion of the dairy and oilseed sub-sectors, and of specific crops in designated areas during the Green Revolution.

Institutional analysis

Throughout this book we talk often of policies and policy-makers. For our analysis we divide policies into four categories: regulatory, promotional, credit and policies for the representation and organization of RNFS producers. Policies are, of course, strongly influenced by the institutional environment, which clearly does not adhere to the restrictive assumptions of the economic model of perfect competition. Moreover, as we suggested above, policies are implemented by organizations, and thus their practical implementation may be very different from the intentions with which they were designed.

In seeking to make sense of this complex interlocking web of policies, organizations and their environment, we draw on neo-institutional economics (see Box 4.1, p. 86). In this theory, 'institution' has a much wider meaning than its common definition as a formal organization of some significance. For example, Douglass North (1990: 3) describes institutions 'as the rules of the game in a society or, more formally . . . the humanly devised constraints that shape human interaction'.

Neo-institutional economics seeks to go beyond the restrictive assumptions of perfect competition by using such concepts as the principal-agent problem and transaction costs. Principals use agents to perform services on their behalf, but the principals cannot ensure that their agents will behave exactly in the way they desire. We use the concept of principals and agents (especially in chapters 4 and 5) to explain distortions between stated and practised policy. We also draw on organizational theory (Israel, 1989, see Box 5.1, p. 116) to assess the wide variation in the performance of agencies implementing policies for the RNFS.

Transaction costs are the costs associated with the process of economic transactions, such as buying and selling. We use them to explain why formal and informal credit markets perform so differently in rural India (Chapter 6). Although transaction costs are rarely measured (but often invoked to explain any apparent market imperfections: Toye, 1995: 65), we provide precise evidence of these costs faced by borrowers and lenders in formal rural credit markets.

We also use transaction costs, although we do not measure them, to explain why RNFS producers do not organize even though the benefits of collective action are substantial (Chapter 7). We analyse issues of power and ideology as part of the institutional environment which influences the extent to which producers organize for their own benefit.

In short, we try to describe and analyse the institutional environment and how it shapes the behaviour of producers, consumers, resource providers and regulators in the rural non-farm sector. As suggested above, we do this at the level of the micro-economy where neo-institutional economics has been applied most effectively (Toye, 1995).

Our pragmatic attitudes to the role of government, which we outlined above, are also in tune with the theory of neo-institutional economics (Toye, 1995: 58):

> The recognition of transaction costs . . . disposes of the automatic preference for provision of goods and services through the market. Equally their presence undermines an ideal view of governments as benevolent and omnicompetent. Market failure is clearly with us, to a greater or lesser extent. But so is government failure. So the questions of public policy become more complicated. Should imperfect governments be used to correct imperfect markets, or contrariwise should imperfect markets be brought into play to improve the resource misallocations of imperfect governments? What the [neo-institutional economics] tells us is that neither answer is invariably correct. Rather, the task is to estimate the respective net changes in transaction costs in comparison with the anticipated allocative improvement, to find out whether policy should be favouring additional government intervention or further privatisation.

Outline of the book

In view of our analysis in this chapter, we have arranged the book as follows. We start where most research has been focused, namely by looking at data on the rural non-farm sector, especially at employment data (Chapter 2 and Appendix 2). Chapter 2 also provides inter-state comparisons, on the basis of descriptions (given in Appendix 3) of the rural non-farm sector in each of the eight states we included in the study. Because we recognize that not all readers will be interested in the detailed data, Chapter 2 begins with a broad overview which summarizes the more thorough analysis given in later parts of the chapter.

While we begin with data-based analysis, we move quickly beyond this by reviewing the different sub-sectors we covered in the eight states (Chapter 3), emphasizing the great diversity of activities within the RNFS. Chapter 3 includes concrete illustrations of the application of sub-sectoral analysis.

Chapters 4–6 focus on policies and organizations or agencies, for regulation, promotion and credit respectively. Chapter 7 then reviews the extent to which rural non-farm producers are organized, especially into cooperatives and industry associations. Each chapter, from 3 to 7, includes some basic theory to give coherence to the analysis, together with illustrations and case studies based on fieldwork. Such illustrative material is important for giving life to our analysis and changing the perceptions that policy-makers and other readers may have of the rural non-farm sector.

It also reflects the fact that our study was more qualitative than quantitative in nature. While we analyse much data in Chapter 2, we did not ourselves gather data in the field which would have statistical validity.

The final chapter gives projections about the potential of the rural non-farm sector for generating rural employment in future, and makes recommendations for developing the RNFS to fulfil that potential.

2 The rural non-farm sector according to aggregate data

This chapter builds up a picture of the rural non-farm sector on the basis of aggregate data at the national and state levels, drawn largely from the Census of India for 1981 and 1991 and the National Sample Surveys for 1977–8 and 1987–8 (GoI, 1981, 1987a, 1990, 1992b). The first section provides an overview and summary, which is then substantiated by more detailed analyses of national data and inter-state comparisons. Readers who are more interested in the general picture of the rural non-farm sector that emerges, rather than the detailed analysis of data, may wish to focus on the overview and summary.[1]

Overview and summary

The current status of RNFS employment

The RNFS in India provides work to between 40 and 50 million rural workers. The sector may indeed generate as much as a quarter of all rural employment in India. However, the percentage of rural workers engaged in non-farm activities varies widely across the different states in India. According to the 1991 Census, Kerala leads with 43.9 per cent, followed by West Bengal (26.5), Haryana (26.2) and Punjab (25.8). At the other end are Bihar (11.7) and Madhya Pradesh (10.7).

Many agricultural households also undertake non-farm activities to generate additional household income. Income from non-farm activities therefore contributes between 25 and 35 per cent of the total income of rural households. The RNFS is particularly important to small and marginal farmers, as well as the landless, who cannot derive sufficient income in the agriculture sector. The sector also serves as an important safety net for many rural households in times of agricultural distress.

A common perception in India has been that the rural non-farm sector largely comprises traditional village industries. This is far from the truth. The sector is very diverse, ranging from mining through manufacturing to services. Only a third of RNFS jobs are in manufacturing, while 60 per cent are in services. The remainder are in construction and mining. The most important activities are manufacturing outside the household, trading and public services, each of which generates about a fifth of RNFS employment.

1. Data sources, however, are not given in the overview and summary.

At a more disaggregated level, 17 sub-sectors account for over 80 per cent of RNFS employment, and we term these 'high employment-share sub-sectors'. In the tertiary sector, these sub-sectors comprise retail trade, education, public administration, personal services, land transport, miscellaneous services, restaurants and hotels, and medical services. In the secondary sector, they comprise many traditional sub-sectors like cotton textiles, and wood, textile, pottery, food, tobacco and metal products, as well as repairs and construction.

Most of these non-farm activities are undertaken in tiny rural enterprises, which number at least 13 million, although on average each provides work to only about two people. Many of these enterprises use basic manual technologies to produce simple and low-quality products or services, so they generate little output and add little value. There are, however, more productive but fewer small, medium and large enterprises, which may invest in more advanced technologies to produce modern and higher quality products. Rural 'directory manufacturing enterprises' (see Figure 2.1, p. 43), employing 11 workers on average, provide employment to two million rural workers, and rural factories to a further two million.

Working conditions in RNFS enterprises are on average better than in the agricultural sector. Wages are higher, child labour less prevalent, and educational attainments better. Indeed, education is an important preparation, even precondition, for rural workers to enter the RNFS.

This does not mean that working conditions in the RNFS are always better. In fact rural non-farm employment can be divided into two types.[2] In most RNFS sub-sectors work is more productive and conditions better, not least when compared to agricultural labour. However, casual labourers, especially in mining and construction, may be little better off than in agricultural labour, and they often have to work in appalling conditions. Specific sub-sectors in the RNFS, such as carpets and *bidis*, are also well known for their low wages and their extensive use of child labour, although they often pay more than agricultural labour and provide vital income to the households involved.

Such issues are particularly important for female rural workers, who make up 23 per cent of RNFS employment (NSS). For them non-household manufacturing trading and 'other services'[3] (especially personal services) generate the most non-farm employment. Much of this work is part-time and low-paid, for example in sub-sectors like *bidis* and matches, or involves casual labour, for example in construction. In some cases, for

2. Models of the RNFS incorporating duality are therefore more realistic (see Ranis and Stewart, 1993). Such duality is seen between casual labour, often taken up by poorer households, and more remunerative businesses in which richer households invest; between household and non-household manufacturing; between tiny and larger enterprises; and between traditional and modern technologies, products and services.
3. 'Other services' usually include all services except trade and commerce, and transport and communications.

example in Gujarat, it is clear that rural female workers are taking over low-paid jobs from male workers as the latter move into more remunerative activities in the non-farm sector. Nevertheless, RNFS employment serves as an important opportunity for many rural women to take up more remunerative work, beyond casual labour and outside the household.

The growth of RNFS employment

Depending on the source, RNFS employment has been growing at 2.8 per cent per annum (Census) or 5.0 per cent (NSS), which is much faster than in the agricultural sector. Thus the proportion of rural workers engaged in the non-farm sector is rising.

The RNFS has in fact been generating between 1 and 1.7 million new jobs a year in rural India. Over the period 1981–91 'other services' (including in the public sector) generated 4.5 million new rural jobs, trade and commerce 2.2 million, and manufacturing outside the household 1.8 million. Household manufacturing on the other hand is the only part of the non-farm sector in which rural employment is declining, undermining further the perception in India that traditional cottage industries are the mainstay of the RNFS.

At the disaggregated level we designate the fastest growing sub-sectors in terms of rural employment as 'high employment-growth sub-sectors'. In the tertiary sector, these include transport, business and legal services, various miscellaneous services and trading activities, and public administration. In the secondary sector, besides construction, many modern manufacturing activities are beginning to emerge, such as electrical equipment, paper and chemicals, as well as iron and steel products, powerlooms and repairs, and some traditional undertakings like silk textiles and country liquor.

Not only is the number of workers engaged in the RNFS rising, but also the income that rural households earn from non-farm activities. During the 1970s, 70 per cent of the increase in real incomes of rural households was derived from non-farm activities. Moreover, a recent study of data from the 15 major states in India from 1957 to 1991 suggests that the growth of per capita real non-agricultural output can have a large quantitative impact on poverty, if such growth exceeds its usual trend. The growth of the rural non-farm sector is therefore benefiting most sections of rural society, although it is also increasing income disparities within rural India, as it is the wealthier households that profit most from increased non-farm incomes.

Comparisons across states, with their widely differing proportions of RNFS workers in the rural labour force, suggest that education, infrastructure and higher agricultural incomes all contribute towards the growth of rural non-farm employment. As we suggested above, education is an important preparation for entry into the RNFS, and assists the mobility of workers within the sector. Better infrastructure promotes RNFS employment, for example by making transport of raw materials and products easier, or by providing electricity to RNFS units. Moreover, rural towns are often the focus of the growing RNFS, as units can enjoy better access to markets, services and infrastructure.

Links between the agricultural and non-farm sectors are of course extensive. Agricultural development provides more produce for processing and trading in the rural non-farm sector, and leads to greater demand for inputs and services supplied by the RNFS. By raising farm incomes, agricultural development also increases demand on the part of rural households for RNFS products. Finally, changes in the labour market in either sector influence the supply and demand for labour in the other.[4]

There is a lively debate within India on whether rural non-farm employment is growing because it has to absorb excess labour that cannot find employment in the agricultural sector ('distress diversification' or the 'residual-sector hypothesis'), or because it is responding to increasing demand as the rural economy develops. The strongest argument in favour of the latter case is that wages in the rural non-farm sector are significantly higher than in the agricultural sector, and the difference is widening over time.

However, the RNFS is not a homogeneous sector, and some parts of it are more productive than others (see note 2). For example, labour in construction and mining, household manufacturing and some trading and personal and miscellaneous services may well be residual activities absorbing excess labour in the rural sector. However, manufacturing outside the household, transport and many services are clearly growing in response to rising demand. Moreover, the largest residual activity is agricultural labour, which is the least remunerative occupation in rural India. The number of agricultural labourers is increasing at the same rate as RNFS employment, and in some states such labourers now account for over 40 per cent of rural employment. As the proportion of cultivators in rural India declines, additional jobs must be generated in the non-farm sector if new entrants are not to swell the ranks of agricultural labourers still further.

The changing composition of rural employment points to wider and ongoing changes in the rural economy in India. What the comparisons across different states in India show is the different results that such changes can bring about. On the negative side, a stagnating rural economy can drive more and more workers to become labourers (especially in agriculture, as well as in construction and mining), to enter the less productive tertiary activities such as petty trading and personal services, to migrate or become unemployed. In Andhra Pradesh agricultural labourers now comprise half

4. However, these inter-sectoral linkages were not the focus of our study, and we do not provide fresh statistical data to assess their impact.

the rural labour force, and employment in personal services is growing faster than in any other part of the non-farm sector. In Tamil Nadu open unemployment rates exceed 8 per cent for rural males and 10 per cent for rural females. In Rajasthan rural employment in manufacturing has been declining. Rural workers from Bihar are migrating to become labourers throughout India. In fact Bihar and Madhya Pradesh are the only two states in India which showed a decline (1981–91) in the proportion of their rural labour force engaged in the non-farm sector. The rural economy in states like these is in crisis, and with the growth of employment as cultivators stagnating, employment in the more productive activities within the non-farm sector seems to provide the only prospect for a resolution to this crisis, as difficult as this may be without significant agricultural growth.

At the other end are the states which demonstrate what positive benefits the growth of productive non-farm employment can bring. In Punjab agricultural development has led to the growth of non-farm jobs, which now make up more than a quarter of all rural employment in the state. Many of these jobs are in the more productive and remunerative service sub-sectors: transport, professional services such as education, health, business and the law, and in public administration. The growth of rural towns dispersed across Punjab has been critical for the dynamism of the rural economy. In Gujarat the secondary sector generates almost half of all employment in the rural non-farm sector, and rural jobs in manufacturing outside the household have been growing at an annual rate of 5.7 per cent. The proportion of agricultural labourers in rural employment hardly rose between 1981 and 1991, Gujarat enjoys low rates of unemployment, and many women are entering the labour force.

The aggregate data thus point to the possibility of two very different scenarios for India's rural economy: stagnation leading to disintegration and crisis, or development leading to dynamic growth and transformation. The more detailed evidence which leads to this conclusion is given in the rest of this chapter.

National data on the rural non-farm sector

Box 2.1: A note on data

There are two main sources of employment data in India: the decennial Census and the quinquennial rounds on employment and unemployment of the National Sample Survey (NSS) (GoI, 1981, 1987a, 1990, 1992b). However, not only do the definitions of employment they use differ, they also classify workers differently. The Census designates those workers who worked for 183 days or more during the year as 'main workers', and those who worked for fewer than 183 days as 'marginal workers'.

The NSS, in contrast, measures employment in three different ways, depending on the reference period preceding the date of survey. The reference period for the 'usual status' is 365 days, for the 'current weekly status' seven days, and for the 'current daily status' each of the seven days preceding the date of survey.

Within the 'usual status', persons are divided into three categories as follows, depending on which they were engaged in for 'a relatively longer period of time' during the year: 1) 'working' or 'employed' (principal status workers); 2) 'seeking or available for work' or 'unemployed'; and 3) 'not in the labour force'. However, when those classified as 'not in the labour force' also undertook some work (but, of course, for relatively less time) they are designated 'subsidiary status workers'.

Data problems are not, however, confined to definitions. The processing and publishing of surveys in India is unbelievably slow. So the latest Census and NSS data available at the time of writing (GoI, 1992b and 1990) comprised some data from the 1991 Census (although not the crucial General Economic Tables) and the results of the 43rd round of the NSS (1987–8), while the data from the next NSS round had not yet been released. Even supposedly published data are often not readily available, and sometimes it took major efforts on our part to gather the results of the various surveys cited in this chapter.

Employment in the RNFS[5]

According to the Census for 1991, the non-farm sector employs 39.4 million rural main workers, which represents 17.7 per cent of all such workers. According to the NSS for 1987–8, 52.4 million rural workers are principally engaged in the non-farm sector, or 23.4 per cent of all principal status workers in rural India. Therefore, depending on the source, about 40 or 50 million workers are primarily employed in the rural non-farm sector in India. This represents between a sixth and a quarter of all rural workers in the country.

However, both the Census and NSS underestimate the extent of rural non-farm sector employment, for three reasons:[6]

5. For definitions of terms used, such as main and marginal workers, principal and subsidiary status, usual and daily status, see Box 2.1.
6. Anderson and Leiserson (1980: 228–32), Breman (1985: 201), Chambers (1988: 22–3), Haggblade *et al.* (1989: 1174–7), Harriss (1989: 160), Hazell and Haggblade (1990: 2–14), Lanjouw and Lanjouw (1995: 6–7), Sen (1994: 576, 579). Micro-level household surveys support these arguments; see Adams (1994), Bliss and Stern (1982), Klennert (1986), Shand (1987), and von Braun and Pandya-Lorch (1992).

(1) The Census and NSS classify people as rural only when they live in locations with less than 5000 population.[7] So workers in rural towns with more than 5000 people are classified as urban (unless they commute to work from rural settlements). Hazell and Haggblade (1990: 4) calculate that if the Census included towns with up to 100 000 population in the rural sector, then 24.3 per cent of rural workers, rather than 18.9 per cent (see note 9), were engaged in the rural non-farm sector in 1981.

(2) Surveys often classify women's work as unremunerative domestic duties, and do not therefore count them as part of the labour force. However, the NSS for 1987–8 (GoI, 1990: S-401) shows that the duties of many women classified as 'usually engaged in domestic duties' include work in kitchen gardens, animal husbandry, food processing, tailoring and education. The Census of India has come in for particular criticism for underestimating women's participation in the labour force (see note 15).

(3) Surveys like the Census and the NSS often fail to capture the true nature and dynamics of much rural employment. Many households, and individuals within households, are engaged in more than one gainful activity at any one time. Their employment patterns also change across different seasons of the year, and across different years. In particular, non-farm activities provide an important source of additional income for many agricultural households outside the peak agricultural seasons. Thus in any one year small farm households, for example, might be engaged in farming, livestock, weaving and construction labour. However, neither the marginal workers of the Census nor the subsidiary status workers of the NSS capture the secondary occupation of their main and principal status workers respectively.

As a result, the extent to which these surveys underestimate rural non-farm employment can be large. As we have seen, Hazell and Haggblade estimate that including rural towns raises the proportion of rural workers engaged in the RNFS by over 5 percentage points. The NSS itself shows that at least 5 million of the workers it classifies as agricultural workers under their principal 'usual' status are engaged in non-agricultural work according to their 'daily' status.[8] This increases the number of persons engaged in the RNFS by 10 per cent. So the proportion of non-farm workers in rural employment given by the 1991 Census (17.7 per cent) must be regarded as the lower limit. It is more likely to be around a quarter of all rural workers.

7. Population densities and even employment profiles are also considered when classifying locations as rural or urban.
8. The calculation is based on NSS data presented in Appendix 2, tables 1 and 2.

Table 2.1: Growth of rural employment (Census, 1981–91)

Category	*Activity*	*Rural main workers (RMWs) in 1981*	*in 1991*	*Annual growth rate %*
I	Cultivators	89 152 963	104 037 619	1.6
II	Agricultural labourers	52 658 046	69 506 105	2.8
III	Activities allied to agriculture	4 143 423	4 230 853	0.2
IV	Mining and quarrying	790 991	1 010 276	2.5
Va	Manufacturing (household)	5 367 827	4 759 598	−1.2
Vb	Manufacturing (non-household)	6 008 388	7 778 757	2.6
VI	Construction	1 786 756	2 251 611	2.3
VII	Trade and commerce	4 882 012	7 039 689	3.7
VIII	Transport, storage and communications	2 327 131	2 659 116	1.3
IX	Other services	8 267 011	12 777 420	4.5
I–IX	Total RMWs	174 979 850	216 053 544	2.1
IV–IX	Total RNFS workers	29 025 418	38 278 967	2.8

Note: Compiled from GoI, 1987a and 1992b. To allow comparisons between 1981 and 1991, Assam and Jammu and Kashmir have been excluded; these figures do not, therefore, tally with those in Table 2.2.

Growth of RNFS employment

Employment in the rural non-farm sector has been growing, not only in absolute terms, but also as a share of total rural employment. According to the NSS, the number of RNFS workers (principal status) grew at 5.0 per cent a year between 1977–8 and 1987–8 (Papola, 1992: 241), and the share of non-agricultural jobs in rural employment rose from 17.9 to 23.4 per cent. The non-farm sector in fact provided the majority of new jobs in rural India during the 1980s (Sen, 1994: 583). Employment in the rural non-farm sector also grew faster than in the urban sector (Chadha, 1993b: 302).

According to the Census (Table 2.1), the number of workers in the RNFS grew at an annual rate of 2.8 per cent during the period 1981–91.[9] This

9. The share of RNFS jobs in rural employment thus rose from 16.6 per cent in 1981 to 17.7 per cent in 1991 (note that our figure for 1981 differs from that of Hazell and Haggblade given on p. 27). The divergence in RNFS growth rates between Census and NSS goes beyond definitional differences. The Census probably underestimates the growth rate (Sen, 1994: 579), while the 1987–8 drought (see note 12) may have increased the NSS growth rate a little, although for the period 1978–83 (principal-status) RNFS employment was already growing at 3.9 per cent a year.

Table 2.2: Distribution of rural main workers in 1991 (Census)

Category	*Activity*	*Total rural main workers (RMWs)*	*As % of total RMWs*	*As % of RMWs in the RNFS*
I	Cultivators	107 568 463	48.4	-
II	Agricultural labourers	70 338 340	31.6	-
III	Activities allied to agriculture	4 940 998	2.2	-
IV	Mining and quarrying	1 039 269	0.5	2.6
Va	Manufacturing (household)	4 810 074	2.2	12.2
Vb	Manufacturing (non-household)	7 903 477	3.6	20.0
VI	Construction	2 318 397	1.0	5.9
VII	Trade and commerce	7 301 392	3.3	18.5
VIII	Transport, storage and communications	2 747 204	1.2	7.0
IX	Other services	13 321 965	6.0	33.8
I–IX	Total RMWs	222 289 579	100.0	-
IV–IX	Total RNFS workers	39 441 778	17.7	100.0

Source: GoI, 1992b: 126–7.

compares to 1.6 per cent among cultivators, and 2.8 per cent among agricultural labourers, the same rate as in the RNFS. These data suggest that, with the declining capacity of agriculture to support additional cultivators, the growing rural labour force can be absorbed either as agricultural labourers or as RNFS workers (see Table 2.18, p. 52). The latter option is clearly preferable. Moreover, in some states such as Andhra Pradesh and Tamil Nadu, agricultural labour already accounts for more than 40 per cent of all rural employment.

RNFS employment by industrial categories and sub-sectors

The rural non-farm sector is diverse and heterogeneous, including primary, secondary and tertiary activities (Table 2.2). Manufacturing accounts for a third of all RNFS jobs, while services account for about 60 per cent. The remainder are in construction, and in mining and quarrying. The largest of the seven industrial categories into which the Census divides RNFS employment are therefore 'other services' (a third of RNFS employment), 'non-household manufacturing' (a fifth) and 'trade and commerce' (just under a fifth).

More than 80 per cent of all rural non-farm sector employment is in fact

Table 2.3: High employment-share sub-sectors in the RNFS (Census, 1981)

NIC code	*Description*	*Rural main workers*	*% of RNFS employment*
65	Retail trade in food, beverages and tobacco	2 636 537	8.8
92	Educational services	2 410 555	8.1
90	Public administration and defence	2 145 762	7.2
96	Personal services	1 910 460	6.4
50	Construction	1 723 151	5.8
27	Wood, wood products, furniture and fixtures	1 585 702	5.3
70	Land transport	1 542 536	5.2
23	Cotton textiles	1 532 897	5.1
26	Textile products	1 378 665	4.6
32	Non-metallic mineral products	1 302 119	4.4
20–21	Food products	1 226 249	4.1
22	Beverages, tobacco and tobacco products	1 180 233	4.0
39	Repairs	1 013 494	3.4
99	Miscellaneous services	835 366	2.8
69	Restaurants and hotels	612 445	2.1
93	Medical and health services	609 640	2.0
34	Metal products and parts	511 336	1.7
	Total	24 157 147	81.0

Source: Table 2.3 is derived from the 1981 Census (GoI, 1987a: Table B12), since disaggregated data were not yet available from the 1991 Census. The equivalent list from the NSS for 1987–8 (Appendix 2, Table 3) is remarkably similar, strongly confirming the broad picture given by the Census.

generated by 17 sub-sectors within these broad industrial categories (Table 2.3).[10] Each of these 17 sub-sectors generates more than half a million rural jobs, or (with the exception of the last) more than 2 per cent of total RNFS employment, and we designate these 17 sub-sectors as the high employment-share sub-sectors.

10. As explained pp. 16–17, we use either the major (two-digit) groups or the minor (three-digit) groups in the National Industrial Classification (NIC) as rough proxies for sub-sectors.

The list of high-share sub-sectors makes clear that substantial employment in rural areas is found within the public sector. We estimate that a fifth of all RNFS employment is generated by public-sector services (Appendix 2, Table 4), primarily in public administration and education. The role of the national and state governments in employing rural workers directly is significant (Sen, 1994).

Over half of all manufacturing jobs in India are in rural areas (Papola, 1992: 242). However, many of the high-share sub-sectors in rural manufacturing are traditional sub-sectors: cotton textiles (especially handlooms), textile products and wood products. Likewise pottery, grain milling and *bidi*-rolling are prominent.[11] Many of these activities are household based (Mathur and Pani, 1993: 334), and their ability to absorb workers is declining. They have, therefore, little capacity to create more productive jobs.

However, most of these industrial groups also include dynamic modern manufacturing activities, such as powerlooms, modern garments, furniture, ceramics and agro-processing, many of which are also making a large contribution to India's exports. In 1993–4, for example, the three largest export items were products in which the RNFS had a substantial share: textile fabrics and manufactures, leather and leather products, and handicrafts, including gems and jewellery and hand-made carpets. Together these products accounted for over 40 per cent of India's total exports, compared to only about 25 per cent from the industrial sector. To get a better perspective on these dynamic components of the RNFS, we use the growth rate of employment as the second criterion to identify prominent sub-sectors.

Growth of employment in RNFS sub-sectors

From 1981 to 1991, other services (see note 3), trade and commerce, and manufacturing outside the household generated the largest number of new jobs in the RNFS: 4.5 million, 2.2 million and 1.8 million respectively (Table 2.1). While the equivalent NSS data for 1977–8 to 1987–8 differs significantly from the Census (see Appendix 2, Table 5), it confirms that manufacturing (4.4 million new jobs), trade and commerce (2.8 million) and other services (2.8 million) were the largest contributors to new rural jobs (principal status), apart from construction. However, rural employment in construction in 1987–8 was high because of the drought in that year.[12]

Many of the 'other services' jobs are in public administration, educational and medical services. Employment in public administration also grew at a high rate between 1977–8 and 1987–8 (Table 2.4). This confirms that the

11. These are the primary activities in the following major groups: non-metallic mineral products, food products, and beverages and tobacco respectively.
12. The drought reduced the growth rate of agricultural employment derived from the NSS (1983–8) to zero, and also significantly reduced the rates for rural employment in manufacturing, transport and services. Some of the surplus labour, however, was absorbed in construction (including of public works), which employed 8.4 million rural workers (principal status) in 1987–8, compared to 4.0 million in 1983.

public sector is important, contributing significantly to the high growth rate of rural jobs in 'other services'. Sen (1994: 585) suggests that between 1977–8 and 1987–8 the public sector provided a fifth of all new jobs in the RNFS.

The large number of new jobs generated by rural manufacturing outside the household is encouraging (Table 2.1). In terms of numbers, it more than compensates for the job losses in household manufacturing. The figures mask a severe social transformation, however. In many cases the workers who could no longer earn a livelihood from household industry would not have been the same as those who found jobs in manufacturing outside the household. Moreover, labour conditions in a number of manufacturing activities outside the household, such as carpet-weaving and *bidi*-rolling, are very poor.

Table 2.4: High employment-growth sub-sectors (1977–8 to 1987–8) (NIC major groups in NSS)

NIC code	*Description*	*Estimated jobs in 1977–8 (000s)*	*Estimated jobs in 1987–8 (000s)*	*Annual growth rate (%)*
36	Electrical equipment	37	239	20.6
51	Activities allied to construction	54	239	16.0
50	Construction	2732	7653	10.9
28	Paper and paper products	94	239	9.8
31	Chemicals and chemical products	195	478	9.4
95	Recreational and cultural services	106	239	8.5
70	Land transport	1488	2870	6.8
82–3	Real estate, business and legal services	127	239	6.5
99	Miscellaneous services	262	478	6.2
60	Wholesale trade in food, animals, textiles and beverages	267	478	6.0
40–2	Electricity, gas and water	272	478	5.8
25	Jute, hemp and *mesta* products	137	239	5.8
90	Public administration and defence	1958	3348	5.5
66	Retail trade in textiles	287	478	5.2
1	Mining and quarrying	883	1435	5.0

Note: Because of the sources, the figures include both principal and subsidiary workers; see GoI, 1981: Table 14 and 1990: Table 57.

In 15 RNFS sub-sectors within the broad industrial categories employment grew at an annual rate of 5 per cent or more between 1977–8 and 1987–8. We therefore designate these sub-sectors as high-growth sub-sectors.[13] They are represented in Table 2.4 by major (two-digit) groups of the National Industrial Classification (NIC), which serve as rough proxies for sub-sectors.

Of these 15 high-growth sub-sectors, only four started from a significant employment base in 1977–8. Construction added 4.9 million new jobs over the decade (once again, exaggerated by the drought in 1987–8), public administration and land transport 1.4 million each, and mining 0.6 million. Since all four of these sub-sectors are already high-share sub-sectors

Table 2.5: High employment-growth sub-sectors (1977–8 to 1987–8) (NIC minor groups in NSS)

NIC code	*Description*	*Annual growth rate (%)*
703	Freight transport by motor vehicles	15.2
262	Embroidery	14.6
236	Powerlooms	13.9
702	Passenger transport (excluding buses and trams)	13.7
973	Repair of motor vehicles and motorcycles	13.2
691	Hotels, rooming houses and other lodging places	12.9
501	Construction and maintenance of roads, railways, ports, etc.	12.9
209	Manufacture of cocoa, chocolate and confectionery	12.2
330	Iron and steel	12.1
800	Banking	12.1
500	Construction and maintenance of buildings	10.7
601	Wholesale trade in foodstuffs other than cereals and pulses	10.2
245	Spinning, weaving and finishing silk textiles	9.5
276	Wooden furniture and fixtures	9.0
503	Construction of dams, canals, tanks, wells, etc.	8.9
223	Production of country liquor and toddy	8.3
653	Retail trade in bakery, dairy, eggs and sweetmeats	8.2

Source: Papola (1992: 243).

13. For this data we rely on the NSS, as the relevant 1991 Census data was not available (see Box 2.1).

(according to the NSS; Appendix 2, Table 3), they are clearly important activities for rural employment.

All the other sub-sectors started from a low base of less than 300 000 jobs in 1977–8. Nevertheless, the data indicate the growing importance for rural employment of some modern manufacturing activities, for example of electrical equipment and paper products. They also point again to the new rural jobs generated in the service sub-sectors, in wholesale and retail trade, in the utilities, in real estate, business and legal services, and in recreational and miscellaneous services.

However, the NIC major (two-digit) groups are only rough proxies for sub-sectors, concealing large variations among different activities in the same group. For example, within the cotton textiles major group, employment in powerlooms is booming, while that in handlooms is stagnant (Papola, 1992: 244). The growth rates in the more disaggregated minor (three-digit) groups thus provide further insights into the growth of RNFS employment (Table 2.5).

The importance of construction, transport, trade, and services like hotels, restaurants and banking is again apparent even at this more disaggregated level. Table 2.5 also points to the more dynamic activities within traditional manufacturing sub-sectors, such as powerlooms, embroidery and silk textiles, wooden furniture and fixtures, and manufacture of confectionery.

Emergent RNFS sub-sectors

There are many sub-sectors which show promise for generating rural non-farm employment in the future, but which do not yet employ many rural workers or may not be growing fast in terms of rural employment (at least according to available data). We call these 'emergent' sub-sectors. Because they are not reflected in past statistical data, we identified them during field visits and in discussion with local officials and organizations working close to the field. Some examples are given in Box 2.2, a number of which have already appeared as high-share or high-growth sub-sectors above. This is because the emergent sub-sectors were identified for particular states, regions or localities. As a result, a sub-sector which is already prominent at the aggregate national level may only be just emerging in certain parts of the country.

Female employment, child labour and educational levels in the RNFS[14]

In 1987–8 only 24.5 per cent of rural women worked in the labour force (as principal status workers,) compared to 51.7 per cent of men (NSS). Many more women in rural India, however, engage in casual and part-time work, concentrated in the agricultural-labour sector in particular. The evidence for this is substantial:

14. For definitions of principal, subsidiary and current daily status, see Box 2.1. For the sources of Census and NSS data, see GoI (1987a, 1990 and 1992b).

Box 2.2: Some emergent sub-sectors in the RNFS in India

- Oilseed processing
- Herbal products and phytochemicals
- Prawn processing
- Fruit and vegetable processing
- Spice processing
- Poultry processing
- Sericulture
- Textile garments (cotton hosiery, woollen knitwear)
- Leather footwear and other products
- Repairs
- Stone quarrying and polishing
- Cutting and polishing precious and semi-precious stones
- Ceramics and glassware
- Structural metal products
- Cement-ware and building materials
- Plastic products
- Agro-services
- Restaurants and hotels
- Rural tourism
- Business services

- Among female workers (principal status), 40.2 per cent are casual labourers, compared to only 32.1 per cent of males, and only 4.9 per cent of women enjoy regular employment, compared to 10.4 per cent of men (NSS).
- The work participation rate for women rises to 32.3 per cent when subsidiary-status workers are included. Over 90 per cent of the 22 million female subsidiary workers are engaged in agriculture (NSS).
- Of all rural marginal workers, 91.5 per cent are women (1991 Census), and most of these marginal workers are agricultural labourers. Of the marginal workers in the RNFS 74.7 per cent are women (1981 Census).
- Unemployment rates among women are higher than among men (Appendix 2, Table 6), especially when measured by current daily status, suggesting that many women are seeking casual employment on a daily basis rather than regular employment.

This evidence suggests that the rural non-farm sector may be even more important to improving employment among women, in particular by drawing them away from agricultural labour, the lowest paid of all rural occupations (see Table 2.9 below).

According to the NSS, 17.4 per cent of rural female workers (principal status) were engaged in the non-farm sector, and 23.3 per cent of RNFS workers were women.[15] Within the RNFS, manufacturing, 'other services'

15. The figures from the 1991 Census are much lower (Appendix 2, Table 8). However, the Census has been criticized for underestimating female work-participation rates, and for classifying women's work too readily as agricultural labour (Hazell and Haggblade, 1990: 10–12; Sen, 1994: 576, 579). On the other hand the NSS for 1987–8 may exaggerate the number of female jobs in construction because of the drought (see note 12).

(see note 3) and trade generate the most jobs for women (Appendix 2, Tables 7 and 8). Almost half of female employment in manufacturing is outside the household. The most important manufacturing sub-sectors are tobacco products (largely *bidi*), cotton textiles, wood products and non-metallic mineral products (largely pottery), which together generate more than a third of all female employment in the rural non-farm sector (Table 2.6).

Table 2.6: High employment-share sub-sectors for rural women in the RNFS (Census 1981).

NIC code	*Description*	*Number of female RMWs*	*Percentage of female RMWs*
96	Personal services	819 879	17.2
22	Beverages, tobacco and tobacco products	633 521	13.3
23	Cotton textiles	409 857	8.6
92	Educational services	395 740	8.3
27	Wood and wood products	310 821	6.5
32	Non-metallic mineral products	279 121	5.9
65	Retail trade in food, beverages and tobacco	272 965	5.7
50	Construction	221 479	4.6
26	Textile products	207 651	4.4
20–21	Food products	198 268	4.2
99	Miscellaneous services	136 470	2.9
93	Medical and health services	122 597	2.6
39	Repairs	118 898	2.5
19	Other mining (not coal, oil, gas or metal ore)	72 511	1.5
69	Restaurants and hotels	59 660	1.3
90	Public administration and defence	58 243	1.2
67	Retail trade in fuel, household utilities and durables	53 959	1.1
31	Chemicals and chemical products	47 136	1.0
(20–59)	Total of secondary sub-sectors given above	2 426 752	50.9
(10–99)	Total rural non-farm sector	4 769 293	100.0

Source: GoI, 1987a: Table B12.

Within 'other services', the public sector does not loom as large in women's employment as it does for men (Appendix 2, Table 4). Women thus make up less than 10 per cent of the rural workforce in public-sector services. Instead, personal services, such as domestic and laundry services, provide most female employment in the 'other services' category.

Unfortunately, the Census and NSS provide very different views of the growth of rural female employment (Table 2.7). The high growth, according to the NSS, of (casual) employment in construction and mining may have resulted from the drought in 1987–8 (see note 12). In effect, these activities were acting as a safety net when there was little demand for agricultural labour. The Census, on the other hand, suggests that 'other services' were the fastest growing segment of the RNFS for female employment, and that female employment in agriculture actually grew faster than in the RNFS. This perhaps reflects a trend of women entering the agricultural labour force to replace men who have found more remunerative employment in the RNFS. However, such conclusions must remain tentative, especially as the Census is notoriously poor at classifying women's employment (note 15). The Census and the NSS do, however,

Table 2.7: Growth rates of female rural employment

Industrial category	*Annual growth rate of female rural main workers (%): Census, 1981–91*	*Annual growth rate of female principal and subsidiary workers (%): NSS, 1977–8 to 1987–8*
Agriculture:		0.9
Cultivators	3.8	–
Labourers	3.1	–
Allied activities	2.0	–
Mining	2.7	8.6
Manufacturing:		2.9
household	0.7	–
non-household	4.4	–
Construction	−4.0	17.7
Trade	3.1	1.8
Transport	−20.5	1.3
Other services	5.3	1.3
Total workers	3.3	1.3
Total RNFS workers	3.0	3.9

Sources: GoI, 1987a: Table B3; 1992b: Table 4; 1981: Table 14; 1990: Table 57.

agree that the growth of female employment in manufacturing, especially outside the household, was significant.

The proportion of children below the age of 15 in the labour force is lower in the non-farm sector than in the agricultural sector, for both boys and girls (Appendix 2, Table 9). It is, however, especially so for boys, suggesting that male children enter the non-farm sector at a later age, presumably because they need more education and skills to work in the RNFS.

Between 20 and 30 per cent of all rural women engaged in manufacturing, construction and mining were below the age of 20. In manufacturing and construction, over 10 per cent of the female labour force were below the age of 15. Child labour among girls is therefore an important issue, including in the non-farm sector.[16]

Education is an important preparation, or even precondition, for rural workers to enter the RNFS. As a result the educational attainment of workers in the RNFS is higher than in the agricultural sector (Appendix 2, tables 10 and 11). According to the 1981 Census, 69.4 per cent of female workers in the RNFS were illiterate, compared to 90.6 per cent in the farm sector; among males 30.8 of RNFS workers were illiterate compared to 63.6 per cent in the farm sector. Educational levels are also higher for manufacturing outside the household rather than within, suggesting that formal learning assists mobility into non-household industry, including for women. In mining and construction, however, the extent of illiteracy among female workers is even greater (at 94.9 and 92.1 per cent respectively) than in the farm sector, which again raises concerns about the quality of casual labour in these activities.

The picture of female rural employment that emerges from the analysis above is mixed. Much of female rural labour is part-time and casual, concentrated in the agricultural labour sector. In 1987–8 there may have been a major shift of female workers into casual labour in construction and mining, which often involve poor working conditions, a lot of child labour, low levels of education and a high incidence of poverty (Sen, 1994: 587). However, such casual labour may have been a vital source of income during a drought when there was little demand for agricultural labour. In some cases rural women seem to be entering the workforce as labourers to replace male workers who are finding more remunerative RNFS employment.

On the other hand, the Census data suggest that female employment in 'other services' and trading is growing fast. They point also to the importance for rural women of the secondary sector, which generates more than half of all female employment in the RNFS (see Table 2.6), much more

16. It is also important for boys. According to the 1981 Census, 58.4 per cent of all rural child workers, in both agricultural and non-farm activities, were boys.

Table 2.8: Daily wage earnings of regular employees (NSS, 1987–8)

Industry category	*Wage earnings in Rs/day*	
	Male	*Female*
Agriculture	14.58	10.65
Mining and quarrying	38.70	23.81
Manufacturing (household)	22.77	9.42
Manufacturing (non-household)	28.69	13.78
Electricity, gas and water	36.16	45.17
Construction	31.58	18.27
Trade and commerce	17.99	18.42
Transport, storage and communications	32.08	26.80
Financial and business services	46.25	38.75
Social and Personal Services	38.54	28.39

Source: GoI, 1990: Table 79.

Table 2.9: Daily wage earnings of casual labourers (NSS, 1987–8)

Activity	*Wage earnings in RS/day*	
	Male	*Female*
Manual work in agriculture	10.73	7.11
Manual work in other cultivation	12.93	9.17
Non-manual work in agriculture	12.31	7.91
Average for agricultural work	11.09	7.32
Manual work in non-agriculture	15.45	8.76
Non-manual work in non-agriculture	15.54	9.12
Average for non-agricultural work	15.48	8.86

Source: GoI, 1990: Table 81 (R).

than for men. Services, in contrast, including in the public sector, are less important for women than for men; moreover, manufacturing employment for rural women continues to grow. In fact manufacturing outside the household is expanding much faster than household manufacturing, shifting women away from being family workers to more highly paid work (Table 2.8) as self-employed single workers, or even employees.

Incomes in the RNFS

Casual labourers earn higher wages in non-agricultural activities than in agriculture (Table 2.9). For male labourers wages are 40 per cent higher; for females the difference is just over 20 per cent.

Papola (1992: 239) calculated that the earnings of regular workers in the non-agricultural sector were 2.4 times higher than that of agricultural workers (see Table 2.8). However, these figures need to be treated with caution. According to the NSS, only 10 per cent of male rural workers, and 5 per cent of female workers, were regularly employed (GoI, 1990: 94–5).

The differences in income between farm and non-farm activities have in fact been increasing (Bhalla, 1994:611–12):

> Per capita incomes in agriculture, during the 40 years from 1950–51 to 1990–91, grew at a compound rate of less than one half of one per cent per year, while per capita incomes in non-agricultural activities grew at the rate of 2.8 per cent compound.

The higher earnings enjoyed by non-farm workers suggest that the RNFS is not just a residual category absorbing excess labour from the agricultural sector (often termed 'distress diversification' or 'the residual-sector hypothesis'). If that were the case, one would expect wages in the non-farm sector to be no higher than in agriculture. But even manual labourers in the RNFS earn more than non-manual labourers in agriculture.

However, there is a lively debate within India around this issue.[17] Recent contributions again suggest that we need to distinguish more carefully among different parts of the heterogeneous non-farm sector. For example, Bhalla (1994: 613–14) argues that poverty (using a variety of measures) is highest among households depending on agriculture, mining and construction; these are also the three activities in which casual labour is most concentrated, so casual labour in agriculture, construction and mining may be acting as a sponge for absorbing workers who cannot find self-employment in agriculture. Some services, such as retail trading, personal and miscellaneous services, in which wages are not much higher than in agriculture, may also be performing this function.

However, other activities, such as manufacturing (outside the household), transport and many other services, are much more remunerative and clearly cannot be regarded as residual categories for absorbing excess labour. Instead they belong to the productive and dynamic part of the rural non-farm sector. On average, wages in the RNFS are therefore significantly higher than in the agricultural sector, and this suggests that the shift from agriculture to non-agricultural activities is more 'demand-induced' than 'simply a fall-out of the inability of agriculture to hold any more workers'.[18] Indeed, even fears about the casualization of the rural workforce may be exaggerated, granted that the major shift in rural employment is from self-employment in agriculture to higher-paid casual work in non-agricultural activities (Papola, 1992: 239–40).

With higher wages in the non-farm sector, it is not surprising that rural

---

17. See, for example, Bhalla (1994), Sen (1994) and Vaidyanathan (1986, 1994), who give many more references.
18. The fact that real wages in agriculture have been increasing significantly also makes the residual hypothesis difficult (Sen, 1994: 588; Vaidyanathan, 1994: 3151).

Table 2.10: Households by land cultivated and RNFS work (NSS, 1987–8)

Households grouped by land cultivated (in hectares)	*Person-days allocated to RNFS by working persons in households (%)*
0.00	45.9
0.01–0.20	33.3
0.21–0.40	25.4
0.41–1.00	19.1
0.01–1.00	24.1
1.01–2.00	*14.0*
2.01–3.00	12.4
3.01–4.00	10.9
2.01–4.00	*11.8*
4.01–6.00	9.1
6.01–8.00	8.9
8.01 & above	8.5
4.01 & above	*9.0*
All	*25.7*

Source: GoI, 1990: Tables 49(R) and 64(R).

households rely more on their non-farm income than the employment data would suggest. Hazell and Haggblade (1990: 3) conclude (from NCAER data) that *the non-farm sector 'normally contributes 25–35 per cent of total income [of rural households] in contrast with its 20–25 per cent share of employment*. The higher income than employment share implies either greater returns to labour in non-farm activity or considerable part-time and seasonal non-farm pursuits uncaptured in the employment statistics' (emphasis added). We suspect both are involved.

The importance of non-farm income to rural households is also growing. Walker and Ryan (1990: 65), also using NCAER data, suggest that:

> Non-agricultural income loomed larger in 1981–82 [than in 1970–71], rising from 20 to 27 per cent of total income; the share of agricultural income fell from 60 to 53 per cent. Seventy per cent of the increase in real household income between the two periods was attributed to the rise in non-agricultural income.

Non-agricultural employment is particularly important for households with little land, and for the landless, who spend between a fifth and a half of their working days on non-farm activities (Table 2.10). The percentage of days spent on non-farm activities in fact rises consistently as the size of landholdings declines. Moreover, part of the rural non-farm sector provides an important employment safety net for poor households in times of agricultural distress (see note 12).

Thus, in a detailed study,[19] Datt and Ravallion (1996: 20) conclude that growth of (real) per capita non-agricultural output can have a large quantitative impact on poverty, if such growth exceeds its usual trend. This suggests that policies that boost rural non-farm employment could have a significant impact in reducing rural poverty.

Rising incomes from non-farm activities may, however, increase income inequalities. Chadha (1993b), Sen (1994) and Thorat (1993) discover, using NSS data, that better-off or landed groups benefit more from the shift out of agriculture than poorer groups, such as the landless or marginal farmers. Non-farm activities also increase gender disparities in earnings (Table 2.9). Among casual labourers, women in agriculture earn 34 per cent less than men, while women in non-agricultural activities earn 43 per cent less. Similar disparities are also found among regular employees (Table 2.8). However, these wage differentials may reflect the underlying gender biases in educational achievement, as male workers have enjoyed more education than their female counterparts.

Non-farm activities therefore enhance incomes, and earnings from such activities are becoming increasingly important to a wide range of rural households. This is an indication of development, not of a sector that acts as a sponge for excess labour agriculture. Parts of the non-farm sector, however, such as labour in construction, mining and some services, do appear to be playing the latter role; moreover, work in the RNFS heightens income inequalities. It remains, nevertheless, a vital source of employment for small and marginal farmers, as well as the landless, and acts as a safety net for poor households in times of agricultural distress. Indeed, long-term data suggest that the rural non-farm sector can contribute significantly to the reduction of poverty.

Enterprises in the RNFS: numbers and size

Enterprises in the rural non-farm sector in India number in the millions, although most are tiny. According to the Economic Census of 1990 (GoI, 1995b), there are 12.6 million such undertakings, employing 29.1 million people, so, on average, each provides work to only 2.3 persons (1.8 males and 0.5 females). Eighty-one per cent of the enterprises run without power, and 18 per cent even without premises. The typical rural undertaking has two people, of whom one is hired, eking out a living with very limited capital investment and without any electricity. Examples are a paddy-

19. Based on evidence from the 15 major Indian states from 1957 to 1991, using net state domestic product (to measure non-agricultural output), and mean consumption per rural person, headcount and poverty-gap indices.

parboiling unit, a cotton handloom, a pottery for earthen utensils, a village shoe-making unit, a small grocery shop, a camel cart, a tea shop or a bicycle-repair shop under a tree. Over three-quarters of the enterprises operate year round, serving as an important alternative or additional source of income to agriculture throughout the year.

Of the 12.6 million units, 39 per cent were in trading and commerce, 28 per cent in 'other services' (see note 3), and 27 per cent in manufacturing. Trade and commerce enterprises were smaller, however, and so employed only a quarter of the total workforce in these units, while manufacturing employed over a third, 'other services' just under a third (GoI, 1995b: Tables 4.2 and 4.8). This broadly confirms our analysis of employment data above.

Surveys focusing specifically on manufacturing enterprises confirm that the vast majority (14.5 million)[20] employ on average only 1.7 persons (Table 2.11). Granted that many operate without power, these undertakings are clearly using simple manual technologies, often to manufacture traditional artisanal products, and generate only a minimal surplus for their workers (Appendix 2, Table 12). However, 86 per cent of the jobs in these 14.5 million enterprises are full-time, and only 12 per cent of own-account enterprises in manufacturing are seasonal (GoI, 1995b: Table 4.4). In short, most provide a full-time occupation throughout the year, not just a little work supplementary to agriculture.

While most manufacturing enterprises in the rural non-farm sector are tiny, some are not (Figure 2.1 and Table 2.11).[21] About two million workers are employed in larger undertakings (rural directory manufacturing establishments, DMEs) and another two million in rural factories.

It is clear that the latter are in a class of their own (Table 2.12). Wages in factories are of course higher than in smaller units, but factories fare poorly in comparison with smaller units (DMEs and SSIs) in terms of the ratios of output and net value added to fixed capital, suggesting that they are not as efficient in their use of capital. The DMEs, on the other hand, are of particular interest. In employing on average 11 workers each they demonstrate some business success. They could also be targeted for promotional inputs more easily than the 14.5 million smaller manufacturing units. The financial data for DMEs given in Table 2.12 probably strongly underestimate their performance (see note to Table).

The census of SSIs (see Appendix 2, Table 14) confirms our earlier analysis that manufacturing jobs are concentrated in traditional sub-sectors, such as pottery, wood and food (although the last also includes modern processed items). However, modern manufactured products are

---

20. Many more than enumerated by the Economic Census (see Table 2.11).
21. Indeed, the predominance of small enterprises may be exaggerated, as many of the relatively larger RNFS enterprises are located in rural towns (which are classified as urban if they have more than 5000 residents).

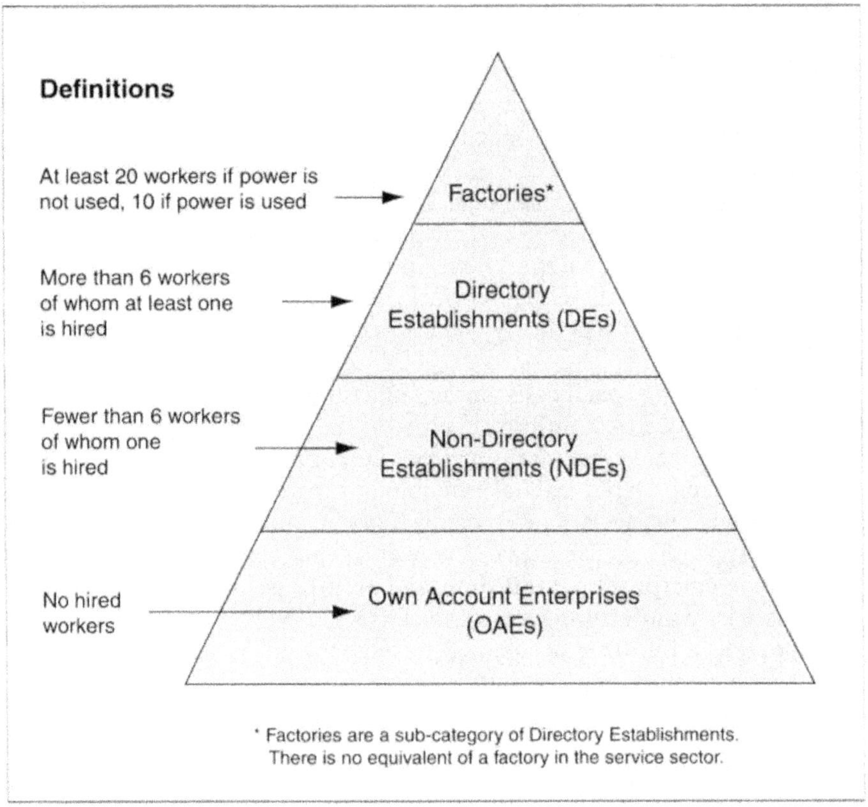

Figure 2.1: Scalar distribution of RNFS units by employment

emerging, including chemical, paper, metal and plastic products, as well as machinery and repairs. These industries have higher fixed investments and consume more energy than traditional manufacturing. With more advanced technologies they can also add more value per worker and so pay higher wages. However, because they use more capital, the number of jobs generated from Rs100 000 of investment is, in many instances, lower.

The data on manufacturing enterprises and on SSIs seem to suggest the traditional trade-off between capital- and labour-intensive enterprises. Many would still argue that the activities which require less capital to generate jobs, even at low wages, are more appropriate to a poor country with a large number of unemployed or underemployed workers. The evidence on these issues is, however, far from conclusive. Reviewing the literature, Uribe-Echevarria (1992: 11–14) states:

Table 2.11: Scalar distribution of RNFS units by employment

Scale category	*Number of units*	*Number of workers (millions)*	*Workers per unit*	*Sources*
Factory	27 073	1.9	71.7	*Annual Survey of Industries, 1987–8* (GoI, 1991a)
DMEs	179 202	2.0	11.1	*Directory Manufacturing Establishments Survey, 1984–5* (GoI, nd: d)
NDMEs and OAEs	14.5 million	24.3	1.7	*Unorganised Manufacturing Survey, 1984–5* (GoI, 1989a)
Rural enterprises (including services)	12.8 million	27.7	2.2	*Economic Census of Enterprises, 1990* (GoI, 1995b)

Table 2.12: Factories, DMEs and SSIs compared

Parameter	*Factory*	*DME*	*SSI*
Fixed capital/unit (Rs000s)	6 640	29	160
Output/unit (Rs000s)	13 068	113	738
NVA/unit (Rs000s)	2 136	35	176
NVA/person engaged (Rs)	29 784	3 119	27 990
Emoluments/person engaged (Rs)	12 515	1 540	6 270
Capital to labour ratio (Rs)	92 573	2 768	25 437
Output to capital ratio	2.0	3.7	4.6
NVA to capital ratio	0.3	1.2	1.1

Note: Financial data in this Table and in Appendix 2, Tables 12 to 14 must be treated with caution. Many figures reflect significant under-reporting. The surveys are old, and some figures would increase dramatically if adjustments for inflation were made. The output and value added per worker would also increase if the number of full-time equivalent jobs were used rather than the number of workers. The survey of factories and the census of SSIs provide, perhaps, more realistic data, because they are more detailed studies conducted for a smaller number of units. The comparison between DMEs and SSIs suggests, therefore, that the figures for the former are understated. For sources, see Table 2.11 and GoI (1992c).

- while small units may generate more direct employment for a given investment in capital, their total employment creation (including jobs generated indirectly) may not be more than for larger units;
- the quality of the employment generated by smaller units may be much poorer; and
- small enterprises are often inefficient users of capital: 'traditional small-scale units use more labour per unit of product but they do not always use less capital per unit of product'.

Little *et al.* (1987: 313), surveying five of the country's industries (shoes, printing, soap, machine tools and metal casting), as well as those in other countries, did not find any clear link between the size of units and their capital and labour productivity:

> There is considerable evidence that many small enterprises, with less than 10 workers, are often not the most labour-intensive and their capital productivity and technical efficiency are very rarely the highest in the whole size range of establishments in the industry. When measured by employment size, firms in the medium-size range of 50–200 workers have the highest capital productivity, and total factor productivity, in most industries in all the countries examined.[22]

The growth of modern compared to traditional manufacturing is confirmed by the available aggregate output data on a few manufacturing sub-sectors in the RNFS (Table 2.13). Production of cotton and woollen *khadi* is barely keeping pace with the rate of inflation, and handloom production is falling behind in real terms. In contrast, the production of handicrafts (especially carpets, and gems and jewellery), and above all of powerloom products, is surging ahead. These products also make a substantial contribution to India's exports. As mentioned above, textile fabrics and manufactures, leather and leather products, and handicrafts accounted for over 40 per cent of total exports in 1993–4. *Khadi* products of silk are also doing better than cotton and woollens. These dynamics are being driven by demand trends, and are reflected in the different rates of employment growth in these activities (see Papola, 1992: 244).

Some inter-state comparisons

Our study was conducted in eight states: Gujarat and Rajasthan in the east, Punjab and Uttar Pradesh in the north, Assam and Orissa in the east, and Andhra Pradesh and Tamil Nadu in the south. The rural non-farm sector in

22. Although they suggest that if enterprises are categorized according to capital used, smaller firms may fare better. However, the Second SSI Census (GoI, 1992c: T-5) does not reveal such a trend in the ratio of net value added to fixed capital, for example, as fixed investment rises.

Table 2.13: Aggregate output of some RNFS sub-sectors

Product or activity	*Output in Rs crores*		*Compound annual growth rate (%)*
	1987–8	*1994–5*	
Khadi	228	390	8.0
Handlooms	3 200	7 234	12.4
Village industries	1 261	3 234	14.4
Sericulture	346	1 276	20.5
Handicrafts	5 350	21 455	22.0
Coir	145	685	24.8
Powerlooms	3 670	293 990	87.1

Source: SIDBI (1996: Table 1).

each of these states is very different (see Appendix 3 for details). However, the eight states fall into two broad groups: the RNFS is more developed in Punjab, Tamil Nadu and Gujarat, and less so in Assam, Orissa, Andhra Pradesh, Rajasthan and Uttar Pradesh.

In Punjab, which has the highest share of RNFS employment among the eight states, agricultural development has clearly contributed to the growth of non-farm employment, especially in the tertiary sector, for example in transport and professional services. Gujarat has also undergone a significant transformation of its rural economy, but through the extensive and rapid growth of rural manufacturing. Tamil Nadu, too, has a large rural manufacturing sector, although it is not growing as fast as in Gujarat, and the state shows some symptoms of rural distress, for example, a stagnant agricultural sector and high unemployment rates.

The five other states show signs of significant rural distress. For example, in Andhra Pradesh agricultural labourers make up almost half the rural workforce. Growth in rural non-farm employment in these states is more dependent on labour in mining and construction (e.g. in Rajasthan), on traditional manufacturing and on public-sector employment (especially in Orissa), and on less remunerative services (e.g. in Uttar Pradesh). However, there are examples of more productive growth, for example in transport (in Assam), in rural tourism (in Uttar Pradesh), and in the coastal districts of Andhra Pradesh. The reliance of these states on their primary economies suggests that the processing of primary products is one of the most promising avenues to develop their non-farm sectors.

The differences in RNFS employment in these eight states correlate also with various other economic and social indicators, suggesting that the

RNFS itself may contribute significantly to overall development (although the correlations do not of course prove such causality). For example, the three states in which the greatest proportion of the rural labour force is engaged in the non-farm sector also have high state domestic products (NSDP) per capita (Table 2.14). Employment in the secondary sector is more extensive in these states, and they have relatively modern manufacturing industries, judged by the proportion of manufacturing jobs which are outside the household. Tamil Nadu, however, still retains a large household manufacturing sector.

Punjab, Tamil Nadu and Gujarat are also the most urbanized, and generally have higher population densities (Table 2.14).[23] Hazell and Haggblade (1990: 19, 27) suggest that rural towns are particularly important for the development of the rural non-farm sector, as many RNFS jobs are found in these locations. As a result, the pattern of urbanization in these leading states may be dispersed, rather than concentrated in a few large urban centres. This would also provide a higher population density in rural areas, which 'may reduce the geographic catchment area necessary [for rural enterprises] to achieve minimum efficient scales of production, reduce transport costs and thereby improve prospects' for the growth of the rural non-farm sector (see also Papola, 1992: 244–5).

Granted the extensive work on the links between the development of agriculture and the rural non-farm sector,[24] it is surprising that there appears to be no correlation between food-grain production per capita and the proportion of rural workers engaged in the non-farm sector (Table 2.15). In fact three of the states with the most extensive RNFS employment (Tamil Nadu, Gujarat and Assam) have low figures for production of food grain per capita.[25]

However, the employment data with their narrow definition of rural may be concealing the changes in the composition of employment in the countryside. Household manufacturing and other activities dispersed in villages may decline with agricultural development, whereas the modern and dynamic parts of the non-farm sector are likely to generate most new jobs in rural towns. This is perhaps why some researchers have found a decline in rural non-farm employment in Punjab, for example (Simmons and Supri, 1994). However, Hazell and Haggblade (1990: 23) find that the

23. Gujarat is an exception as it is divided between districts with high population densities, where most economic activity is also concentrated, and those which are sparsely populated. UP is another exception.
24. See, among many others, Mellor (1976), Hazell and Haggblade (1990), Kumar (1993), Singh (1993), and Lanjouw and Lanjouw (1995), who provide many other references.
25. Vaidyanathan (1986: A-143), Hazell and Haggblade (1990: 18–26) and others (see Basant, 1993: 362) found a positive relationship between crop output per capita and RNFS employment, but others have failed to do so, at least in terms of a linear relationship (Sen, 1994: 588–9).

Table 2.14: RNFS employment, population and net state domestic product in 1991

State	*RNFS workers as % of RMWs*	*Secondary workers as % of RMWs*	*Manufacturing jobs outside the household (%)*	*Rural population as % of total*	*Population density per sq. km*	*NSDP per capita in Rs/ year 1991–2*
Punjab	25.8	8.5	82.4	70.5	403	9643
Tamil Nadu	20.6	9.5	63.5	65.8	429	5078
Gujarat	19.6	9.6	83.5	65.5	211	6425
Assam	18.6	3.9	71.2	88.9	286	4230
Orissa	17.5	5.7	38.4	86.6	203	4068
Andhra Pradesh	17.1	7.5	48.2	73.1	242	5570
Rajasthan	15.6	5.3	58.9	77.1	129	4361
Uttar Pradesh	14.9	5.5	60.7	80.2	473	4012
India	17.7	6.8	62.0	74.3	273	5583

Sources: Census, 1991 (GoI, 1992b: Table 4); GoI (1992d); Drèze and Sen (1995: Statistical Appendix).

Table 2.15: Agricultural production and RNFS employment

State	*Food grain production p.c. in kg, 1989–90*	*RNFS workers as % of RMWs, 1991*	*Tertiary workers as % of RNFS workers, 1991*
Punjab	1526.9	25.8	66.9
UP	347.1	14.9	63.7
Rajasthan	344.7	15.6	59.8
Orissa	264.1	17.5	63.0
Tamil Nadu	259.4	20.6	52.8
AP	239.6	17.1	55.3
Gujarat	193.9	19.6	49.5
Assam	175.1	18.6	76.9
India	198.7	17.7	58.7

Sources: Census, 1991 (GoI, 1992b: Tables 3 and 4), CMIE (1996: A103–A108).

correlations between agricultural income and rural non-farm employment are negative, but that they become strongly positive when employment in rural towns is included.

Indeed the links between agricultural income and non-farm income seem more robust. The model that Hazell and Haggblade (1990: 29) test suggests that:

> a one-hundred rupee increase in agricultural income will generate about an additional 64 rupees in rural non-farm incomes, 25 rupees in rural areas and 39 in rural towns.

Moreover, higher agricultural production per capita seems to induce a higher proportion of tertiary employment within the rural non-farm sector (Table 2.15) (although tertiary employment is also strongly influenced by public-sector jobs). This may suggest that the states which are most advanced agriculturally need more service jobs within their non-farm sectors to support their agricultural development. The economies of Gujarat and Tamil Nadu, on the other hand, rely less on agriculture and more on industry.

The provision of rural infrastructure, such as railways, roads and electricity, is clearly vital for the development of RNFS employment (Table 2.16). Thus rural infrastructure is much more highly developed in those states which have the highest share of RNFS employment. In some cases causality may also flow in the reverse direction: as incomes rise with the

Table 2.16: Rural infrastructure and RNFS employment

State	*RNFS workers as % of RMWs, 1991*	*Railways: km per 1000 sq.km 1989–90*	*Villages connected with all-weather roads, 1987–8 (%)*	*Rural households electrified, 1990–91 (%)*	*Goods vehicles per million population, 1988–9*
Punjab	25.8	0.44	99	77.0	2311
Tamil Nadu	20.6	0.31	63	44.5	2137
Gujarat	19.6	0.27	74	56.4	2575
Assam	18.6	0.28	65	12.4	2354
Orissa	17.5	0.13	15	17.5	675
AP	17.1	0.19	43	37.5	1113
Rajasthan	15.6	0.17	21	22.4	1368
UP	14.9	0.32	43	11.0	489
India	17.7	0.20	41	30.5	1557

Sources: GoI (1992d); Drèze and Sen (1995: Statistical Appendix).

development of the RNFS (as well as of agriculture) there is more capital to invest in infrastructure.

We have argued that workers in the RNFS are more educated than in the agricultural sector, and that education is important in allowing workers to enter RNFS employment. Inter-state comparisons appear to support this argument (Table 2.17). Differences in female educational attainments are particularly sharp.

Finally, we look at changes in rural employment over time. Comparisons across states are highly revealing when dividing the rural workforce into three major groups: cultivators, agricultural labourers and the non-farm sector (Table 2.18). In all states the proportion of cultivators in the rural workforce is declining. The question is: what compensates for the falling proportion of cultivators – agricultural labour or the non-farm sector?

Three states, Andhra Pradesh, Tamil Nadu and Uttar Pradesh experienced a sharp decline in the proportion of cultivators between 1981 and 1991. These states differed, however, in their capacity to increase the proportion of their rural workers in the non-farm sector. Obviously, the greater the ability of states to enhance the proportion of RNFS jobs, the less the proportion of agricultural labourers rises.

This is revealed even more strongly in Rajasthan, Punjab and Orissa, states which have not experienced such a sharp decline in the proportion of cultivators, but have had very different rates of expansion of their RNFS employment. While the proportion of cultivators in Rajasthan is

Table 2.17: Education and RNFS employment

State	*RNFS workers as % of RMWs, 1991*	*Rural literacy rate (aged 7+) (%), 1991*		*Completed primary education (aged 6+) (%), 1992–3*		*Never enrolled rural children (aged 12–14) (%), 1986–7*	
		Male	*Female*	*Male*	*Female*	*Male*	*Female*
Punjab	25.8	60.7	43.9	51.6	41.0	22.6	33.3
Tamil Nadu	20.6	67.2	41.8	58.7	40.1	11.5	26.3
Gujarat	19.6	66.8	38.7	53.6	33.5	22.5	38.7
Assam	18.6	58.7	39.2	41.2	28.5	22.9	28.5
Orissa	17.5	60.0	30.8	42.8	23.0	34.0	54.7
AP	17.1	47.3	23.9	45.3	26.4	32.7	59.7
Rajasthan	15.6	47.6	11.6	41.8	15.6	26.1	81.7
UP	14.9	52.1	19.0	47.3	21.4	27.2	38.8
India	17.7	57.9	30.6	48.6	28.1	26.4	50.7

Sources: Census (GoI, 1992b: Table 4); Drèze and Sen (1995: Statistical Appendix).

Table 2.18: Changes in the composition of rural employment (1981–91)

State	*% point change in proportion of cultivators to RMWs*	*New jobs in RNFS as % of jobs lost in cultivation*	*Change in proportion of agricultural labourers to RMWs (%)*
Andhra Pradesh	−6.0	3	5.8
Tamil Nadu	−6.0	18	4.9
Uttar Pradesh	−5.6	40	3.3
Rajasthan	−2.1	−51	3.2
Punjab	−2.7	19	2.2
Orissa	−2.4	72	0.7
Gujarat	−4.7	82	0.8
India	−3.4	33	2.3

Source: Compiled from Census data (GoI, 1987a: Table B3 and 1992b: Table 4).

declining more slowly than in Andhra Pradesh, Tamil Nadu and Uttar Pradesh, the growth in the proportion of agricultural labourers is almost as high because Rajasthan has failed to expand its non-farm sector. In contrast in Orissa the proportion of agricultural labourers in the rural workforce hardly increased over the decade because of the absorption of workers within the RNFS.

Gujarat confirms this analysis. While the decline in the proportion of cultivators in the state falls between the above two groups, the proportion of agricultural labourers has hardly increased because of the expansion of the RNFS, particularly in manufacturing.

Clearly the rural non-farm sector is not simply a sponge absorbing excess agricultural labour.[26] We believe, instead, that the agricultural-labour sector serves this function. Moreover, the extent to which agricultural labour has to do so depends on the ability of the economy to generate more productive jobs in the RNFS. This is very much in accord with the data on wages, which show that agricultural labour is the lowest-paid occupation in rural India, making it the last resort for finding rural employment. As our arguments above made clear, however, there are some residual categories within the RNFS, such as construction, which may also be absorbing excess labour from the agricultural sector.

Conclusions

The rural non-farm sector may already be generating as much as a quarter of all rural employment in India. It also provides secondary employment to agricultural households, and is particularly important for small and marginal farmers, as well as for the landless. Non-farm activities are not confined to traditional village industries, which are declining in many areas, but comprise a highly diverse set of activities ranging across the primary, secondary and tertiary sectors.

Employment and incomes in the rural non-farm sector are growing faster than in the agricultural sector, so that the importance of the RNFS is only increasing. In many cases this growth reflects the development of the rural economy, rather than the result of rural distress pushing workers out of the agricultural sector. Indeed, in view of the on-going transformation of the rural economy in India, the RNFS plays a critical role in generating more productive employment and providing rural workers with better work opportunities than in agricultural labour in particular.

There are, of course, a number of concerns. For example, in some RNFS sub-sectors working conditions are appalling, wages low, educational attainments poor, and child labour extensive, especially among girls, although on average workers in the RNFS are better paid and educated, and not as poor as in the agricultural sector. There is also less child labour in the rural non-farm sector. While many of the tiny units which predomi-

26. If it were, RNFS employment might be correlated with work-participation and unemployment rates, which, if higher, would put pressure on the RNFS to absorb excess labour (Vaidyanathan, 1986: A-143, Sen, 1994: 586–87). Our eight states did not reveal such correlations.

nate within the RNFS are hardly productive and show little potential for expansion, there are many small enteprises which are more productive.

On the whole, therefore, the growth of the RNFS brings many benefits, in addition to contributing to the goal of full employment. It enhances rural incomes, reduces the incidence of poverty, and builds a skill-base in the rural population, and adds significantly to exports, for example of textile, leather and handicraft products.

3 Sub-sectors in the rural non-farm sector

In Chapter 2 we looked at data on the RNFS from the Census of India, the National Sample Survey and various enterprise surveys. A significant impression derived from the data is the great diversity of rural non-farm activities. In this chapter we explore this heterogeneity further by reviewing many of the different sub-sectors that make up the RNFS.

We first set out a framework for analysing sub-sectors, adapted from Michael Porter's *The Competitive Advantage of Nations* (1990), and describe one sub-sector (leather) in detail. We chose this sub-sector because it illustrates many important themes for the RNFS, including the close links between economic and social structures within India.

We then summarize our analysis of the 80 sub-sectors, ten in each of eight states, that we covered during the study. We review them in the following five groups: food-processing, other primary processing, traditional manufacturing, modern manufacturing, and service sub-sectors. Box 3.1 provides another concrete example of an RNFS sub-sector (rural tourism) to emphasize the importance of rural services, which have often been ignored by policy-makers. Figure 3.2 provides an example of a typical cluster (in the stone-processing sub-sector) to illustrate this form of industry structure, which is common to many RNFS sub-sectors.

While our evaluation of sub-sectors is based on extensive fieldwork in all eight states, we did not seek to gather quantitative data that would have statistical validity. Our analysis in this and subsequent chapters is qualitative in nature, providing a wealth of examples and illustrations, but continuing to cite supporting quantitative data from primary surveys and secondary sources.

After reviewing the different groups of sub-sectors, we look at one important component of all the sub-sectors: technology. In this chapter we confine our discussion largely to illustrations and insights, derived from fieldwork, on the state of technology and of skills and training in the RNFS, while we examine the dynamics of technology change and development in the following two chapters on regulation and promotion.

In concluding this chapter we revert to the categorization, developed in the previous chapters, into high-share, high-growth and emergent sub-sectors, to see whether our analysis points to important differences among these categories of sub-sectors. Above all, we emphasize the importance for policy-makers of taking into consideration the demand trends faced by different sub-sectors.

Competitive versus comparative advantage

Michael Porter's (1990) ground-breaking research on ten nations (USA, Britain, Germany, Italy, Denmark, Sweden, Switzerland, Japan, Korea and Singapore) presents a useful model for understanding which industries of a nation's economy can become competitive, and how. Porter identified four determinants (1990: 71) that shape the macro-environment in which local firms compete and that promote or impede the creation of competitive advantage:

(1) *Factor conditions* The nation's position in factors of production, such as skilled labour or infrastructure, necessary to compete in a given industry.
(2) *Demand conditions* The nature of home demand for the industry's product or service.
(3) *Related and supporting industries* The presence or absence in the nation of supplier industries and related industries that are internationally competitive.
(4) *Firm strategy, structure and rivalry* The conditions in the nation governing how companies are created, organized, and managed, and the nature of domestic rivalry.

The determinants are presented in the form of a diamond (Figure 3.1). The diamond is a mutually reinforcing system; advantages in one determinant can create or enhance advantages in others. Porter found that the advantages most critical for success are in his second and fourth determinants respectively: the existence of a large and discerning domestic market, and the existence of a large number of firms with intense competitive rivalry among them. The resulting competition itself leads to the creation of supporting industries and services which further enhance the innovation and competitive advantage of the industry.

It follows from this that factor conditions, which in classical economic theory were considered the basis for the comparative advantage of nations, are not the most critical determinant for competitive advantage. Porter found that in many examples he studied, traditional factor conditions (such as raw materials) were in fact adverse to begin with (for example in the steel industry in Japan and ship-building in Korea). Basic raw materials were often imported. Other factors such as skilled manpower, technology, specialized infrastructure, design and marketing skills were created by firms either singly or through trade associations, under pressure not to fall behind.

This shift in the paradigm from comparative to competitive advantage is

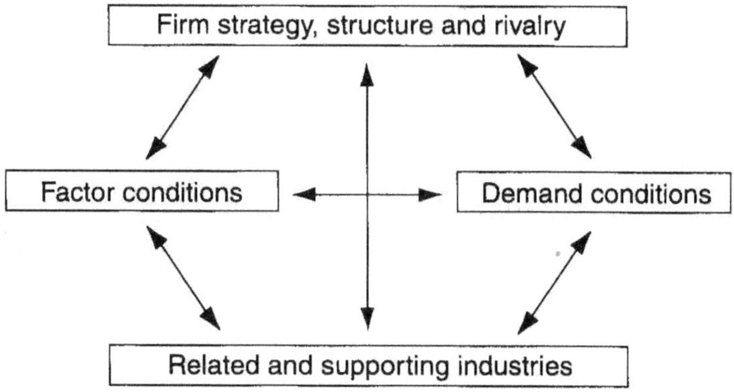

Source: Porter, Michael E. (1990), *The Competitive Advantage of Nations,* Macmillan, London

Figure 3.1: The determinants of national advantage

fundamental to thinking about how economic growth is fuelled. Traditional wisdom about focusing on those industries in which a country has a cost advantage is no longer valid since, according to Porter, others will innovate to increase their productivity and lower their costs.

An important point to note in Porter's model is that government does not appear as a determinant in its own right (see Chapter 12 in Porter). Instead, 'the proper role for government policy toward a nation's industry is to stimulate . . . dynamism and upgrading . . . [and] to unleash and even amplify the forces within the "diamond". This creates opportunities, and pressures, for continued innovation' (Porter, 1990: 618–20).

Government can influence each of the four determinants either positively or negatively. For example, government policies can affect factor conditions by influencing capital markets, education, research and infrastructure, or by providing subsidies. Government can also play a role, though a subtle one, in shaping domestic demand conditions, for example by establishing product standards or through its own purchasing policies.

Government policies can also affect related and supporting industries. Porter found, for example, that unconstrained and innovative media – television, radio, magazines, newspapers, and so on – were a source of competitive advantage in marketing and in reducing information and communication costs. Finally, government policies influence the way firms are created, organized and managed, and how they compete.

Thus the goals of individuals and firms, though often shaped by social attitudes and structures, can none the less be influenced by government policies, such as regulation, fiscal measures and promotional initiatives. However:

> Government policy toward industry must recognize that the 'diamond' is a system, which makes policies in many areas interdependent. The weakest link constrains the development of an economy, so that progress is needed on each determinant. (Porter, 1990: 682)

We used Porter's framework, slightly adapted, for analysing the strengths and weaknesses of each of the RNFS sub-sectors we studied. In each case we looked at the following aspects under the four determinants in the diamond:

(1) *Factor conditions*

- Physical raw-material availability
- Human-resource availability and skills
- Knowledge base and research capability
- Capital availability
- Availability of infrastructure

(2) *Demand conditions*

- Size of domestic demand
- Number of buyers
- Sophistication of buyers
- Presence of multinational buyers
- Growth rate of domestic demand

(3) *Size and structure of firms*

- Number of firms
- Size of firms (is the size efficient?)
- Existence of rivalry among firms
- Formation of new firms (are there barriers to entry?)
- Congruence between sub-sector and firm goals

(4) *Related and supporting industries*

- Design and product development
- Marketing, market research and advertising
- Training
- Research and development
- Component and machinery suppliers
- Existence of producer associations
- Existence of promotional agencies.

We used a rating system to identify, for each sub-sector, which of these components are unfavourable and need to be strengthened in order to promote the sub-sector. In this book we cannot include the detailed analysis for each of the sub-sectors we studied. Instead, in this chapter, we first illustrate the use of the framework by comparing the leather sub-sector in two states, Uttar Pradesh and Rajasthan. We then summarize our analysis, based on the framework, for various groups of sub-sectors, and provide another specific example (of the rural tourism sub-sector) in Box 3.1.

The leather sub-sector

The leather sub-sector is defined by its primary raw material rather than its product. Because of religious and cultural restrictions on killing cattle in India, many of the raw hides come not from slaughter houses but from flaying animals that have died (although some Indian states do allow the slaughter of cattle). There are also many other animals which are flayed for their hides, such as buffalo, sheep and goats. Most raw hides are sold through well-developed marketing channels to tanneries using chemical processes, although some hides are processed through traditional methods using vegetable material. The primary product for which the leather is then used is footwear, although other items such as belts, bags and sportswear are also produced. Before comparing the leather sub-sector in Uttar Pradesh and Rajasthan, we first explain some of the broad characteristics of the sub-sector throughout India, which also serve to illustrate important themes for the rural non-farm sector in general.

The transformation of a sub-sector Traditionally animals were flayed, the hides tanned using vegetable material, and leather products made and marketed, all by the same artisans in a locality. With growing markets and especially export opportunities the sub-sector has changed radically, however. Three main centres for tanning have developed (Calcutta for cattle hides, Kanpur for buffalo, and Madras for goat and sheep); there are relatively few tanneries elsewhere. The units in all these centres use chemical-tanning processes, which are particularly capital-intensive during the finishing stages. Some traditional vegetable tanning does survive, to supply local markets and particular industries such as sports goods which need the tougher vegetable-tanned leather. As hide prices rise, however, vegetable tanning in villages is becoming increasingly untenable.

Because of the concentration of tanning, coupled with the fact that many animals are flayed only when and where they die, a lucrative trade in raw hides from throughout India to the tanning centres, then back to producers of shoes and other leather products, has evolved. Manufacturing leather products is also concentrated in clusters, most notably Agra, the largest centre in Asia for producing shoes, but most leather products are produced by artisans or small manufacturers using traditional manual technologies.

Production processes in the leather sub-sector range, therefore, from those of rural self-employed artisans to urban capital-intensive factories, which are linked by highly developed trading channels. This demonstrates the absurdity of trying to enforce a rigorous division between rural and urban components of a sub-sector.

Social stratification Many economic activities in India are structured according to social status, particularly in the caste hierarchy, and the leather sub-sector is no exception. Traditionally those involved in flaying, tanning and making leather products belonged to the very lowest castes (such as Chamars, Raigars and Madigas). While leather was processed largely in villages, the same leather workers were involved in all three activities. However, as leather tanning evolved into a centralized capital-intensive process, a hierarchy developed even within the existing caste structure, with leather workers, (vegetable) tanners and flayers in descending order. At the same time there was a social movement to encourage traditional workers to move out of the sub-sector because of its low social status. As a result, many from these castes no longer practise their traditional profession, and leather work, tanning and even flaying have disappeared from some areas altogether.

Those who trade in hides and tanned leather may also be defined by their social status. For example, many of the primary traders who purchase hides directly from the flayers are Muslims who entered this activity as the sub-sector grew because they do not face the same social restrictions as Hindus. Moreover, traders throughout the trading chain may be close-knit socially, with the large traders often appointing their relatives and friends as agents. This is one of the primary barriers against outsiders seeking to enter this lucrative trade. The traders in fact make up the most powerful group within the sub-sector.

Finally, most producers of leather products belong to the traditional lower castes or to Muslim communities. It is only in the large urban tanning units that the social boundaries have to some extent been broken down.

The political economy of the sub-sector is therefore clearly defined in terms not only of economic activity but also of social status, and policy interventions cannot ignore the power relations that arise from this stratification (compare Knorringa, 1994).

Government regulation Government regulation has in fact provided a powerful mechanism for traders to exercise control over the flayers of dead animals. Traditionally flayers were allowed to strip the skin off dead animals for free, thus helping in the disposal of the beasts, and then to use or sell the raw hides and other parts of the carcasses. However, in the

1970s *panchayats* began enforcing a public-health law which requires those stocking and trading in raw hides and bones to have a licence. With the growth of the leather sub-sector, auctioning these licenses for blocks (a sub-unit of districts) has now become an important source of local revenue. However, this method of implementing the law has proved extremely regressive socially. Because the *panchayats* sell the licences to the highest bidder who must pay up-front, traditional flayers, who cannot put together the necessary capital, have been excluded. Traders have therefore captured the licences and, because the flayers cannot sell raw hides to anyone apart from the licence-holder in a particular block, the traders are able to determine the price of hides to their advantage. So in UP, the primary trader, who does little more than take the hide to the wholesale market at the block level, is able to capture some two-thirds of the value of the raw hide, and only a small proportion of this margin (about a tenth) can be regarded as recouping the cost of the licence which he had to pay up-front.

The other main area of regulation in this sub-sector concerns environmental protection. Unfortunately, because such environmental controls have had little impact, the results have again been pernicious. Pollution in the three main tanning centres is extensive, and even court injunctions to close tanneries in Kanpur (and thereby to protect the holy River Ganges) have failed to stop it. Small tanneries outside these centres also pollute the environment, but they are at least dispersed rather than concentrated in one location.

Uttar Pradesh and Rajasthan compared We reviewed the leather sub-sector in these two states, and Table 3.1 provides a comparison using our adaptation of Porter's framework. The sub-sector in these two states is strikingly different. UP has the largest number of buffalo and cattle, one of the main tanning centres (Kanpur), the main shoe cluster (Agra) and an important cluster for sports goods (Meerut) which require vegetable-tanned leather. Competition among the numerous units in the leather sub-sector is intense. Because of its large population (180 million in 1991) UP also has a substantial domestic market for leather products, and because of Kanpur and Agra many large buyers of leather products, including from abroad, come to the state. Rural employment in the leather sub-sector in UP grew, therefore, at 10.8 per cent a year between 1982 and 1987 (NSS).

The main constraints in UP centre around research and development and the supply of technology, machinery, components and finance to upgrade the tanning industry in particular, including improvement of its appalling environmental record. As in most other sub-sectors in the RNFS, marketing research, information and advertising are weak, and India as a whole has failed to exploit the substantial potential for marketing its leather goods abroad.

Table 3.1: Application of Porter's Model to the leather sub-sector

Determinant	*Uttar Pradesh*	*Rajasthan*
1. Factor conditions		
Raw-material availability	4	2
Human-resource availability and skills	5	2
Knowledge base and research capability	4	1
Capital availability	3	3
Availability of infrastructure	3	3
2. Demand conditions		
Size of domestic demand	5	3
Number of buyers	5	2
Sophistication of buyers	4	2
Presence of multinational buyers	5	1
Growth rate of domestic demand	5	2
3. Size and structure of firms		
Number of firms	4	3
Size of firms	4	1
Existence of rivalry among firms	4	3
Formation of new firms (entry barriers)	4	2
Congruence between sub-sector and firm goals	4	2
4. Related and supporting industries		
Design and product development	4	2
Marketing, market research and advertising	2	1
Training	4	2
Research and development	2	1
Component and machinery suppliers	2	1
Existence of producer associations	4	1
Existence of promotional agencies	4	2

Note: 1 = highly unfavourable, 2 = unfavourable, 3 = neutral, 4 = favourable, 5 = highly favourable.

The picture in Rajasthan is very different. Rajasthan has the largest number of sheep and goats, as well as a substantial number of cattle, but only one modern tannery in the whole state. In some areas flaying, tanning and leather work have died out completely. In consequence, almost all raw hides are exported out of the state. However, there is no clear information on the extent of trading in raw hides or on how many animals are not even flayed in spite of the rising value of raw hides. The lack of water is a constraint on tanning, and the small and dispersed population does not offer a large market for leather products either.

As a result Rajasthan has not attracted any attention from the many promotional programmes for the leather sub-sector, such as the National Leather Development Programme. Until recently the state government had also done little to promote the sub-sector.

Under these circumstances it might be argued that the sub-sector has no potential in Rajasthan. However, in 1981, according to the Census, the leather sub-sector was still among the ten largest in rural Rajasthan, employing 3.3 per cent of rural main workers. Moreover, the large number of raw hides that could be made available for processing remains an unexploited resource. To promote the sub-sector the state will have to assist the establishment of larger-scale tanneries (an endeavour which the state government initiated in 1995) which can boost the local demand for raw hides. The state will also have to attract the relevant specialized technical institutes to undertake research, development and promotion appropriate to Rajasthan, for example of tanning processes which use less water.

Other sub-sectors

To provide an overview of the other sub-sectors covered by the study we arrange them into the following five groups: (1) food-processing; (2) other primary processing; (3) traditional manufacturing; (4) modern manufacturing; and (5) services.

For each sub-sector we specify (in brackets) the state(s) in which we studied that sub-sector. For the process that we used to select sub-sectors in a particular state, see Appendix 1.

Food processing

We studied many food-processing sub-sectors, covering:

- grains and pulses (AP, Gujarat, Orissa)
- oilseeds (Gujarat, Rajasthan)
- *khandsari* and *gur* (forms of unrefined sugar) (UP)
- spices (Orissa)
- tea from small plantations (Assam)
- fruit and vegetables (AP, Assam, Punjab, UP)
- milk (Gujarat)
- fish and prawns (AP, Assam, Orissa)
- poultry (Tamil Nadu)

Food-processing employs about 4 per cent of the RNFS workforce (Census), engaging almost two million rural workers (NSS), and is thus among the high-share sub-sectors. Growth rates in employment have been more modest, however, at 1.4 per cent a year between 1977–8 and 1987–8 (NSS). Only processing of cocoa, chocolate and confectionery (and of country liquor and toddy) were among the fastest-growing activities for rural employment, as well as trading in these and other foodstuffs (see Table 2.5, p. 33).

Demand prospects for most processed foods are promising, with the growth of population and of the middle classes, and with urbanization, although many households still prefer fresh rather than processed foods. Some processed items also enjoy good export opportunities, especially rice, tea, spices, castor oil, fruit and prawns. Food for processing is also abundantly available. However, while grains, pulses, edible oils, sugar and tea are all processed, less than 1 per cent of fruit and vegetables are, and very few spices, fish, poultry and eggs. Constraints are the seasonal supply of many fresh foods and their poor quality, price controls and the restriction on movements of 'essential commodities', underdeveloped storage and transport facilities, the lack of credit for working capital in particular, backward technologies, unreliable power supplies and a weak packaging industry. Productivity in the industry is, as a result, generally low and quality indifferent.

The numerous government agencies, departments and directorates, state corporations and specialized institutes for this sub-sector have failed to make a major difference. Some corporate entities are now investing in various food-processing plants, which should upgrade technology levels in the industry. The central government has also launched various quality standards (such as the Food Products Order), and some of these are now recognized at the top end of the market. To have a significant impact, however, these quality standards need better monitoring and enforcement, as well as greater consumer awareness.

The overall impression of the sub-sector is therefore of wasted potential, especially in the light of good demand prospects and abundant raw materials. This might explain the modest growth rates of rural employment in food-processing activities. Nevertheless, the potential for food processing remains enormous, and more successful cases, like the rapid development of edible oils (see p. 74), show that the potential can be realized.

Other primary processing

This heading groups the following diverse sub-sectors:

- mining, quarrying and stoneware (AP, Orissa, Rajasthan)
- sericulture and silk processing (AP, Assam, Orissa, Tamil Nadu)
- processing of fibres (Assam, Orissa)
- floriculture and phytochemicals (Orissa, UP)
- *bidi*-rolling (AP, UP)

Processing of primary products, including food, featured prominently in our selection of sub-sectors in Andhra Pradesh, Assam and Orissa, reflecting the importance of these activities for the less-developed economies of these states.

Some of the sub-sectors face very good demand prospects. With the boom in construction, demand for stone products is growing; India is also the third largest exporter of natural stone. Domestic consumption and exports of silk goods have been expanding rapidly, and there is growing domestic and export demand for herbal products and phytochemicals (chemicals extracted from plants). On the other hand, demand prospects for jute fibres and for *bidis* (tobacco rolled in *tendu* leaves) are more uncertain. Jute faces competition from synthetic fibres, and *bidis* from cigarettes.

The adequacy of raw materials for these sub-sectors varies. For example, stone is abundantly available, although reserves have not been adequately explored. The rearing of mulberry silk has been promoted in India since the 1970s and output is rising steadily, although it is of poor quality and not enough attention has been given to other types of silk traditional to states like Assam and Orissa. On the other hand, production of roses and mint for phytochemicals is limited and some fibres such as *sabai* grass (made into ropes) are not even cultivated systematically. Only a small fraction of the coconuts available in Assam and Orissa is processed into coir, a fibre made from the coconut husks.

Processing activities are limited as well. For example, apart from traditional stone carvers, most processing of stone comprises crushing it for construction material rather than cutting and polishing it for higher-value products. Most stone which is exported is unprocessed. Herbs are simply dried, graded and packed. The primary distilling of roses and mint by local farmers leaves many impurities, necessitating further purification elsewhere.

Even more than with food-processing, these sub-sectors demonstrate clearly wasted potential in the face of good demand prospects and reasonable supplies of raw materials. This is particularly disturbing, as these areas of activity are important for many poor producers and workers. Mining and quarrying provide extensive employment to migrant labourers, and *bidi*-rolling to women, many of whom have no alternative sources of work; many fibres are cultivated and herbs gathered by tribal peoples. The potential of these sub-sectors is clear from the fact that rural employment in processing jute, hemp and *mesta* fibres grew at 5.8 per cent a year between 1977–8 and 1987–8, and in mining and quarrying at 5.0 per cent (see Table 2.4, p. 32). In the *bidi* sub-sector prospects are more uncertain, however, and here a major focus of policy must be to develop alternative employment opportunities for the workers.

To fulfil their potential, these sub-sectors need a complete package of promotional inputs ranging from raw-material cultivation through processing technologies to designing and marketing of products. Only in the case of sericulture has this been attempted. Even here promotion needs to go much further, by improving storage facilities, introducing forward markets and lifting restrictions on the movement of cocoons and raw silk across state borders in order to reduce fluctuations in their prices.

In addition to measures to upgrade productivity and enhance value addition in these sub-sectors, however, workers and the environment need to be protected, especially in quarrying and *bidi*-rolling, where labour conditions are appalling and slaughter-mining is common.

Traditional manufacturing

Many RNFS sub-sectors that provide employment to a substantial number of rural workers involve traditional manufacturing jobs. These activities therefore form an important part of the RNFS, and have indeed received considerable policy attention. We looked at the following sub-sectors:

- handloom and/or textile products, of cotton and/or silk (in all eight states apart from Punjab)
- carpets (UP)
- leather (Rajasthan, UP; see detailed analysis above)
- wood products (Assam, Punjab, Rajasthan)
- pottery (Gujarat, Rajasthan, UP)
- gems and jewellery (Rajasthan, Tamil Nadu)

Four of these sub-sectors alone, namely wood products, cotton textiles, textile products, and non-metallic mineral products (pottery and related activities), generate almost 20 per cent of rural non-farm employment (see Table 2.3, p. 30), although some of this work is in modern activities within the sub-sectors concerned (such as powerlooms, ceramics and exported gems and jewellery). Two of these sub-sectors (wooden furniture and fixtures, and silk textiles) also feature among the sub-sectors with high growth rates of employment (see Table 2.5, p. 33).

Many of these traditional products face strong competition from substitutes, such as synthetic fibres, modern ready-made garments, plastic, metal and stone items. In almost all cases there are, however, potential niche markets, generally for higher-value products. Silk textiles have been particularly successful, and rural employment in this sub-sector grew at over 9 per cent a year (Papola, 1992: 243). There are also some larger markets, especially for cotton- and silk-textile products, from which rural producers can benefit. Exports are important for all the products we looked at with the exception of pottery and wood items. Indeed, the carpet and the gem and jewellery industries are highly dependent on overseas sales, although consumer concerns about the extensive use of child labour have constrained carpet exports.

So the demand prospects for these traditional manufacturing sub-sectors are uncertain. While there are market opportunities to exploit, it is clear that few of the sub-sectors will be able to sustain the large number of workers they currently engage. The greatest challenge is therefore to upgrade manufacturing processes and products for specialized markets, including exports, and to find alternative employment opportunities for those producers who can no longer find remunerative work in their traditional crafts.

These sub-sectors also face major constraints in terms of the supply of raw materials. Despite many regulations, the textile industry cannot meet the demand for handloom yarn, and supplies of wool, clay and especially wood and bamboo are declining. Only silk production is rising significantly, although supply lags far behind demand. On the other hand, some sub-sectors, such as carpets and gems and jewellery, have expanded using imported raw materials.

Many of the artisans in these sub-sectors belong to castes or communities that have traditionally specialized in their respective crafts. The craft people are highly skilled, but often lack the technologies, expertise, exposure and information to supply non-local markets directly. Improved technologies have been developed but not widely adopted. The lack of bank finance, especially for working capital, is a further constraint. As a result, many artisans have become piece-rate employees of traders in a putting-out system in which the traders supply the raw materials and buy back the finished products.

The organization of traditional producers into cooperatives has largely failed to reduce their dependence on traders and master-craftsmen, and the cooperatives have often been exploited by state governments (see Chapter 7). In general, the numerous promotional activities and agencies for these sub-sectors have focused on preserving existing employment, rather than upgrading the sub-sectors so that they become competitive and independent. They have often failed to take account of demand trends in particular.

A few of the sub-sectors are being upgraded, usually by private actors seeking to exploit export opportunities: in the carpet industry those manufacturing processes, such as dyeing, which are most important for quality control have been centralized and improved; and exporters, traders and private companies are introducing better technologies and training for gem processing. A few dynamic clusters have also been able to upgrade their manufacturing, for example from red-clay pottery to ceramics.

Modern manufacturing

The long-term prospects of many traditional sub-sectors, particularly in terms of employment, are uncertain. In contrast, rural employment in the manufacturing of many modern products is growing rapidly. We covered the following sub-sectors:

- powerlooms (Tamil Nadu, UP)
- knitwear and ready-made garments (Gujarat, Tamil Nadu)

- matches (Tamil Nadu)
- ceramic products (Gujarat, UP)
- bricks (Gujarat, Punjab)
- metal products and small engineering (Gujarat, Punjab)
- repairs (AP, Gujarat, Rajasthan)
- cement products, plastic products and diamond processing (all in Gujarat)
- construction (AP, Assam, Gujarat)

Gujarat features prominently in this list, because it is the most industrialized state among the eight we covered. The only other state comparable to Gujarat in terms of rural industrialization is Maharashtra, which we did not include in our study.

Describing the above sub-sectors as modern is to some extent arbitrary. Many of them, for example knitwear, ceramics, metal products and repairs, have roots in traditional activities such as pottery and blacksmithery. However, all have been transformed, largely post-independence, with the introduction of modern technologies and machinery. It is this transformation that marks out most of these sub-sectors as modern. (The match sub-sector is an exception; see Chapter 4, p. 90).

We have also included construction in this category because many of the above sub-sectors supply the construction industry and because the development of infrastructure is vital for a modern economy. Much housing construction in rural India, however, especially in states like Assam, still uses traditional materials and methods which are often appropriate to the local conditions.

What is immediately apparent from an analysis of these modern manufacturing sub-sectors is that they are being driven by growing demand. Domestic demand prospects are good for all the sub-sectors concerned, except perhaps matches. Output in some of these sub-sectors has therefore seen phenomenal growth. For example, cloth output from powerlooms grew at about 5 per cent a year from 1988 to 1993 (compared to about 1 per cent for handlooms). Export demand has also been growing rapidly, especially for garments, diamonds and plastic products.

The influence of growing demand is clearly revealed in the employment data (see Tables 2.3, 2.4 and 2.5, pp. 30–33). Construction, repairs and metal products are already among the high-share sub-sectors in terms of rural employment. Powerlooms, repair of vehicles, construction, iron and steel products are among the high-growth sub-sectors: rural employment in these sub-sectors is growing at between 9 and 14 per cent a year (Papola, 1992: 243). In rural Gujarat employment in processing diamonds grew at an annual rate of 12.5 per cent over the same period.

The availability of raw materials for many of these sub-sectors has improved with liberalization, including the decontrol of cement, iron and steel, and the reduction of duties on many imports. Machinery and spare parts are also readily available. The regulatory environment is generally lighter than in other sub-sectors (matches and land transactions for construction being major exceptions). Bankers have also been more willing to lend to units in these sub-sectors.

These areas have also seen some of the most successful promotional activities. In the public sector, examples include the inputs provided by the Central Glass and Ceramics Research Institute and the UP Small Industries Development Corporation in developing ceramic clusters; the promotion of rural industrial estates in Gujarat; and the role of the export promotion councils in promoting exports of apparel and plastic products.

The private sector has also played a major part in promotion. Because the entrepreneurs often run larger units in dynamic clusters many of these sub-sectors have active associations of entrepreneurs. Some supplier industries, such as plastic and cement manufacturers and diamond traders, have also played an important promotional role.

Some of these sub-sectors, such as repairs and small engineering, serve as an important entry point for new entrepreneurs to launch themselves in the RNFS. Traditional castes and communities are not so significant in these sub-sectors, and new entrants can learn through informal apprenticeship in existing units. The machinery and raw materials are readily available. And initial investments are either small or can be met more speedily through bank finance.

There remain many constraints on the further development of these sub-sectors, however. While raw materials and spare parts are readily available, their quality is not always high. Upgrading technologies is hampered by the relatively poor standard of much machinery produced in India, the low skill levels, the lack of adequate and up-to-date training, and the lack of reliable sources of energy. More sophisticated technologies are being introduced only in those sub-sectors which face the most competition internationally, particularly in knitwear and diamond processing.

Upgrading production processes is not only important for the quality of the products, but also for labour conditions. Almost all the sub-sectors have poor working conditions, whether in terms of physical effort (for example in construction), health hazards (bricks, ceramics and cement products), child labour (matches and knitwear) and bonded labour (construction). Some production processes are also environmentally damaging, for example brick kilns, recycled plastic and repairs.

Smaller units have less ready access to bank finance, and almost all producers complained that bankers set working-capital limits that are too low. Promotional agencies have been weak in providing inputs for design and innovation which are important in addressing growing but changing markets.

In terms of industry structure, these modern sub-sectors have relatively more industrial units, employing about 10 to 20 workers, and fewer tiny or own-account enterprises. Clusters of such small units which both compete and collaborate with each other are particularly common, although less so in bricks, construction and repairs. Such groupings are often dynamic, specializing in specific products, but also constantly experimenting and innovating. (For an illustration of a cluster, see Figure 3.2. p. 82.)

Services

The analysis in Chapter 2 revealed that services account for 60 per cent of RNFS employment. Tables 2.4 and 2.5 (pp. 32–3) have shown that freight and passenger transport, wholesale and retail trade, hotels, business and legal services, recreational and cultural services are among the fastest growing sub-sectors in terms of rural employment. Our study covered the following service sub-sectors:

- agro-services (AP, Assam)
- retail trade (Assam)
- restaurants (Tamil Nadu)
- mechanized transport for freight or passengers (Assam, Punjab, Rajasthan, Tamil Nadu, UP)
- communications: public call offices and courier services (Punjab)
- private health care (Punjab)
- private educational services and vocational training (Gujarat, Punjab)
- rural tourism (Orissa, Rajasthan, UP)

In Punjab we gave particular attention to services, because in that state two-thirds of RNFS workers are employed in this sector, while economic development is leading to the rapid growth of many professional and business services. Box 3.1 provides details on rural tourism as an interesting composite service sub-sector. Here we look at some insights from other services.

As the economy expands and incomes rise, the prospects for many service sub-sectors are good; many are already growing rapidly, so have considerable potential for employment generation, both for educated workers in professions like education and health and for less-educated workers in such activities as trading and transport. Moreover, many services are predominantly supplied by tiny enterprises, employing perhaps only two workers, which are widely dispersed in rural areas. A few, such as transport and trading, and the fast-expanding telecommunications, have active associations, although most private-service providers, especially when dispersed widely, are not well organized.

The public sector has been deeply involved in providing many of the services we studied, especially agro-services, transport, communications, education and health. Private enterprises have, on the other hand, been relatively neglected in terms of promotion. This has meant that there are

Box 3.1: Rural tourism

Rural tourism is a composite service sub-sector, made up, for example, of travel and transport; hotels and restaurants; supplying food and other inputs; entertainment; and sale of handicrafts. It covers a wide range of activities: religious, cultural and historical tourism, festivals, fairs and markets, wild-life and adventure tourism, tourism to the desert, mountains and beaches.

Demand conditions There is substantial demand for rural tourism, ranging from about 90 million domestic tourists, mostly religious pilgrims, to two million foreign visitors in 1995, some of whom travel to rural destinations. Demand is growing. The number of tourists entering UP, for example, has been increasing by around 5 per cent a year (1984–90). The long-term prospects are therefore promising.

Factor conditions These are less favourable. While India is rich in rural tourist sites and events, many of these suffer from poor infrastructure, for example transport and accommodation, although telecommunications have improved significantly. State governments and local authorities have a major role to play in developing better tourist destinations and infrastructure, although with greater emphasis on encouraging private investment than in the past.

Skilled workers are in short supply. Indeed, there is often little recognition of the need for skilled labour to provide high quality services. There are also few quality standards beyond the classification of the better hotels. Bank finance is limited as well. At one end, tiny loans for tea-shops and roadside *dhabas* are available under the IRDP; at the other end, the Tourism Finance Corporation of India provides loans of Rs50 lakhs or more. But many banks are reluctant to lend, for example to hotels.

Size and structure of firms Rural tourism is characterized by a large number of small businesses which compete vigorously with each other. At the upper end of the market the public sector has been prominent, but some public assets are now being sold off to the private sector. The lack of bank finance acts, however, as a barrier to entry for larger businesses.

Supporting agencies The primary support for developing tourism has come from central and state tourism departments and development corporations. These have tended, however, to focus on developing public-sector facilities rather than providing support services for private activities and coordinating the diverse components of this composite sub-sector. There are only a few relevant research and training agencies, such as the network of public-sector institutes of hotel management. There are many local membership organizations of hotel and restaurant owners, and some national and state-level associations, but few of these have played any significant role.

almost no promotional agencies of relevance to them in rural areas. This has led to a limited amount of bank finance available for such services, except for tiny IRDP loans and a few large ones from state finance corporations. Above all, private services, especially transport, agro-services, telecommunications and education, have faced a complex regulatory environment in terms of licensing, price controls and so on. Most of these regulations have given unfair advantages to public-service providers. In spite of complex controls, however, state governments have been unable to guarantee any reliable standards for private-service provision, even in sub-sectors such as health which have a direct impact on consumers.

Removing the unfair advantages (such as large subsidies on capital and operating costs) enjoyed by public-service providers, simplifying the regulatory framework for many services, but also introducing measures to improve quality and skills, and to promote standards for consumer protection, are therefore some of the key issues for government action within the service sub-sectors.

Technology

Having analysed various groups of sub-sectors, we now look at the status of technology, as well as of training, across all of them. This review provides important background for our analysis of technology change and skill development in the following two chapters on regulation and promotion.

Almost all sub-sectors in the RNFS are characterized by the existence of technological dualism. There are simultaneously a large number of small producers, often engaged in the artisanal mode of production and using traditional technology, and a small number of larger units in the capitalist mode of production, using modern technology. This is reflected in the aggregate figures on enterprises (see Table 2.11, p. 45): in the mid-1980s there were fewer than 30 000 rural factories, and fewer than 200 000 rural (directory) manufacturing establishments (employing 11 workers on average). In contrast there were over 14 million tiny units employing, on average, one or two workers each.

Box 3.2 provides some examples from our fieldwork of backward technologies. The vast majority of producers operate with traditional tools which were suitable for the earlier conditions of localized markets. With trading to more distant markets becoming widespread, and demanding greater sophistication and product variety, the existing technologies and skills (see Box 3.3, p. 76) can often no longer cope. That is why household manufacturing is the only part of the rural non-farm sector in which employment is declining.

The fieldwork also identified some exceptions in this catalogue of backward technologies. For example, some modern rice-milling units are being

Box 3.2: Examples of backward technologies in the RNFS
Stoneware and granite mines often use only manual labour and handtools for mining, resulting in poor quality stone and low productivity. The average yield of granite mining in India is about 1 cubic metre/person/day compared to 30 to 40 cubic metres in Italy and Spain. Primitive 'slaughter-mining', in which sometimes less than 10 per cent of the mineral is extracted from the material excavated, causes huge wastage and environmental damage. Working conditions are also appalling.

Cottage-based paddy-processing units, such as single-huller units, use inefficient technologies, leading to the wastage of paddy, by-products and fuel. Even in agriculturally developed Punjab, almost two-thirds of paddy-processing units are single-huller units. Even the mill sector often fails to utilize by-products, such as rice-husk boards, for which proven technology is available.

Handloom technologies are still primitive. For example, according to the state Commissioner of Handlooms, in Tamil Nadu 77 per cent of machines are traditional pit-looms; frame-looms account for 22 per cent of the total; while the share of semi-automatic and other looms is negligible. Few technologial improvements have been made even for powerlooms; many of them are simply looms purchased from textile mills which have closed down.

Continued use of traditional wooden wheels by potters, and of traditional methods for making kilns and firing pottery, leads to damaged products, low productivity and hard manual labour.

Poor-quality brick-kiln furnaces produce weak and brittle bricks, and a high percentage of damaged output. Poor-quality machinery and tools also lead to low-quality products and services in light engineering and repairs.

introduced in Andhra Pradesh and especially in Punjab. Other illustrations include:

- In Andhra Pradesh some corporate firms have invested in imported machinery and equipment for prawn farming and granite mining and processing. Large corporations, including multinationals, are also establishing modern plants for food processing, for example in Punjab. In the poultry industry, companies like Venkateshwara are investing heavily in training, research and development.
- In synthetic-gem cutting, modern machines have been introduced to a limited extent. For example, Trichy Gem Park in Tamil Nadu is supply-

ing imported Korean machines and providing training in gem-cutting. Other producers, however, still work on antique wooden wheels, on which they cannot produce well calibrated stones.

- The growth of plastic manufacturing in rural industrial estates in Gujarat requires modern machinery, with initial capital investments ranging from Rs10 lakhs to crores.
- The advances in telecommunication technology, along with regulatory changes, have led to the boom in telephone services provided through public call offices (PCOs).

The oilseed processing sub-sector in Rajasthan provides an interesting example of technology change. Because of ever-increasing demand for edible oils, it had become one of the largest contributors to India's import bill. The growth in demand has drawn in large investors, which the central government, concerned about imports, has actively supported. The government has therefore promoted cultivation of oilseeds (through the National Oilseed Development Programme), removed oilseed processing using solvent-extraction technology from the reserved list for small-scale industry, and provided fiscal incentives and some capital subsidies.

The establishment of new solvent-extraction units, as well as modern expeller units, has, however, made many of the small village-based *ghani* units unviable, because the traditional method cannot compete with the more efficient technologies. The residual oilcake from *ghanis* contains 10 to 15 per cent oil, compared to 7 to 8.5 per cent from expellers and only 1 per cent from solvent extraction. Nevertheless, because of the sharp growth in demand the sub-sector continues to grow, even in terms of employment, although some of this employment is in urban centres where most solvent-extraction units are located. The growth of oilseed production has in fact been so fast (at a compound growth rate of 16 per cent a year between 1969 and 1991) that the traditional *ghani* technology could not have kept pace.

The establishment of expeller and solvent-extraction units does not mean, however, that all technological problems in this sub-sector have been solved. For example, the productivity of oilseed cultivation in the country is low by international standards; there is little or no post-harvest grading and cleaning of oilseeds; and expeller plants generate intense heat, which can be harmful for workers.

The most advanced technologies are, however, found in those sub-sectors which rely heavily on exports. The outstanding example is diamond processing in Gujarat where, in spite of having some of the most skilled workers in the world, the industry is introducing the latest laser-cutting machines to retain its position in world markets. In the knitwear sub-sector some entrepreneurs are importing advanced machinery in spite of high import duties. However, even here technology generally lags behind international standards, in spite of a large textile-machinery industry in the country, which has been overprotected from foreign competition to the detriment of the textile industry as a whole.

Three features distinguish clearly the sub-sectors with more efficient technologies:

- Their growth is a response to growing demand, either domestic (for example for poultry, garments, plastics and telecommunications) or foreign (for prawns, processed foods, garments and diamonds); moreover, demand in these sub-sectors is more discerning about product quality.
- New investment is largely being made by the private sector, by corporate entities (for example in mining, poultry and food processing), by traders (in diamonds and other gems), and by individual entrepreneurs (in prawns, rice processing and garments).
- The government has recently assisted the growth of the sub-sectors concerned by relaxing regulatory restrictions, for example in mining, oil processing, garments (for export), diamonds and telecommunications. This has often been coupled with fiscal incentives; reducing import duties on high-quality machinery is particularly important.

Our analysis does not mean that 'modern' technologies are intrinsically better. In some sub-sectors, basic labour-intensive methods are appropriate granted India's factor conditions. In many traditional sub-sectors, such as handlooms, carpet-weaving and other handicrafts, the putting-out system is extensive, whereby traders deliver raw materials and inputs to home-based producers and take back the finished or semi-finished products. Such a system makes use of India's comparative advantage in labour which is cheap but skilled in traditional crafts.

In other cases there is a clear trade-off between more efficient technologies and traditional livelihoods, as we illustrated above for oilseed processing. Another example was the Tatas proposal to enter the fish sub-sector on Chilka Lake, Orissa, which would have significantly developed fish processing in the state, but threatened the traditional livelihoods of many fishermen. The protection of these livelihoods was one of the main reasons for reserving many traditional products, such as handlooms, textile products and pottery, for small and tiny-scale industries.

Technologies should not of course be upgraded purely in the pursuit of some vague goal of modernization; equally, traditional workers who often belong to weaker sections of society need to be ensured employment. Our study suggests, however, that the policies on traditional technologies pursued so far have largely failed (see chapters 4 and 5). All too often it has been assumed that such technologies are appropriate, regardless of their efficiency and productivity. As a result, India has sought to preserve low capital–labour ratios within traditional sub-sectors through reservation, fiscal concessions and subsidies, and attempts to upgrade skills among traditional workers have been lamentable (Box 3.3). The result has often been to condemn traditional workers to poor working conditions, low productivity and hence low wages. Far less has been done to upgrade technologies and products for changing markets, and to enhance basic education and skills. At the other end of the spectrum, as India becomes more integrated into the world economy, it cannot afford to fall too far behind in the technologies it uses. Export sectors need sophisticated methods to compete in international markets.

Box 3.3: Training and skills in the RNFS

There are many formal training programmes and institutes in India, but the number of trainees that graduate from these is fairly limited. Thus in 1993–4 the TRYSEM programme (Training of Rural Youth for Self-Employment) sought to train only 300 000 youth all over the country. Many training programmes for village producers and artisans are limited to those identified by the District Industries Centres and Khadi and Village Industries Boards. Training at Industrial Training Institutes is more suited to larger urban units rather than the all-purpose small manufacturing or repairs that many rural units have to undertake. The formal training institutes we saw in, for example, the agro-processing, coir, leather and tourism sub-sectors are also more oriented to larger urban units. Many NGOs provide training as well, but in terms of the overall size of the RNFS their coverage is limited. Some exceptions are, for example, in traditional garments in Gujarat and in gem cutting in Tamil Nadu, where NGOs have had a larger impact.

There are also many private vocational training institutes that receive no support from the government. Few of these have fully qualified staff, and the quality of the training they provide is not always high. In the case of computer training the Department of Electronics has introduced a system of recognizing institutes (although these are found largely in urban areas), and has removed recognition from those that have not met the required standards. Such a system has not been applied to other training activities, however, although the All-India Council of Technical Education has framed regulations to give recognition to training establishments for various professional programmes. The National Council for Vocational Training has made similar efforts for vocational training.

With such inadequate formal training available for the rural non-farm sector, most workers learn the necessary skills on-the-job, often from family members or through informal apprenticeship. In some cases such on-the-job training can be of a high order, for example in diamond processing and ready-made garments, both of which need to ensure quality for exports. In other cases the lack of training opportunities may cause problems in upgrading skills to deal with new and modern materials, products and services. It is thus entrepreneurs in modern sub-sectors that complain most about the lack of skilled human resources. This applies, for example, to fisheries, stone processing, silk reeling, modern garments, plastics, small engineering and tourism.

The situation is no better in the service sub-sectors. There are no training programmes for business services. In private health care many of the medical practitioners are not fully qualified and there is no system for ensuring standards among them. Even in education no specific training institutes or courses exist, apart from such courses as the B.Ed., and most graduates from these courses seek employment in government and recognized schools where remuneration is higher. Most teachers at private schools learn on the job, even though such schools teach a substantial proportion of children.

One of the difficulties is the technology dualism in so many sub-sectors, and thus the enormous gap between larger modern units and the vast majority of tiny enterprises. There are several ways to bridge this gap.

First, intermediate technologies are needed, which are descaled from modern manufacturing processes, but which would allow small rural producers to enhance their productivity significantly. Some examples of such intermediate technologies are oil-expeller units, hydraulic crushers for *khandsari*, wet-blue tanneries, and even powerlooms. In the transport sector examples include the improvised 'Jugadi' or 'Maruta', and various three-wheelers for goods and passenger transport. The public call offices (PCOs) are an outstanding case of labour-intensive telecommunications.

Second, closer links need to be established between small producers and large corporate entities. Examples of this are the Common Production Centre of the UP Small Industry Development Corporation for ceramic manufacture in Khurja, which has some 80 dependent units, and Deejay Hatcheries, which is vigorously promoting small-scale poultry rearing in Tamil Nadu.

Both the above proposals may require dividing manufacturing processes into different stages, only some of which need more advanced technologies. A good example of this is carpet-weaving in UP, where traders purchase raw materials in bulk, household producers weave the carpets using traditional technologies, and finishing is done in larger factory units, which may be mechanized. This is also possible in garment manufacturing and gem processing.

Liberalization, through the lowering of tariff barriers, is, however, gradually aligning domestic and international prices, and this is leading to cost-driven restructuring in many sub-sectors. Some rural industries may benefit from such changes if they enjoy certain cost advantages. First are those, such as silk textiles, in which the wage share of the total value added is high, and thus rural industries have the advantage of cheaper labour. Second are those industries, such as sugar and stone processing, which use bulky raw materials found in rural areas, and rural enterprises therefore enjoy the benefits of lower transportation costs. Third, as space costs in many urban centres are rising, some industries may relocate to cheaper rural areas. New policies have, therefore, to recognize the need to adapt to such changes, and take advantage of them, rather than seeking to preserve the *status quo*.

Conclusions

Different types of sub-sectors

In this chapter we have given an overview of the 80 sub-sectors covered in our study, ten in each of eight states, which we analysed using a framework adapted from Michael Porter's *Competitive Advantage*.

As we have seen, food-processing sub-sectors enjoy good long-term demand prospects and abundant raw materials. However, this potential is often wasted, especially because of restrictive regulations, backward technologies and poor infrastructure. The processing of other primary resources, such as stone, fibres, silk and flowers, is often only emerging, and many will require a full package of promotional inputs to fulfil their considerable potential for generating rural employment. The rapid growth of oilseed processing is the outstanding example of a dynamic primary-processing industry.

The demand prospects, and the raw-material supplies, for many traditional manufactured products, for example of textiles, pottery, leather and wood, are uncertain. Few of these sub-sectors will be able to sustain the large number of workers they currently engage, even though many of them are highly skilled. However, some activities and clusters have been upgraded, for example in the manufacturing of silk products, carpets and gems, to meet niche, urban and export markets.

In contrast, rural employment in modern manufacturing, for example of garments, metal, ceramic and plastic products, has been growing rapidly. These sub-sectors enjoy growing demand, improved availability of raw materials, a generally lighter regulatory environment and effective promotional inputs, especially from the private sector. The challenges they face are to improve the quality of inputs and products, to upgrade technologies

Table 3.2: Different RNFS sub-sectors covered in eight states and categorized as high-share, high-growth and emergent

High-share	*High-growth*	*Emergent*
Mining and quarrying	Mining and quarrying	Poultry processing
Plantation products (Assam)	Processing of fibres	Prawn processing
Processing of grain, paddy, sugar and fish	Powerlooms	Sericulture and silk
Bidi-rolling	Silk textiles	Floriculture and phytochemicals
Cotton textiles	Textile products	Spice processing
Textile products	Carpets (UP)	Oilseed processing
Wood, cane and bamboo products	Wooden furniture and fixtures	Fruit and vegetable processing
Leather (Rajasthan)	Leather (UP)	Ceramics
Pottery	Ceramics	Stone-ware
Matches (Tamil Nadu)	Diamonds (Gujarat)	Cement-ware
Metal products	Metal products	Plastic products
Repairs	Repairs	Gem cutting
Construction	Construction	Business and communication services
Land transport	Land transport	Rural tourism
Retail trade	Retail trade	
Restaurants and hotels	Restaurants and hotels	
Educational services	Business and communication services	
Health services	Rural tourism	

and skills, to obtain reliable sources of energy, and to improve working conditions.

Services employ the majority of rural non-farm workers, and as the economy expands and incomes rise, they are likely to continue to grow rapidly. However, private-service providers have often been neglected in the face of extensive public-sector involvement and regulation. This needs to be reduced, the quality of services improved, and consumers protected.

In concluding this chapter, we revert to the categorization of sub-sectors developed in the previous chapter:

- *high-share*: those sub-sectors which already generate a high share of employment in the rural non-farm sector;

- *high-growth*: those sub-sectors in which RNFS employment is growing at a rapid rate; and
- *emergent*: those sub-sectors which are only just emerging as part of the RNFS, and thus do not feature prominently in past data.

Table 3.2 lists some of the sub-sectors we have reviewed in this chapter as high-share, high-growth or emergent. This categorization should not be treated rigidly. Some sub-sectors may fall into different categories depending on how narrowly they are defined. For example, cotton textiles is a high-share sub-sector, but powerlooms is one of the fast growing sub-sectors in terms of rural employment, while employment in handlooms is stagnating. Some sub-sectors, such as construction, are both high-share and high-growth. Others may fall into different categories, depending on which region or state within India is under consideration.

We now compare these different groups of sub-sectors according to the four determinants that contribute to competitive advantage: factor conditions, supporting industries, size and structure of firms, and demand conditions.

Factor conditions and supporting industries

Factor conditions are often favourable in high-share sub-sectors. For example, agricultural produce and other raw materials are readily available through highly developed trading channels. The skills and knowledge for basic processing, traditional manufacturing and basic repairs are widespread within the rural population, and formal and informal apprenticeship provides easy access to these skills for new entrants. There are also plenty of unskilled labourers. Access to capital from the formal banking system and the availability of infrastructure are generally less favourable, although this applies equally to high-growth and especially emergent sub-sectors.

Likewise, in high-share sub-sectors supporting industries are often well established, for example for machinery and tools. There are also many promotional agencies for assisting with raw-material supplies, technology development and marketing. And producers, or at least traders, in these sub-sectors are often well organized.

Similar comments could be made about many high-growth sub-sectors. For example, metal, leather, yarn and, increasingly, silk are readily available, and diamonds are easily imported. Basic skills and knowledge, for example for textile products, diamond processing and transport, already exist or are being developed through private or public initiatives. Unskilled labour is abundantly available for mining and construction. In some high-growth sub-sectors there are also many promotional agencies, for example for textile products, ceramics and leather.

The picture is often very different for emergent sub-sectors. The growth of some of these has been assisted by public or private promotion, or both.

Examples include prawn and poultry processing, plastic products and gem-cutting. In others, changes in the regulatory environment, such as decontrolling supplies of cement or franchising telephone services to small PCOs, have allowed the sub-sectors to emerge.

But for many emergent sub-sectors factor conditions and the supporting environment are unfavourable. Less than 1 per cent of fruit and vegetables produced in India are processed, partly because of weak storage and transportation facilities. The cultivation of flowers and herbs is not highly developed in spite of potentially high returns. In many cases the necessary skills and knowledge as well as tools and machinery are in short supply, either for new activities, such as phytochemicals and plastic products, or for upgrading traditional activities, such as sericulture and stoneware, to access modern markets.

In some cases bankers are unfamiliar with these emergent activities, and so are unwilling to take risks to finance them, although some of the industrial units in modern manufacturing have better access to formal financial channels. Related industries for packaging of processed foods, for supplying quality machinery and components, for providing design inputs, and so on, are underdeveloped. And some emergent sub-sectors, such as stone and cement-ware, have received little attention from public agencies or private corporations.

Size and structure of firms

The vast majority of RNFS enterprises are tiny, often using traditional artisanal technologies, while there are only a few larger units with more modern machinery. Granted this huge number of enterprises, and the size of the Indian economy, many of the high-share and high-growth sub-sectors are extremely competitive. Existing enterprises even in emergent sub-sectors, while fewer in number, are often unable to establish barriers to prevent new entrants.

Competition can be particularly intense in dynamic clusters where many units in the same sub-sector come together in one locality. Such clusters are characteristic of many sub-sectors, whether high-share, high-growth or emergent, although they are particularly common in some of the most dynamic and growing activities. Figure 3.2 provides an illustration of one such cluster in the stone-processing sub-sector in Betamcherla in Kurnool District (AP). Note that the different types of enterprises in the cluster extend well beyond the stone-polishing units themselves to include many of the supporting industries, such as equipment suppliers, finance and transportation companies. The cluster has also given rise to a series of producer associations. Such industrial clusters (or districts) have recently attracted considerable policy attention in developing countries as an effective structure for small industries which compete and collaborate with each other, and are sufficient in number to attract the necessary related and

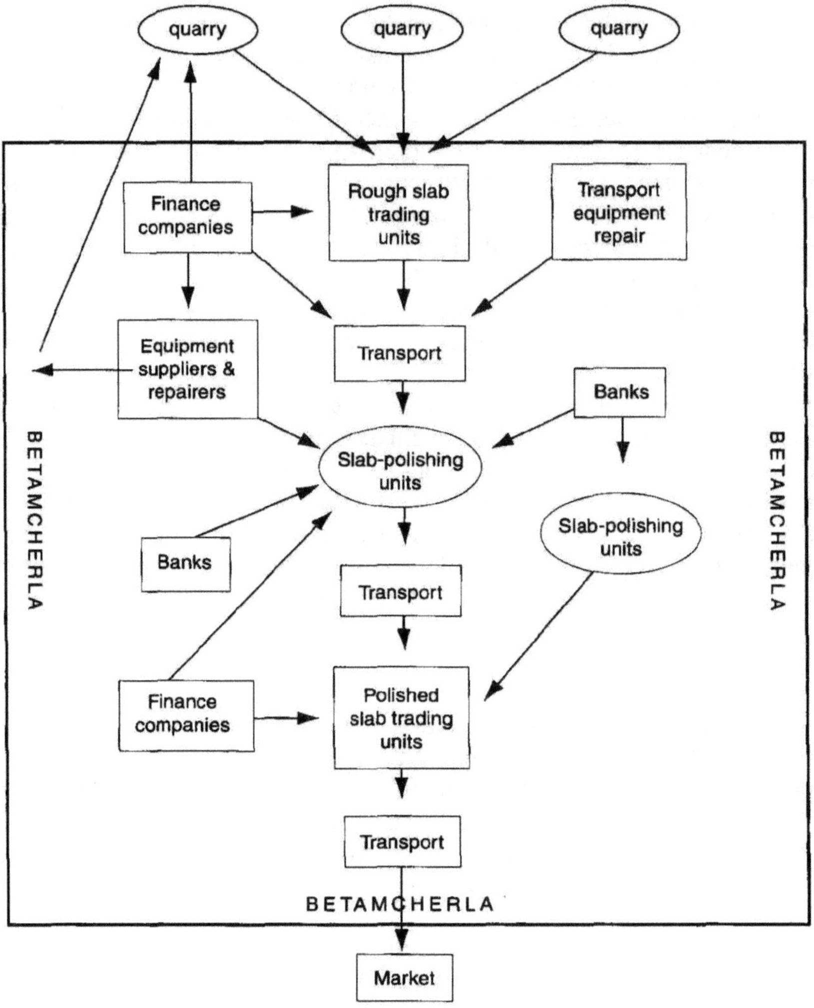

Unit type	No. of units	Workers
Quarry	400	10 000
Transport (rough slab)	200 lorries	1000
Transport (polished)	200 lorries	1000
Rough-slab trading	50	200
Transport repair	15-20 shops	60-80
Equipment supply and repair	5 shops	15-20
Stone polishing	250	3000
Polished-slab trading	100	400
Private finance companies	55	150
Banks	3	15

History of growth

Year	No. of units
1912	First unit established
1975	5 units
1985	15-20 units
1995	250 units

Producers' associations

Rough-slab traders association
Slab-polishing units association
Lorry owners' association
Polishing workers' association
Slab-loaders' association

Figure 3.2: A stone-processing cluster in Betamcherla, Kurnool District, in Andhra Pradesh

supporting industries (IDS, 1992; Holmstrom, 1994; Pedersen *et al.*, 1994; Humphrey and Schmitz, 1995).

Constraints on competition are found mostly in those sub-sectors in which government regulation has been extensive, for example in the processing of 'essential commodities', in sericulture and textiles, in mining and public construction, in matches and *bidis*, in telecommunications and transport (see analysis in the next chapter). Many of these are high-share sub-sectors, although some, such as mining, construction and textile products, are also high-growth, and a few are emergent.

Competition within some sub-sectors is also restricted by the close links between economic and social structures. We illustrated this with the case of the leather sub-sector, in which traders in raw hides and tanned leather are close-knit socially; this forms a strong barrier against outsiders seeking to enter this lucrative trade.

Demand conditions

We have seen that factor conditions and supporting industries are generally favourable for both high-share and high-growth sub-sectors, even though rural employment in the former is often stagnant while it is growing rapidly in the latter; nor do clear distinguishing features emerge when comparing the size and structure of firms across high-share, high-growth and emergent sub-sectors.

The determinant that most clearly distinguishes sub-sectors in these three different categories is, therefore, demand. Almost all high-growth and emergent sub-sectors enjoy increasing demand. Demand in the former tends to be large and growing; stone, powerlooms, garments and metal products are all good examples. Demand in the latter tends to be growing fast, although it may not yet be substantial; examples of this include processed fruit, vegetables and poultry, phytochemicals and cement-ware.

In contrast, demand prospects for products from high-share sub-sectors are much less certain. In some cases, such as processed grains, textile products and construction, demand is large and growing, not least because of the growth in population. In other cases, such as handloom products and pottery, demand may be declining in the face of competition from substitutes. In other cases future demand prospects are uncertain, for example for *gur* (a semi-processed sugar) and *bidis*. Prospects may be better within niche markets, for example for silk textiles and glazed pottery, but such demand is unlikely to sustain the extensive employment in these sub-sectors.

Our conclusions therefore confirm Porter (1990) in suggesting that demand conditions are a more important determinant than factor conditions. In most sub-sectors domestic demand is the key. Although strong export demand is driving a number of high-growth and emergent sub-sectors, such as prawns, garments, leather and diamonds, the strength of export demand varies a lot within all three categories of sub-sectors. For example, India is a major exporter of stone (and quarrying is a high-share sub-sector) while wooden furniture, metalwork and cement-ware (high-growth and emergent sub-sectors) enjoy very little export demand.

Hence our analysis suggests the primary importance of demand conditions. The most striking example is the phenomenal growth in the output from powerlooms despite a hostile policy environment designed to protect handloom weaving. This does not mean that the other determinants (factor conditions, the size and structure of firms, and supporting industries) are not important. As Porter argues, rightly, his diamond is a mutually reinforcing system. Demand trends have so often been ignored among Indian policy-makers, however, that they deserve special emphasis.

Promotional resources and activities are wasted if they fly in the face of the underlying demand trends, and this has led to a series of major policy failures within the context of the RNFS. A notorious example is the way in which policy-makers have regarded the lack of credit rather than of demand as the ruling constraint, and devoted vast resources to financing unproductive activities. This diversion of resources and attention to unproductive purposes has caused Indian policy-makers to miss opportunities to promote other sub-sectors, where demand trends are promising but where constraints are faced in the other three determinants of the diamond. With adequate resources these constraints could have been addressed by public action or by supporting private initiatives.

In the next three chapters we look at public action in regulation, promotion and the provision of credit respectively. We look both at policies and at the bodies that implement these policies. Later we assess the extent to which producers and other actors are organized, before summarizing our overall analysis of the RNFS, assessing its future prospects for generating rural employment, and recommending alternative policies and organizational structures for promoting the RNFS.

4 Regulatory policies and agencies

India has an elaborate framework of laws, with further rules and regulations under those laws, for controlling economic activities and enterprises. In this chapter we analyse these laws and the agencies responsible for implementing them, using some of the theoretical insights described in Box 4.1. Assuming for the most part that the rationale for these laws is reasonable, we review whether the laws meet their objectives in practice, and in particular what impact they have on the rural non-farm sector. Do they promote or hinder the growth of the RNFS? If they do not meet their objectives in practice and have an adverse impact on the RNFS, how can the laws and regulations, as well as their implementing agencies, be changed to contribute more positively to rural development?

To this end, we divide the chapter into four sections. The first describes the various types of laws and regulations that apply to, or impinge on, the rural non-farm sector; the second provides an overall assessment of these regulatory policies and their impact; the third analyses the regulatory agencies responsible for implementing the laws and regulations; and the final section offers some conclusions and recommendations for reform.

Specific regulatory policies

Table 4.1 lists the different types of laws that we review in this chapter, along with the various rationales for designing them. We describe each of these types below, so that we can draw on this analysis for our overall assessment of regulatory policies in the second section of this chapter.

Incorporation In the RNFS the vast majority of units are proprietary and do not therefore need any formal incorporation. This applies in particular to household 'own-account enterprises' (see Figure 2.1, p. 44) or cottage industries. A few RNFS units, on the other hand, are partnership firms, which require an appropriate deed drawn up by a lawyer or chartered accountant.

The major disadvantages of a proprietary or partnership firm are that there is no limit to the liability of the owner(s) if the firm suffers from a sustained loss, nor can the owners seek equity capital from a wider set of individuals. These disadvantages are strongly outweighed, however, by the ease with which entrepreneurs can establish such firms, and the lack of

Box 4.1: Neo-institutional economics

Neo-institutional economics is a branch of economics that attempts to go beyond the restrictive assumptions used in the model of perfect competition, assumptions such as perfect information, a large number of producers and consumers, and no barriers to entry and exit. Neo-institutional economics acknowledges market imperfections due not only to monopolistic and monopsonistic competition, but also to institutional constraints. It handles these by using the concepts of 'transaction costs', 'property rights' and imperfections therein, due to the unenforceability of 'contracts', and the 'principal-agent problem' (Eggertsson, 1990).

In this theory the term 'institution' has a much wider meaning than its common definition as a formal organization of some significance. For example, Douglass North (1990: 3) describes institutions 'as the rules of the game in a society or, more formally, . . . the humanly devised constraints that shape human interaction'.

We draw on neo-institutional economics to analyse different types of policies and agencies which impinge on the rural non-farm sector. In this chapter we use the principal-agent problem, as well as the theory of transaction costs, to explain some of the features of regulatory policies and agencies in India, including why distortions take place between stated and practised policy. North (1981: 201–2) explains the meaning of principals and agents as follows:

> Institutions are a set of rules, compliance procedures, and moral and ethical behavioural norms designed to constrain the behaviour of individuals in the interests of maximising the wealth or utility of principals. . . . A key distinction in this model is between agents and principals. Put simply, agents work for principals, or, in the more formal terminology of Meckling and Jensen, the principals 'engage another person (the agent) to perform some service on their behalf which involves delegating some decision-making authority to the agent'. . . . There is some latitude in decision-making power by the agent as a result of the inability of the principal to perfectly constrain the agent's behaviour. Most individuals are agents in one role as employees and principals in another role as consumers.

Table 4.1: Laws and their rationale

Laws	*Rationale*
Incorporation	To allow enterprises to derive benefits as legally recognized entities, and to protect owners, investors and debtors
Registration	To gather information for governing economic activities and allocating resources and services
Licensing for production	To control modes of production, and to protect weaker economic actors (especially traditional and small producers), as well as workers, consumers and the environment
Licences and quotas for raw materials	To control inter- and intra-sectoral resource allocations, and to allocate public or quasi-public goods
Taxation (income and sales tax, excise, *octroi*)	To gather revenue for the various tiers of government, from local to central; sometimes to change relative prices
Labour laws	To ensure fair wages, welfare and safety for workers
Environmental laws	To protect the environment
Consumer laws	To protect consumers by ensuring quality and standards for products
Laws applying to specific sub-sectors	All the above rationales may apply, depending on the specific laws introduced

visibility and accountability to public authorities that such entities entail. Nevertheless, a new form of incorporation of 'limited partnership', which would limit the liability of the partners, would be advantageous for many partnership firms.

The currently available forms of limited-liability incorporation, the private- and public-limited company, are beyond the reach of the vast majority of RNFS entrepreneurs, because of the legal formalities and transaction costs involved. Even in a town such as Tiruppur in Tamil Nadu, where the hosiery industry is booming, only 12 out of an estimated 3000 units are registered as private-limited companies. Nevertheless some larger modern factories in the RNFS, for example for food processing in Punjab, granite processing in Andhra Pradesh, or for plastics and ceramics in Gujarat, are being incorporated as limited companies.

One mode of incorporation which is of special relevance to the sector is the industrial cooperative society. Such organizations are common in many sub-sectors, for instance in traditional crafts such as handlooms, and in processing primary products such as silk, milk, oil and fish. We discuss the success or otherwise of cooperative societies in Chapter 7. Here we focus on the legal framework.

Under most state cooperative acts, the state can exercise a high degree of control over industrial cooperative societies. The Registrars of Cooperatives thus have powers to call for and suspend elections, supersede an elected Board of Directors, and audit the books of accounts. In state after state we came across extensive political abuse of these powers. In some states the Khadi and Village Industries Board, or specific state directorates (e.g. for sericulture), act as the registrar for cooperatives in the sub-sectors that fall under their remit. These registrars have sometimes been less eager to interfere politically in the management of cooperatives. And in some states, notably Gujarat, the strength of the cooperative movement has reduced the extent of government interference.

For many years efforts have been made to free the cooperative sector from the yoke of bureaucratic and political control. A committee chaired by Chaudhary Brahm Prakash (GoI, 1991c) has submitted a model cooperative bill which enhances cooperative autonomy considerably. Other suggestions have been to add a separate chapter on 'independent' cooperatives (which do not use substantial government resources) to existing cooperative laws, or to insert a chapter on 'cooperative companies' under the Companies Act. A major breakthrough in cooperative legislation came in 1995 when the first state government adopted a new cooperative law, the Andhra Pradesh Mutually Aided Cooperative Societies Act, based on Prakash's model bill, and there is now hope that some other states may enact similar legislation (Cooperative Development Foundation, 1996: 2–5).

Cooperative societies enjoy many special benefits and concessions, such as the preferential allocation of scarce raw materials, concessional credit and exemption from certain taxes. As a result, many dummy cooperatives have been formed, which are in essence private businesses run by individual entrepreneurs. For example, most silk handloom weavers' cooperatives in Andhra Pradesh are in practice owned by master-weavers.

A further problem with the existing laws is that they do not allow executive committee members to draw any salary from the society, as in most cases the executive members are also worker members of the organization. However, since the executive members cannot therefore be compensated for their additional duties, a lot of business of even genuine cooperative societies is conducted outside the purview of their legal books of account.

In summary, the vast majority of RNFS units remain unincorporated and therefore unable to seek outside capital for growth or protect the owners' personal assets against liquidation if their businesses fail. The most common form of incorporation, cooperatives, has turned out to be rife with bureaucratic and political interference.

Registration Larger RNFS units which employ ten workers, if using generated power, or twenty workers, if not, fall under the purview of the Factories Act. This act involves considerable micro-regulation, requiring not only registration (to be renewed annually) and approval of the factory premises, but also the submission of a half-yearly return (Form 21), a yearly return (Form 22), and even that a change of manager be intimated (Form 23). Since the advent of liberalization, however, many states, such as Gujarat, Punjab, Rajasthan and Uttar Pradesh, have simplified or reduced inspections under the Factories Act. Moreover, most RNFS units are too small to fall under the purview of the act. Nevertheless, it remains a powerful incentive for expanding units to stay below the stipulated limits. This is one of the primary reasons cited by RNFS entrepreneurs for promoting multiple firms, often in the same premises.

In many sub-sectors producers have to register with agencies specific to that sub-sector. For example, small tea estates in Assam need to register with the Tea Board if they want access to subsidized credit, while private schools usually need recognition from the state Department of Education if they wish to receive state grants. Many small RNFS units also register with their District Industries Centre (DIC). Although such registration is not compulsory, it is needed, for instance, for applying for an electricity connection, obtaining quotas of controlled raw materials, and informally even for obtaining a bank loan.

Entrepreneurs who have derived benefits from registering with DICs or with specific state directorates did not air many complaints about the process. In some cases, however, obtaining even a provisional registration at the DIC can take several visits (a journey which may be over 100km in some of the larger districts of Rajasthan, for example!).

Moreover, many entrepreneurs who do not want to make their units visible to the authorities do not register with the DICs and other agencies, even though they forgo thereby the benefits to be derived from such registration. Indeed, due to the dispersed nature of the RNFS, it would not be possible to achieve a policy goal of registering all rural enterprises, which number in the millions (see Chapter 2). As a result the practice of restricting mandatory registration to the larger factory type of units is appropriate in terms of setting realistic goals and pursuing administrative efficiency.

The benefits to the authorities derived from registration need to be considered. One objective is to keep track of economic activities, so that data for policy-making can be collected, which is reasonable enough. A second objective is to plan systematically for local raw material, infrastructure and manpower requirements in order to allocate scarce resources efficiently. This assumes, however, that such micro-planning is good for rural units in terms of allocative efficiency, of which there is no evidence, and also that it can be done by local planners. But in practice the DICs (which control raw material supplies) and the Industrial Training Institutes (which train skilled workers), for example, rarely take data from the factory and other surveys into account.

Licensing for production

Since the recent liberalization, licensing for production is now confined to only a few products or sub-sectors. The items relevant to the RNFS are (GoI, 1995a: 32–4):

- distillation and brewing of alcoholic drinks
- sugar
- animal fats and oils
- cigars, cigarettes and manufactured tobacco substitutes
- asbestos and asbestos-based products
- plywood, decorative veneers, and other wood-based products
- raw hides and skins, leather, chamois and patent leather
- tanned or dressed fur-skins
- matches
- paper and newsprint, except when *bagasse*-based

This list of products suggests that important objectives of licensing are to control environmental pollution, to ensure safety standards for workers, and to protect consumers (each of which we discuss further below).

Licensing for production has also been used to protect traditional employment from competition from more modern units. For example, traditional textile products, pottery, paddy and groundnut-kernel processing are restricted to small or tiny units. However, such licensing has rarely proved effective. In particular, it has failed to protect handloom weaving from powerlooms and the mills. Little, Mazumdar and Page (1987: 303–4) argue forcefully that the boom in output from powerlooms has undermined the objectives of extensive government interventions in the textile sector since the 1950s:

> It is not even certain that handlooms have, on balance, benefited at all from the government's policies, for their production was also rising slowly throughout the first half of this century, being 'protected' as now by low wages and, to some extent, specialization in certain markets.

Production licensing in the match industry, reinforced by a structure of excise duty highly favourable towards cottage units, has also had perverse effects: employment conditions are poor, and the industry relies heavily on child labour. Moreover, technology remains primitive and cannot be upgraded without being penalized by the excise duty structure; hence labour productivity is low and units cannot reap the benefits of economies of scale. Many of the cottage units are in any case not genuine, but are simply larger units which have been broken up to enjoy lower excise-duty rates. The industry is in fact dominated by some 18 families who run many small-scale units each. If the licensing system were abolished, the cottage sector would suffer a setback in employment, but it might also lead to the emergence of a more productive and competitive intermediate sector.

A further drawback of production licensing is that it increases the transaction costs involved in establishing new units in the relevant sub-sectors. At worst, production licensing has contributed, for example, to the stagnation of leather tanning in Rajasthan or plywood in Assam, even when raw materials are abundantly available. In Uttar Pradesh horizontal crushers for *khandsari* production require a license, but vertical crushers do not. This has led to a technology shift within the sub-sector in favour of vertical crushers.

There is also some licensing in the tertiary sector, for example of trading in what are deemed essential commodities, such as paddy. Ironically, such restrictions have led to speculative hoarding and the formation of cartels among traders, which the regulations were designed to prevent. Indeed Harriss-White (1996: 301) states that 'it is the collaboration of merchants in the implementation of the array of measures designed to curb their economic power which helps to increase this power'.

In general, therefore, production licensing has not served the intended purposes of more equitable income distribution or consumer protection. Instead pervasive violation has led to the growth of strong vested interests among powerful producers and officials.

Licensing for raw materials As with licensing for production, this practice is being reduced. Until recently, steel and non-ferrous metals, as well as coal, were available at administered prices through controlled channels, but there were also flourishing black markets for these inputs. For example, the cornering of licences or quotas for scarce raw materials was a lucrative side business in the cases of coal used by pottery producers in Khurja, Uttar Pradesh, and of aluminium used by handicraft producers in Jodhpur, Rajasthan.

However, licensing for raw materials remains a ruling constraint in a number of important sub-sectors. This applies, for instance, to the import of roughs, based on import licences, for the flourishing gem-polishing sub-sector. But the most notable raw material whose production and distribution is still tightly controlled is cotton yarn for handlooms. It has been suggested (Jaitley, 1992) that the export of raw cotton and of yarn has affected traditional weavers adversely. The fact is that only a small fraction of either is exported. The main reason why the handloom sector is unable to obtain yarn is paradoxically the result of the very policy designed to ensure that cheap yarn is available to it. Under the government's policy, no excise duty is levied on hank yarn used for handlooms, and it is for this reason that hank yarn is diverted to the powerloom sub-sector.

That removing such regulatory restrictions can allow a sub-sector to grow is clear, for example, from the emergence of small units manufacturing metal, cement or plastic products since steel, cement and plastic raw materials were decontrolled (import duties on some of these raw materials were also reduced).

There are, however, a number of sub-sectors where the primary raw material is essentially a public good which is allocated through some form of licensing. The central and state governments grant leases for mining; the *zilla parishads* in Uttar Pradesh auction licences for lifting raw hides; the Revenue Departments and other agencies in Orissa and Assam auction the rights to fishing in public-water bodies; the Forestry Departments in Assam and other states auction licences for timber harvesting, bamboo and other forest produce.

In each of these cases the prevailing relations of power and control over resources may prevent the most desirable economic or social allocation of such raw materials. In mining, collusive behaviour between existing mine-owners and the leasing authorities allows the mine-owners to corner licences at well below the market value; in the flaying of dead animals for hides and in fishing, the traditional producers cannot compete with contractors or traders who have sufficient capital to buy up the licences; and the traditional wood, cane and bamboo workers cannot collect the necessary raw materials themselves, while there are thriving parallel channels for supplying these raw materials. In many of these cases traditional producers lose control of their customary livelihoods when more powerful economic interests enter the sub-sector. The licensing systems provide an important mechanism for the new entrants to gain control.

Taxation There are at least three types of tax that the RNFS potentially faces: customs and excise levied by the central government; sales and entry taxes levied by the state governments; and *octroi* tax imposed by municipal bodies. Income tax of course also applies to owners of units and the better-paid employees, although there is widespread evasion and most incomes in the RNFS in any case fall below the minimum taxable level.

With liberalization, import duties on many raw materials and products are being reduced. However, restrictions on imports, often enforced by imposing high duties, continue to have a significant impact on many sub-sectors. For example, imported metal sheets from Japan are restricted, reducing quality standards in the metal-product sub-sector. High duties on imported synthetic stone affect the gem-processing industry adversely, and in the sericulture sub-sector there is still significant disagreement about whether silk yarn should be imported, a measure which would benefit producers who use finished silk, but not the cocoon farmers.

Many manufacturing units are affected by high import duties on capital goods, which do not allow them to import machinery to upgrade their production. This is particularly difficult for modern manufacturing units, for example in the food processing, garment, plastic and repair sub-sectors. The import duties have partly been imposed to protect the machinery

Table 4.2: Excise-duty structure (simplified)

Product or item	*Rate of duty* *Basic*	*Additional*
Preserved and prepared vegetables	15%	
Cotton yarn	Rs15/kg	
Cotton fabrics woven on handloom and processed in registered co-operative or other government-approved factory	0%	
Cotton fabrics woven on powerlooms	20%	
Cotton knitwear	8%	1.5%
Embroidery:		
(a) cotton	20%	20%
(b) wool	25%	-
(c) silk	20%	5.1%
Grain (milled)	15%	
Leather	10%	
Tanning industry products	0%	
Footwear:		
(a) manufactured with aid of power	20%	
(b) other	10%	
Leather articles, suitcases, etc.	35%	
Fur-skin garments	15%	
Structural wood	15%	
Plywood	30% + Rs10/ mm thickness/ sq.m	
Furniture	30%	
Iron and steel	15%	
Diamonds, cut and polished	0%	
Articles of jewellery	15%	
Oils and perfumes	20%	

Source: Kohli *et al.* (1992).

industry in India, which is substantial. For the future growth of other manufacturing industries, however, the machinery industry itself needs to be upgraded. Generating more competition by gradually lowering duties on imported machinery is probably the key to this.

Table 4.2 provides a (highly simplified) account of excise due on various raw materials and products. However, as with other small-scale industries (SSIs), no excise is due when the total value of excise clearance is less than Rs3 crores (GoI, 1995a: 137) in any financial year. Beyond this limit excise is levied on a progressively increasing basis. However, such differing rates of tax have encouraged the fragmentation of RNFS units, and in the case of matches have played a major part in determining the very structure of the industry (see p. 90).

Table 4.3: Sales-tax rates under the General Sales Tax Act and Schedules on food stuffs in Andhra Pradesh

Item	*Rate (%)*
Bran and husk of rice	4
De-oiled bran of rice	8
Paddy and rice products such as murmuralu, pelalu and atukulu	8
Maida, atta, ravva and bran obtained from wheat	4
Ravva obtained from rice that has been taxed under this Act	4
Ravva obtained from rice not covered above	9
Ravva obtained from maize	4
Parched and fried Bengal-gram or dhal, and flour of gram or dhal, from gram and dhal that has been taxed under this Act	4
Bengal-gram or dhal not covered above	9
Noodles of wheat or maida that has been taxed under this Act	4
Noodles not covered above	8
Vegetable oils and oil cakes	2
Hydrogenated oils	10
Other articles of processed foods prepared from flour of gram, cereals, pulses or oil seeds	10
Molasses	50
Coconuts other than tender coconuts, and copra	4
Coconuts other than above	8
Cashew nut (with shell)	9
Cashew nut kernel	10
Butter and ghee when sold by a registered organization	10
Other butter and ghee	9
Cheese	10
Milk foods and powders such as Horlicks, Viva and the like, condensed milk, baby milk and baby foods	8
All other food stuffs or products when sold in sealed or tinned containers such as Bournvita, Ovaltine, Ragimalt, Boost and the like	10
Tinned, canned or preserved food in sealed containers	15
Ice, ice-cream and kulfi	10
Cakes, biscuits, pastries, toffees, chocolates and confectionery	15
Sugar-candy	10
Articles of cooked or baked food	9

Source: Krishna Murty (1996: 46–81).

RNFS units pay sales tax on some raw materials, and have sales tax imposed on some of their products (although leather, wood, pottery and other products made by rural artisans are often exempted). In Andhra Pradesh there are some 250 listed items in the General Sales Tax Act and Schedules, with 16 different rates ranging from 1 to 50 per cent. Table

4.3 shows the sales-tax rates for various food products in the state. As can be seen, the level of taxation is erratic and the code leaves a lot of scope for arbitary interpretation.

The major problems faced by producers with sales tax are twofold: first, the complicated systems followed by most states for assessing tax (Table 4.3 is highly simplified and cannot reflect these complexities); and, second, the pervasive corruption in the Sales Tax Departments. In addition to regular visits by the sales-tax inspector, producers and traders have to put up with the surprise checks of the sales-tax inspector (mobile) and the sales-tax inspector (vigilance). And so, while most of the less organized non-farm sector escapes paying sales tax, there may be substantial fear of the inspectors' visits. Moreover, transporters, though not liable for sales tax themselves, suffer from the system of check-posts established at state borders because of the different tax rates imposed by states on the same products. These check-posts can hold up goods vehicles for many hours.

Some attempts to reform the sales-tax system are now being considered. For example, at the request of the Confederation of Indian Industries (CII), the Chief Ministers of states in northern India met to try to harmonize the sales-tax structures across their different states, and sales-tax check-posts between Punjab and Haryana have been abolished.

Octroi is the most problematic of all the taxes for the RNFS, as it affects even small producers. Implementation is often arbitrary and corruption at the check-posts rampant. Small producers often have to pay *octroi* even while in transit through a particular city, since they do not have the necessary documentation to prove that they are in transit. Assessing the value of unpriced goods becomes a problem for small producers, and reclaiming *octroi* paid on unsold goods taken back is near impossible. In addition, transporters are extremely critical of *octroi* because of the frequent hold-ups it causes, and have gone on strike on several occasions in protest. Again, some reforms are underway. For example, in Rajasthan the collection of *octroi* in some selected municipalities has been auctioned out to private contractors, and the municipalities have already raised far more revenue this way than they did before.

And so the small size and physical dispersion of many RNFS units ensure that the majority of taxes do not apply to them. However, the units are affected by taxes on inputs produced by large industrial concerns, for example yarn produced by mills, and by various taxes like sales tax and *octroi* that cause considerable disruption to the transportation of rural products. At the same time, even when taxes do apply, there is widespread evasion among producers in the RNFS, as elsewhere in the Indian economy (see, for example, the account of tax evasion by traders in Harriss, 1991). While small producers may escape the reach of the tax authorities, larger producers may use the very complexity of the tax laws to their own advantage in evading tax dues: 'The unrealistic economic assumptions upon which commercial law is made are as clear as the unwillingness of the state to close the loopholes of evasion' (Harriss-White, 1996: 296).

Labour wages, welfare and occupational safety There is a whole series of labour laws which may apply to RNFS units.[1] The objectives of these laws are to ensure that workers get a fair wage and benefit entitlements and that the physical conditions of work are safe and healthy; to prevent illegal practices such as bonded, contract and child labour; to support labour rights; and to govern industrial disputes.

All of these laws apply to the industrial sector in general, and most have a lower limit below which they do not apply. Thus the majority of RNFS units fall outside their ambit. In the field it became clear that there is little regard for labour legislation even when it does apply to RNFS units.

There are numerous examples of child labour, for example in the carpet, knitwear, match and diamond-processing industries, as well as in service sub-sectors like restaurants and hotels. A study by the Madras Institute of Development Studies (MIDS, 1985) on child labour in the match industry points out that while many male workers are unwilling to work at the wages paid to unskilled workers, there are still sufficient women willing to work at these rates, as well as households willing to provide child labour, thus ensuring that wages do not rise. Direct intervention may therefore be the only way to increase wages. The difficulty is that many of the smaller units may go out of business as a result, and there is currently no alternative work for the households; in some cases earnings from child labour in the match industry exceed 50 per cent of total household earnings.

However, there is relatively less child labour in some sub-sectors such as *bidi*-making, partly because of the high political profile and organization of the workers in this industry. Likewise the high political visibility of labour in the plantation industry in Assam (two ministers in the government are from tea tribes) may have resulted in child labour being used more sparingly there.

Few units in any of the sub-sectors we covered pay benefits to workers, such as employees' state insurance, bonus, provident fund, gratuity or

1. Acts for Minimum Wages, and Payment of Wages; for Employees Provident Fund, Employees State Insurance, Payment of Bonus, Payment of Gratuity, and Maternity Benefits; for Factories, Mines, and Workmen's Compensation; for Bonded Labour System (Abolition), Child Labour (Prevention and Regulation), and Contract Labour (Abolition and Regulation); for Equal Remuneration, and Industrial Employment (Standing Orders); and for Industrial Disputes.

maternity benefits. Many units in fact pay workers daily wages or piece rates precisely to avoid having to pay benefits. Many other labour laws are flouted. As just one example, in the trade sub-sector long hours are maintained by staff, well beyond those declared in the forms displayed in the premises under the Shops and Establishments Act.

In summary, labour policies are mostly ignored in the RNFS, by both producers and regulators. Only in larger factory units in some of the more organized sub-sectors (e.g. in jute mills) do labour laws have a greater impact. But even many large units flout the regulations by under-reporting the number of workers employed and the number of days worked. Avoiding labour legislation is, in fact, one of the primary motives behind entrepreneurs dividing their units into multiple smaller units.

The reason that labour laws are ignored so much is not far to seek. The RNFS is dominated by tiny units, most of which employ both family and hired labour. For many unskilled workers the RNFS is the entry point into the labour market, while for others it may be a lean-season part-time source of employment. Workers in the RNFS are, therefore, rarely willing or in a position to bargain for better wages, benefits or working conditions.

Moreover, the sheer number of labour laws, each with numerous stipulations, does not help producers or regulators to focus on the most critical labour issues. In one of our case studies, a labour inspector found that a leather-tanning unit in Rajasthan was in breach of labour regulations on over 40 different counts. These included infringements on the almost petty grounds that there was no soap and plastic mug in the bathroom. Under such circumstances it becomes almost impossible for producers fully to implement the laws, even if they wanted to. Even the regulators themselves have to choose what to give more attention, and it is not surprising that they can thus use the regulations to harass producers.

In the final analysis, however, wages and benefits will equal the marginal productivity of labour, and if the technology used is such that the productivity of labour cannot exceed a certain level, wages will also remain low. This is why woollen *khadi*-yarn spinners in Rajasthan earn as little as Rs600 a year as wages (although they do not work full-time), and why the wages of handloom workers trail those of powerloom workers by a factor of two or more. The *bidi* sub-sector also employs a large number of low-paid workers, mostly home-based women in remote regions. In export-driven sectors such as diamond processing and ready-made garments wages are, however, higher. The long-term solution for better wages therefore appears to be higher productivity. While this would lead to a fall in employment in specific sub-sectors, it does not mean that rural employment overall would necessarily fall. Both employment and real wages in rural India have been increasing since the mid-1970s (Vaidyanathan, 1994: 3154).

Environmental protection The main policies for environmental protection are embodied in the Environmental (Prevention and Control of Pollution) Act, the Water (Prevention and Control of Pollution) Act, and the Air (Prevention and Control of Pollution) Act. These laws are implemented by the state and central Pollution Control Boards (PCBs); in addition, the Forest Conservation Act addresses environmental issues for activities carried out in forest areas.

In practice the implementation of these acts is highly erratic. While it is becoming more and more difficult for new units to receive clearance from the PCBs, existing units, and even new units once they somehow get clearance, can continue to cause pollution without being questioned. The statutory powers to fine and prosecute defaulting units is inadequate, and the PCBs have only limited infrastructure and reach to enforce the regulations.

Environmental problems in the RNFS are, however, limited to a few sub-sectors. The list of industries for which licensing is compulsory (see p. 90) includes some industries, such as sugar, leather-tanning and wood products, for environmental reasons. Other RNFS activities may also damage the environment, such as construction, manufacturing bricks and cement products, recycling plastics and dyeing textiles. Most RNFS units, however, are small and dispersed, which reduces the pollution problem (though not necessarily to their local neighbourhoods).

Nevertheless, some sub-sectors are particularly damaging to the environment. For example, in the minor minerals sub-sector in Rajasthan mine-owners operate the mines and quarries without concern for the environmental damage being caused. But this itself was partly a result of the regulatory framework. Because mining leases were until recently awarded only for small areas and for short time periods, mine-owners could not develop their mines systematically and dispose of over-burden properly. Slaughter-mining and waste dumping have therefore been the norm.

There are clusters of units, such as tanneries, dyeing units and quarries, which together generate substantial pollution. Likewise, in the coastal districts of Andhra Pradesh many of the fertile paddy fields have been converted into prawn farms, resulting in the incursion of salinity into neighbouring fields and even into village drinking-water wells (although in most cases it is local farmers who are converting their fields voluntarily in pursuit of higher profits). There are, however, examples where clustering has been used to advantage to treat polluting effluents. For instance, clusters of textile processing and dyeing units in Balotra in Rajasthan and in Tiruppur in Tamil Nadu are establishing common effluent treatment plants.

Consumer protection: quality and standards

The Consumer Protection Act and the Prevention of Food Adulteration Act, along with the Food Products Order (FPO), are some of the laws designed to protect consumers. In addition, each state has a Directorate of Weights and Measures to ensure that packages contain as much product as claimed on their labels. There are also regulations about stamping on the price and the date of manufacture.

Compliance with these regulations on the part of RNFS units depends largely on which markets are being catered to. Undertakings which sell their output in local markets usually do not bother about the regulations, although this does not necessarily mean that their products are inferior or under-measured. For example, *gur* units in Uttar Pradesh always sell their produce loose, unpackaged and unbranded, yet they command a premium price in the local *haats*.

In contrast, units which produce for non-local (domestic or export) markets are more conscious of quality as well as regulations. In Rajasthan even many of the small oilseed crushing or expeller units sell edible oil in branded tin packs, with a guarantee of purity linked to the brand name. Units which supply fruit and vegetable products to government organizations, as well as for export, need an FPO licence. However, only a very small proportion of units have such a licence, and once a unit receives one, there are few follow-up inspections to check that quality standards are being maintained.

Certain exported textile items require certification by the Export Inspection Agency of the Ministry of Textiles to ensure that the products comply with international regulations on the use of fibres, hand operations, and so on. Where such certification is necessary, there is much greater awareness of quality standards. Carpets in Uttar Pradesh are another example. In this case consumer pressure in importing countries has led to attempts within the industry to certify that no child labour has been used.

However, there are many cases where regulations are deliberately flouted. Packets of *bidis* may contain fewer than stated on the label; some traders in fertilizer adulterate phosphatic fertilizers with ash (which has the same appearance); a number of food products may be wrapped in packaging which is not made of food-grade plastic, even though it is poisonous. In some sub-sectors there are no quality controls at all, for example, matches, potentially dangerous, and poultry products (whether eggs or meat). Perhaps most astonishing is that until recently most states had no effective regulations governing private hospitals or nursing homes, even though the importance of consumer protection in this sub-sector is obvious.

Likewise, where compliance with standards is voluntary, it is only sporadic. This is true of Agmark, which certifies compliance with purity and flavour standards of the Directorate of Agricultural Marketing and

Inspection, of the ISI mark, which certifies compliance with standards laid down by the Bureau of Indian Standards, and of the Ecomark, promoted by the Ministry of Environment for products which are environmentally friendly. The experience with the *Kaleen* brand name certifying that carpets are not made using child labour has been more successful, because it was in response to pressure from overseas buyers.

In summary, it appears that so far most effective efforts to ensure quality and standards are market-driven, rather than due to regulatory pressure. This has the advantage of greater reach and reduced transaction costs, but it does leave a substantial proportion of consumers, particularly poorer consumers, open to the possibility of purchasing sub-standard goods and services. Until more consumers become more conscious of quality and safety, this situation is unlikely to change.

Sub-sector specific policies There is also a plethora of laws and regulations which apply to specific sub-sectors in the RNFS (Table 4.4). Each of the sub-sectors given in the table either has a high share of current rural employment or has experienced a high growth rate of employment in 1978–88. Not only is regulatory control pervasive in some of these important RNFS sub-sectors, but many laws are also old and may no longer be appropriate.

An overall assessment of regulatory policies

Our review points to some common characteristics of laws and regulations that may apply to the RNFS. We look at four in particular: the disparity between highly regulated sub-sectors and those that face almost no regulation; the many laws that have failed to achieve their objectives; the highly complex regulatory environment; and the many laws that are out-of-date or inappropriate for the RNFS.

Disparity Some sub-sectors in the RNFS are highly regulated, while others seem to escape almost all regulation. This chapter itself reflects this divergence by featuring frequent examples of heavily regulated sub-sectors: mining, leather, wood, all kinds of food processing, textiles and textile products, *bidis*, matches, transport, and educational services. There are obvious reasons why these sub-sectors have received such regulatory attention. Some involve primary products for which the state has to assign property rights; some generate substantial employment; and some may have a significant impact on the environment or on consumers. Other RNFS sub-sectors, however, face very little regulation: spices, poultry, traditional textile products, metal products, repairs, cement products, rural construction, and many services, including small retail trade, business services and even health services.

Table 4.4: Some laws applying to specific sub-sectors in the RNFS

Sub-sector	*Laws and regulations*
Food products	Food Products Order, 1955
	Rice Milling Industry (Regulation) Act, 1959
	Wheat Roller Flour Mills (Licensing and Control Order), 1957
	Food Grain (Prohibition of Use in Manufacture of Starch) Order, 1966
	Fruit Production Order, 1955
	Vegetable Oil Products (Control) Order, 1947
	Sugarcane Control Order, 1966
	Sugarcane Press Mud (Control) Order, 1969
	Cold Storage Order, 1961
	Milk and Milk Products Order, 1976
	Coffee Act, 1942
	Meat Food Products Order, 1973
	Maritime Zones of India Act, 1981
	Marine Product Export Development Agency Act, 1972
Retail trade in food	Essential Commodities Act, 1955
	Prevention of Food Adulteration Act, 1954
Tobacco	Tobacco Act, 1978
	Bidi and Cigar Workers (Conditions of Employment) Act, 1966
	Bidi Workers Welfare Fund Act, 1976
	Bidi Workers Cess Act, 1976
Cotton textiles	Textiles (Production by Handlooms) Control Order, 1956
	Handlooms (Reservation of Articles for Production) Act, 1985
Wood and wood products	Indian Forest Act, 1927
	UP Protection of Trees in Rural and Hill Areas Act, 1979
	UP Transit of Timber and Forest Produce Rules, 1978
	Tamil Nadu Sandalwood Possession Rules, 1970
	Tamil Nadu Hill Areas (Preservation of Trees) Act, 1955
	Orissa Forest Act, 1972
Paper	Paper (Control of Production) Order, 1978
Chemical products	Drugs and Cosmetics Act, 1940
	Drugs (Price Control) Order, 1970, 1979, 1987
Minor minerals	Mineral Regulation and Development Act, 1957
	Tamil Nadu Minor Mineral Concessional Rules, 1959
Land transport	Motor Vehicle Act, 1988
	Motor Cars (Distribution and Sales) Control Order, 1959

Sources: *Nabhi's* (1991: 102–4); PRADAN (1988: 154, 180, 203).

Ineffectiveness It is striking how many of the laws have failed to achieve the objectives for which they were enacted (see Table 4.1, p. 87). The livelihoods of traditional workers have not been protected against competition or against control by powerful interests,[2] and the state has failed to guarantee such workers raw materials by controlling their supply. Labour conditions within the RNFS often remain poor, and in some cases appalling, including extensive child labour (as in the carpet and match sub-sectors). Local economic planners have not made use of information generated by registration and other such regulatory requirements. Environmental and consumer protection remains weak. A significant proportion of the potential tax revenue is not collected or is diverted through corruption.

Complexity The third notable characteristic of the regulatory environment is its sheer complexity. For example, some 15 different labour laws may apply to any one factory, and until recently most of these statutes had a separate inspector. Some sub-sectors, such as food processing, are subject to a vast array of legislation. Sales-tax rates, as well as excise rates, vary enormously across different products, even within the same sub-sector, and across states, leaving plenty of scope for arbitrary application and generating severe problems for goods crossing state borders.

The complexity arises partly from the degree of micro-management the central or state governments have sought; for example: to restrict horizontal *khandsari* crushers from operating more than 100 days a year; to know who the current manager of each factory is; to ensure there is a plastic mug in the bathroom; and so on. Many regulations seek to replace market mechanisms: to control the rates charged for cold storage; to purchase inputs on behalf of cooperatives; to ensure adequate and cheap supplies of hank-yarn for handlooms; to plan for raw material and manpower requirements of the local economy; and so on. On top of all this, there are numerous exemptions for small, tiny or village industries, for particular products or technologies.

It is hardly surprising, therefore, that a severe information asymmetry prevails between producers and regulators, allowing the latter to exercise considerable power over the former. Even some regulators are not fully conversant with all the details of the laws they are supposed to enforce.

Outdated and inappropriate Many of the laws and regulations are either out of date or inappropriate. In the former case laws introduced in very different circumstances have not been revised or taken off the statute books. For example, the parameters laid down for edible oils in the Prevention of Food Adulteration Act were stipulated over 40 years ago, and

2. Some sub-sectors are in fact dominated by small and well-known groups: collusive coalitions of contractors in (public) construction and mining; the *bidi* and the match 'kings'; the 'special officers' and others who control handloom and other cooperatives.

cause problems for new types of oilseeds. Regulations for construction are based on out-dated parameters and technologies, and they have not kept up with present-day needs for greater safety, sanitation and environmental protection. (For more examples, see Table 4.4.)

Laws are often inappropriate for the RNFS because they have been devised with larger units in the organized sector primarily in mind. For example, there is no form of formal incorporation below private- or public-limited companies, except partnerships, which do not limit the partners' liability or allow them to raise equity finance. But when laws are clearly inappropriate for smaller units, a size limit is set so that any unit falling below this limit is exempt. This applies to almost all the labour laws, even though labour conditions in the RNFS are often poor. In some cases ideological concerns have clouded practical considerations. For example, the egalitarian philosophy underpinning cooperatives does not allow executive members to be remunerated for their additional duties on behalf of their cooperatives.

Below we analyse some of the institutional reasons for the failure of many laws and regulations, but first, the question remains whether the regulatory framework, as complex and inappropriate as it may be, has much impact on the RNFS at all. Three arguments could be put forward to suggest that it does not:

- As we have seen, some sub-sectors have largely escaped the attention of the regulatory authorities.
- Tiny and small units predominate in the RNFS, and are dispersed over vast geographical areas. It is impossible for the regulatory authorities to cover more than a tiny proportion of them, and most are in any case exempted from many of the laws.
- Even if the reach of regulation does extend to RNFS units, it only imposes some additional costs, which can be treated quite simply as business costs. During field interviews many producers stated that they pay off inspectors when the latter visit, and that such costs have become routine.

The validity of these arguments is questionable, however. Many sub-sectors do face extensive regulation, and even the smallest and remotest units are affected by taxes and other regulations that influence prices and markets. Moreover, many of the most dynamic units within the RNFS are not small,[3] and are clustered, often in rural towns, where regulatory enforcement becomes much easier. And so some of the more dynamic sub-

3. Although they may appear so if deliberately fragmented to be exempted from relevant legislation or to capture special benefits.

sectors with the greatest potential for generating new and productive jobs may be particularly affected by the regulatory framework.

Nor can extra-legal payments to inspectors be considered only as routine business costs. For a producer to comply, or to avoid compliance, with various regulations involves transaction costs.[4] And these transaction costs become more significant the smaller the scale of operations and the more bureaucratic the regulatory agency. Thus regulations may cause substantial delays, which can become a significant barrier to entry for new units. For example, to open a cold storage in Assam requires a licence or permission from three different departments: industry, horticulture and agriculture. Once established, RNFS units then face a multiplicity of regulatory agencies, many of which have several representatives. As one producer put it, he goes by the rule of thumb of 'an inspector a day' (for a list of these inspectors, see ILO, 1994: 40).

Moreover, our analysis of different sub-sectors reveals clearly that the regulatory environment has had concrete impacts, often adverse, which go well beyond mere red tape, harassment and corruption. These impacts are sufficiently important that we describe them in Box 4.2. They demonstrate that the effects of the regulatory environment are a matter not merely of slightly increased business and transaction costs. Barriers to entry are created, and the availability of raw materials, the structure of industries, the choice of technologies and labour conditions affected. In some cases a combination of these factors has contributed to the stagnation of a whole sub-sector, such as handlooms and matches.

Regulatory agencies

The above assessment of the regulatory environment is highly critical. In this section we seek to address why so much of the extensive regulatory framework has failed or been distorted.

Regulatory enforcement in India is regarded by government authorities as their exclusive preserve. Most regulatory policies are implemented by central- or state-government departments, directorates or special offices. The influence that such agencies have on the rural non-farm sector varies according to the sub-sector and the size of operations of a unit.

- Regulatory agencies have greater influence over those sub-sectors which depend on them more, for example for access to a critical resource, such

4. Entrepreneurs themselves distinguish between additional but predictable business costs imposed by regulation and the more uncertain transaction costs of, for example, red tape and unexpected delays. Thus entrepreneurs in Gujarat and Punjab maintain that for every law and regulation officials have a price. However, the difference with other states is that once that price is paid, decisions are taken fast and the work gets done. The pace of decision-making by regulatory officials in Gujarat and Punjab thus came in for praise by businessmen.

Box 4.2: Some impacts of the regulatory framework on the RNFS

Controlling raw materials led to flourishing black markets. Even now much cheap hank-yarn intended for handlooms is diverted to powerlooms, and regulations designed to prevent traders hoarding 'essential commodities' and manipulating their markets have, perversely, encouraged such behaviour. It was the powerful well-connected producers who obtained most subsidized materials, while small producers often paid more than the free-market price, and sometimes failed to purchase vital raw materials at all.

The regulatory framework has resulted in the use of backward technologies in numerous sub-sectors, such as food processing, textiles and matches (see Chapter 3, pp. 72–8). High import duties on capital goods have also prevented entrepreneurs from investing in machinery to compete in international markets. Such backward technologies have contributed to stagnant sub-sectors, poor-quality products and low wages.

Many larger units have been broken up into smaller components to avoid the reach of regulations (such as labour laws) and to enjoy benefits (such as tax exemptions) granted to smaller concerns. This often prevents them from integrating production and management functions, from deriving economies of scale, and from upgrading technologies.

The industrial structure of some sub-sectors, such as textiles and matches, is determined largely by the regulatory framework, regardless of economic efficiency or even social benefits. Among services, regulations in Gujarat, for example, have restricted competition among schools and made it almost impossible for them to be financially viable without government grants.

Some regulations have had perverse environmental effects: regulations on mining leases have actually encouraged environmental damage; regulations directed at conserving forests are not only ineffective, but even discourage farmers from growing trees.

Many regulations, especially on taxes, have caused serious delays for transportation, which increases costs in every subsector. Many state governments have also hindered the growth of private transportation by reserving the most profitable routes for state-owned companies.

Regulations which allocate what are essentially public goods are particularly potent. In Orissa the licence to good land in Chilka granted to the Tata Aqua Farm, rather than to local fishermen, was controversial. Licences for trading raw hides, and the large lots in which the Forestry Department sells wood, are beyond the reach of traditional producers. Only those with substantial spare capital and good government connections can obtain mining leases. In many cases the powerful, often in collusion with the authorities, are cornering licences at below the full market value in order to extract the maximum rent possible from the resources secured. In the process many traditional producers are disempowered.

Some regulations have also become mechanisms for political control. For example, state governments have blatantly abused cooperatives to distribute patronage and manipulate them as vote-banks.

as fish, raw hides, mining and forest produce, or to critical finances such as state grants for schools.

- Regulatory agencies can extend their reach more easily to those sub-sectors which are clustered in an area, such as *bidi* units in Nizamabad, Andhra Pradesh, silk handlooms in Sualkuchi, Assam, rice-milling units in Bargarh, Orissa, and plastic product units in industrial estates in Gujarat.
- The larger the size of the unit, the more easily they can be covered by regulatory agencies. Many small units do not even have to register and may therefore be invisible to regulatory authorities.

Thus the smaller, the more dispersed and the less organized the sub-sector's enterprises are, the more difficult it is for regulatory agencies to cover them. The importance of the sub-sector to the government may also affect the extent to which regulators go to enforce regulations. Sub-sectors may be important because of their potential as vote-banks (handlooms and *bidis*) or as sources of revenue (stoneware, other minerals and wood). The state has also invested heavily in sub-sectors such as sericulture and education.

Many of the agencies entrusted with regulatory functions maintain that they do not have the reach or powers to implement the laws effectively. For example, sales-tax officials believe that a majority of traders do not pay any sales tax and that they, the agents, are helpless to do anything about it. The PCBs maintain that they do not have adequate powers to prosecute for non-compliance, and that they can only withhold giving the initial clearance. The Directorates of Transport complain that they lack the resources to enforce regulations on the rapidly expanding transport sub-sector, and so often leave supposed enforcement to the police. The administrative machinery of the Food Products Order, run by the Directorate of Fruit and Vegetable Preservation, is limited, with only four regional offices, some deputed state officials, and fewer than 100 qualified food inspectors in all of India. Thus, in spite of a strong ideological commitment in the country to an active role for the state, the enforcement machinery available remains weak, as well as being corrupt. The very complexity of the regulatory framework exacerbates this weakness: laws and regulations have not been designed with the ability to enforce them in mind.

Within regulatory agencies, salaries, which are low and often fixed regardless of performance, poor working conditions, the need to comply with bureaucratic procedures, and the difficulty of producers seeking redress against harassment, act as incentives for officials to use regulations to obtain extra-legal payments. The very complexity of the laws often allows them to do this, as regulators enjoy considerable discretion, for example in determining tax rates on goods, which can in some cases involve differences of lakhs of rupees.

What help does the theory from neo-institutional economics, as described in Box 4.1 on p. 86, give in explaining this distortion by implementing agencies of policies with ostensibly good rationales? Let us start by thinking of the regulatory officials as agents of the state, which is the principal. The state has appointed regulators as its agents to perform certain tasks on its behalf, among them, for example, the collecting of taxes, enforcing of labour laws, and ensuring that units do not pollute the environment or sell products which may harm consumers.

The 'rational' profit-maximizing (or cost-minimizing) producer will try not to follow any of these regulations, since they reduce his profits. The rational producer further weighs the costs of being penalized, if caught, against the benefits of higher profits if he gets away with it. In an institutional environment where regulation is sporadic and whimsical, most producers opt for evasion. This explains, for example, the widespread tax evasion in the RNFS. The solution might be to tighten enforcement, but soon the incremental costs of additional machinery for collecting taxes may outweigh the additional revenue raised. The spatial dispersion and the low average tax revenue likely from individual RNFS units therefore prevent much further expansion of the tax net.

On the side of the regulatory officials, a 'rational' agent would like to keep as much as possible of the revenue he collects on behalf of the state to himself. This tendency is curbed only by the possible penalties (such as fines, dismissal or imprisonment) his agency might impose if he is caught. Because in many regulatory agencies 'distributional coalitions' (Olson, 1965) have emerged, the probability of such penalties is low (although the benefits have also to be shared). This gives the regulatory agent an incentive to collude with a producer, by taking as bribes part of the revenue that the producer would have paid to the state.

This transaction is 'rational' for the producer as long as his pay-out is lower than the legitimate tax payment. The acceptable difference is based on his subjective assessment of the probability of being caught and the penalty he might thereby incur. The transaction is also 'rational' for the regulatory agent, as long as his net take (after sharing it with his protectors) exceeds his subjective assessment of any likely costs on being caught, despite protection.

In the case of the RNFS, however, the spatial dispersal and small size of units constrain a regulatory agent's rent-seeking by increasing his trawling costs. He tends to focus on the bigger, road-side, peri-urban units. This explains why fieldwork showed relatively little harassment of cottage units by regulatory officials.

This is not to say that the cottage sector has been spared from rent extraction: it is just that the logic of transaction costs has led to more 'economic' ways of obtaining it. In the case of handlooms, for example, while the individual weaver is not harassed, the subsidies meant for handloom weavers are siphoned off through dummy cooperative societies, effectively owned by the staff and political masters of the various state handloom development agencies. We were given a detailed insight into this 'distributional coalition' by an officer of one such state agency, and the essentials were reconfirmed in interviews with a senior official and the politician chairman of that agency. There is no reason to believe that this practice does not prevail in other states as well.

The theory outlined in Box 4.1 sheds light on possible solutions also. One answer to tax evasion is the imposition of a value-added tax, where it is in the interest of producers to declare their transactions to reclaim the tax they paid on their inputs.[5] Another possibility could be to use non-state intermediaries for tax collection – not the equivalents of RNFS *zamindars*, but producers' associations for example, whose incentive to collect taxes could be the right to retain a part of the revenue for developmental purposes.

As for the regulatory agents, it is neither exhortation nor moral training which will reform them, but rather a change in their incentives. On the one hand, to encourage regulators to perform better, appropriate performance incentives and bonuses could be developed. Currently there are no obligations upon the regulatory authorities to perform which correspond to the obligations on the part of producers to adhere to regulations. On the other hand, to discourage regulators from malpractice like harassment of producers, the costs of such practices to the officials need to be increased, both their actual costs in the present and their potential costs if caught.

New industrial policies in various states already move in this direction. For example, in its industrial policy of 1994, Rajasthan introduced provisions restricting the possibility of harassment by inspectors. There will now be one common return and a common notice for all the labour laws. Compliance with all such laws (except the Factories Act) will be checked through a single inspection. Moreover, only 5 per cent of small-scale units,

5. The Chelliah Committee (GoI, 1992a) concluded that a 5 per cent VAT on cotton yarn was efficient, equitable and implementable.

selected at random, will be inspected. Even here, the officials will need written permission from their departmental head before visiting a unit (except in the case of complaints). Such measures not only increase the officials' immediate costs but also enhance the possibility of internal supervision, thereby strengthening their subjective assessment of the potential costs of being caught.

Simplifying regulations also enhances the possibilities of identifying malpractice. With a uniform tax, such as a sales tax across all products, it is less easy for inspectors to earn extra-legal income by wrongly classifying particular products. Such a uniform tax would also make internal supervision of revenues collected easier. Again, steps in this direction have already been taken when Chief Ministers from different states in northern India met to try to equalize sales-tax rates across state borders.

However, the subjective assessment by officials of the likelihood of not only being caught but also being penalized needs to be increased as well. The latter ultimately requires reforms in the laws governing the security of tenure of public servants (emanating from Article 311 of the Constitution), and reforms in the judicial system, which has not been able to defend the spirit of the law in the face of legal subterfuge and judicial misconduct. Some recent judgements by higher courts, however, have at last come down heavily on corruption and lax enforcement.

While some regulations will always be needed, it does not follow that state functionaries should be the only ones to enforce them. There are at least four other possible regulatory channels: (1) regulation through third-party professionals, such as auditors, chartered accountants, company secretaries and cost accountants; (2) self-regulation by producers' associations; (3) regulation of owner entrepreneurs by worker trade unions; and (4) regulation of producers by consumer and citizen groups. Unions and consumer organizations can act as important and effective countervailing forces to entrepreneurs and producers, as well as to regulatory officials. For example, in the *bidi* sub-sector the unions hold regular meetings with the manufacturers and government representatives.

If such countervailing forces are to become active, however, the transaction costs of exercising vigilance need to be reduced. This has happened already to some extent with unions, whose rights have been enshrined in various laws. More recently consumer courts have been established at various levels. Compared to going through the former cumbersome legal procedures, these new courts have radically reduced consumers' costs in putting forward complaints. Once developed, this system will provide an important additional channel for enforcing regulations relating to food safety, for example, and give considerable support to the state officials.

However, the transaction costs of producers exercising vigilance over regulatory officials also need to be reduced significantly. At present complaints get bogged down in legal procedures, and as a result most producers prefer to make extra-legal payments. Once again, simplifying the regulatory framework is an important method for reducing such transaction costs. The current regulations are often so complex that the producer cannot hope to be aware of all the clauses and stipulations that apply, thereby giving the advantage to the regulator. Simplified regulations, including easier reporting requirements, will reduce this information asymmetry and make it easier for producers both to comply with the regulations and to fight against unfair treatment on the part of regulators.

Producer associations could also be an effective channel for exercising vigilance, as the small-scale industry associations already demonstrate. Such bodies can take up similar complaints from different members, and it is more difficult for officials to harass groups in contrast to individual producers. A more effective system of ombudsmen who could deal swiftly with complaints against government departments and directorates would further reduce the transaction costs to producers. In 1995, for example, the Reserve Bank of India appointed state-level ombudsmen to hear complaints against banks.

As sub-sector after sub-sector is opened up by liberalization to greater domestic and external competition, the economics of mutually-reinforcing patronage by politicians, rent-extraction by officials, and evasion of taxes and other laws by producers begin to crumble. There are already in place new national and state-level policies on minerals (GoI, 1995a: 135), for example allowing for the mortgaging of mining leases in order to obtain loans. Once mining companies obtain loans from formal financial institutions, rather than being dependent on their own capital or on private financiers, their accountability is bound to rise, since the new contractual arrangements demand more careful documentation of production costs and revenues. This in turn will make informal pay-offs on a regular basis more difficult, though by no means impossible. Moreover, the patronage-dependent system of awarding leases, ostensibly on a first-come, first-served basis, will be replaced by a more transparent and competitive auction or tendering system. Above all, the entry of new types of actors in mining will disturb the balance of the distributional coalition between the existing mine-owners and the leasing authorities in the various state Directorates of Mines and Geology and their political masters.

What we have illustrated for mining applies also to other sub-sectors, such as construction. Traditional artisanal sub-sectors, such as handlooms, wood, pottery and leather handicrafts, however, face increasing competition from substitutes and so their profitability is on the decline. After a while regulators may not find much to pick on.

In short, competition, whether internal to the sub-sector or from other sub-sectors, seems to reduce extra-marginal profits and hence the willingness and the ability of producers to make extra-legal payments to regulators. It also results in incentives for collective action to change or remove taxes and laws, compliance with which is costly. If successful, this reduces the need for evasion and thus the necessity to gratify regulators. In sum, greater economic competition among producers is an effective route to better performance by regulatory agencies.

This does not mean that competition will solve all the problems of regulatory policies and agencies we have analysed in this chapter. Rent-seeking is as much a part of unfettered markets as of government interventions (Streeten, 1995: 224–6). Reducing regulations will therefore open up economic activities to greater competition and remove specific mechanisms for powerful interests to exercise their power. But without perfectly competitive markets the underlying power relations may remain. Nevertheless, there can be little doubt that easing the current heavy regulatory burden and increasing competition will lead to a more positive institutional environment for productive economic development in the rural non-farm sector, as the outstanding achievements of China in promoting village and township enterprises (see Box 1.1, p. 4) make clear. In contrast to China, however, India enjoys a strong judicial system which has recently demonstrated its independence in taking up a series of corruption cases brought by private individuals and organizations through public-interest litigation. This change is itself partly a product of the more liberalized environment.

Conclusions

The continuing rationale for regulation

India has a plethora of laws to regulate economic activities, including the rural non-farm sector. Many of these have, however, not only failed to achieve their objectives but also distorted and hindered the economic development of the RNFS. Laws and regulations are also widely flouted by RNFS producers and units, and are used by regulators for rent extraction and by powerful interests to further their own ends. The previous section on regulatory agencies has shown that these outcomes often arise from 'rational' responses by regulators and producers to the incentives provided by the regulatory environment. These conclusions do not, however, lead to the recommendation that all regulations should be abolished, for four reasons:

(1) Some regulation is obviously necessary, and the rationale for many of the laws (as described in Table 4.1, p. 87) remains valid. The various tiers of governance need sources of revenue. Entrepreneurs need to reduce their personal liability through formal incorporation. Workers need to be protected from exploitation and hazardous working conditions. Citizens need to be protected from defective products and pollution. The state needs to gather socio-economic data to be able to govern appropriately.

(2) Some regulation has had a positive impact. It may have helped to preserve employment in traditional sub-sectors like handlooms, pottery and fisheries. Regulation (and promotion) of sericulture, including protecting the industry from cheap imports, appears to have been successful. Some industries have provided substantial tax revenues to various tiers of governance.

Moreover, many laws, even those more often honoured in the breach, help groups to fight for their entitlements or rights. This applies to regulations specifying that preference in the allocation of resources, such as raw hides and brackish-water lands, must be given to traditional producers or small farmers. It also applies to the labour laws, which assist trade unions and NGOs to fight for labour rights. Similarly, laws to protect the environment and consumers give a handle to citizens and citizens' groups to file suits, which can act as a deterrent to other enterprises. Regulations on quality, such as the Food Products Order, have also provided a useful mechanism when market pressures from discerning consumers have demanded guarantees of product quality.

(3) Substantial progress has already been made in reducing the regulatory burden. With liberalization much licensing of production and control of raw materials has been abolished. Many import duties have been radically reduced. Some states have introduced new industrial policies, and have moved towards more uniform rates of sales tax with neighbouring states. Significant regulatory reforms have also been introduced in specific sub-sectors, which we illustrated above in the case of mining; in other sub-sectors, such as transport, more private-sector involvement has been allowed.

There is also evidence that a lighter regulatory environment can indeed assist economic growth and employment generation. For example, small units manufacturing metal, plastic or cement products have emerged since steel, plastic and cement raw materials were decontrolled, while easing the regulatory environment has allowed the diamond processing sub-sector to grow rapidly and become one of the most dynamic activities in the RNFS.[6]

(4) It is important that the authorities do not succumb to special pleading on the part of particular industries, all of which would like to see their tax burden reduced. Those who enjoy special benefits and concessions, as well as members of the many distributional coali-

6. Diamond roughs which are exported after processing are not subject to tax, import duties on machinery have been reduced, the convertibility of the rupee on the trade account has encouraged most traders to turn to legal and accounted trade, while processing units, which do not enjoy such benefits, are able to keep regulatory officials contented with payments.

tions that have grown up around particular regulations, would of course like to maintain their access to such special privileges.

Recommendations for reforming regulations

The barest rationale for regulation, to protect the rights of citizens and ensure the smooth running of the economy, is accepted even among those who favour a minimalist role for the state. Many others would also accept the justification for a more active state to use regulation to protect weaker sections of society and to pursue economic growth. The issue is not so much the rationale of regulation as how to achieve the objectives for which regulations are designed. Currently the impact of regulations is often perverse in undermining their stated objectives. Moreover, the current situation of extensive legislation coupled with pervasive violation prevents progress towards a more positive institutional environment, not just in terms of formal laws but also of informal constraints such as norms of behaviour or self-imposed codes of conduct (North, 1990: 4). Various recommendations follow from this analysis.

- To change the institutional environment from one of extensive regulation with pervasive violation to one of reduced regulation but universal compliance, the regulatory framework needs to be reviewed and simplified, and then more rigorously enforced. The current complexity of the regulatory environment leads to significant information, and hence power, asymmetries between regulators and the regulated; it also goes beyond the ability of the regulatory machinery to enforce. This agenda for reform is one for all levels of governance. It certainly cannot be undertaken by the central government alone, but must be implemented state by state, sub-sector by sub-sector, as each entity has an array of policies specific to itself.
- In spite of some liberalization, the central and state governments in India still retain considerable control over many parts of the economy. Liberalization needs, therefore, to be pushed much further. In particular, regulations which restrict competition must be curtailed in order to break powerful distributional coalitions. The growing competition among states in India will assist this process.
- Any reforms need, however, to consider how regulations will be implemented. A value-added tax has an in-built self-regulatory mechanism; flat-rate taxes allow less arbitrary application, harassment and corruption and involve fewer transaction costs in order for small producers to comply; regulations should place the onus of proof on the regulator, not the producer; and so on.
- As important for implementation is the need for a simplified regulatory framework to be transparent to those who are expected to abide by its laws and stipulations. Governments should seek to create greater aware-

ness through greater openness, publicity, public education and media channels. Transparency will also provide information to producers and workers about their obligations and rights, thereby reducing the power that regulators enjoy over producers, or entrepreneurs over workers, on account of asymmetrical access to information.

- Market mechanisms and countervailing forces are important, too, for the effective implementation of regulations. So the state needs to reduce its control, and place greater emphasis on supporting market mechanisms, strengthening and balancing countervailing interests, guaranteeing quality and protecting rights. Unions are already protected by law (although little labour in the RNFS is unionized). The new consumer courts will contribute significantly to enhancing consumer pressures. In addition, producer associations need to be strengthened. Producer representatives should also be extensively involved in reviewing and reforming regulations that affect them.
- The interests of weaker sections need to be supported, and regulation should continue to protect traditional rights. Due recognition should, however, be given to the fact that the current laws which ostensibly protect such rights have often perversely served as tools for powerful outside interests to exercise control over the resources concerned.

Only with such measures will the regulatory environment support the healthy growth of the rural non-farm sector and of productive rural employment, rather than hinder that development as at present.

5 Promotional policies and agencies

The rural non-farm sector has often been treated as a residual category. Promotional policies[1] have been formulated for agriculture and industry as a whole and have been further broken down into policies for specific crops or industries; for example, India has a textile policy, including policies for textile mills, powerlooms and handlooms, but historically there has been no comprehensive framework for promoting the rural non-farm sector. At best there have been, within broad industrial policy, strategies for promoting rural enterprises clubbed together under '*khadi* and village industries' and, within agricultural policy, strategies for promoting agro-processing activities. It was only the National Bank for Agriculture and Rural Development (NABARD) that formulated rural credit policies separately for the farm and non-farm sectors.

One problem with having a framework for promoting the RNFS as a sector, compared to specific sub-sectoral policies, is its diversity, encompassing, as it does, many different primary, secondary and tertiary activities. Another problem has simply been the failure to see the rural non-farm sector as a critical growth area having the potential to meet national goals of employment and equitable income distribution.

The absence of a comprehensive policy framework for the sector does not, however, imply the absence of any policy influence. To some extent it has been the reverse, with multiple sets of policies impinging on the RNFS. As these policies are not integrated, they often have contradictory impacts on the sector. The objective of most policies directed explicitly at parts of the RNFS has been to preserve employment rather than to increase productivity. Thus policies for *khadi* and village industries, as well as the Integrated Rural Development Programme (IRDP), have not looked at the RNFS as a potential high-growth sector but as one requiring subsidies to meet welfare goals. Other policies influencing the RNFS are a spill-over of the policy framework for the small-scale industries (SSI) sector (including the tiny sector).

The statement on industrial policy issued by the Government of India in 1991, and which still applies today (GoI, 1995a: 23–7), is an example of this scattered approach to policy for the RNFS. The sector appears under various sectoral headings, such as tiny, handloom, handicraft and 'other

1. And regulatory and credit policies also; in practice policy-makers in India rarely distinguish carefully between these different types of policies. For example, protecting industries through regulation has been a favourite 'promotional' strategy.

Box 5.1: Organizational performance

In his book (*Institutional Development: Incentives to Performance*, 1989) Arturo Israel considers variations in performance among organizations. He concludes that the most important contributory factors are:

- the specificity of an organization's objectives and methods;
- the existence of competition or competition surrogates; and
- an organization's management, including structure, decision-making style and personnel policy.

Performance is better among organizations which have a higher degree of specificity in their mission, or which make efforts to increase that specificity by translating their broad goals into agreed concrete objectives and delineated methods. Performance is also better among bodies which have to compete with other similar bodies, or, if external competition is not feasible, among organizations that are either subject to competition surrogates, such as pressure from clients or regulators, or have high internal competition. In such cases the pressure on management to enhance performance is reduced. Israel also points to the importance of freedom from political interference for organizations to perform well.

village industries'. While the term 'non-farm employment' is at least mentioned, the rest of the text seems to follow the typical approach by Indian policy-makers of equating the RNFS with the *khadi* and village-industries sector. Rural services, including trade, transport and financial services, are not mentioned at all. Nevertheless this industrial policy continues to be the overarching framework under which policies for sub-sectors and functional areas are formulated. We give the main features of the policy affecting the rural non-farm sector in Box 5.2.

As with regulation in the previous chapter, it is not feasible to discuss in detail all the promotional policies and agencies for each sub-sector within the RNFS. Instead, we select a few for more detailed analysis, as follows:[2]

- the Rural Industries Projects (RIPs);
- promotion of traditional rural industries;
- technology development, training and technology institutes; and
- infrastructure, raw materials, marketing and the relevant promotional agencies.

2. The Integrated Rural Development Programme (IRDP) does not appear in this chapter. The IRDP was originally conceived as an integrated programme to promote self-employment among the poor, including within industry, services and business. But in practice it has been reduced to a subsidized and targeted credit programme. We analyse it in the next chapter on credit.

Box 5.2: Features of the Industrial Policy of the Government of India (6 August 1991) affecting the RNFS

- The investment limit in plant and machinery for tiny enterprises to be increased from Rs2 lakhs to Rs5 lakhs, irrespective of the location of the unit.
- Tiny enterprises to be eligible for continuing support, including easier access to institutional finance, priority in the government-purchase programme and relaxation from certain provisions of the labour laws.
- To provide a boost to ancillarization and sub-contracting, equity participation by large-scale industrial enterprises in a small-scale unit to be permitted up to a limit of 24 per cent of the total shareholding.
- The Small Industries Development Bank of India (SIDBI) to establish a 'factoring' service to ensure prompt payment of small-enterprise bills.
- A scheme of integrated infrastructural development (including technological back-up services) to be introduced to facilitate location of enterprises in rural and backward areas.
- Tiny and small-scale units to be given priority in the allocation of indigenous raw materials.
- The National Small Industries Corporation to concentrate on marketing, under a common brand name, mass-consumption items produced by tiny and small enterprises.
- The defininition of 'women enterprises' to be simplified. The former stipulation that women workers be in a majority to be dropped; instead, units in which women entrepreneurs have the majority shareholding and management control to be defined as 'women enterprises'.
- Functional industrial estates to be established in areas where agricultural or horticultural produce is concentrated.

On the basis of this analysis we then provide an overall assessment of promotional policies and agencies, before drawing conclusions and making broad recommendations in the final part of the chapter.

Selected promotional policies and agencies

The Rural Industries Projects

One of the earliest initiatives to promote rural industries, particularly in backward regions, was the Rural Industries Projects (RIPs), which began in

1962. According to an evaluation (GoI, 1978) there were many lacunae in the implementation of the projects.

> The central objective before the RIPs was to evolve effective techniques, methods and programmes for promoting intensive development of village and small industries. The choice of industries to be encouraged and the level of technology to be sponsored, were to be related to the economy of the selected areas. . . . [Right from the outset, the surveys conducted by the project staff] used a generalized pro forma which did not permit a satisfactory appreciation of the local economy or of potentialities of the regions covered by the projects. The units which actually came up bore no relation to the so-called potential brought out by the surveys.

The tendency to standardize policies, even across a sub-continent, rather than adapt them to local economic environments, has been repeated often by policy-makers in India. Indeed, as our analysis will show, policy-makers have learnt few lessons from the mixed record of the RIPs, and have made many of the same mistakes, even though these lessons have been apparent for two or more decades.

The RIPs themselves were merged in 1977 into the District Industries Centre (DIC) programme. This was in many ways a replication of the RIPs in every district, but shedding any rural pretensions. The DICs were created to house under one roof various promotional and regulatory activities, such as the registration of small-scale units, and the offices of the many state corporations and departments for different aspects of industrial development. However, the experiences of entrepreneurs we surveyed indicate that DICs do not fulfil their coordination role effectively.

Promotion of traditional rural industries

Traditional sub-sectors such as *khadi*, handlooms, handicrafts and other village industries have received special policy attention since independence. Indeed, policy-makers have often equated the rural non-farm sector with these traditional activities. The main thrust of policy has been to protect employment in these sub-sectors against competition. Thus *khadi* and handlooms have both been protected, the former through subsidized credit and rebates to consumers on purchases, the latter by not imposing excise on hank-yarn for handlooms. Other policies have included promoting weavers' cooperatives, supplying raw materials, providing concessional credit and marketing assistance, and establishing welfare schemes for weavers.

It is worth illustrating the extent of this protection and support with the case of Tamil Nadu (Box 5.3). In the Seventh-Plan outlay for village and small industries in the state over 50 per cent was allocated to *khadi* and handlooms (MIDS, 1988: 221), even though in 1981 handlooms employed only 8.6 per cent of rural main workers outside of agriculture (Census). During fieldwork in that state we identified 27 different policies, programmes or organizations to support the handloom sub-sector.

Box 5.3: Policies for *khadi* and handlooms in Tamil Nadu

The Directorate of Handlooms and Textiles is the primary agency in the state for implementing policies and programmes for *khadi* and handlooms. The performance budget of the directorate suggests that in 1991–2 the agency spent Rs124 crores, the vast bulk to aid cotton- and silk-handloom cooperatives. Indeed, over 80 per cent of this budget was spent on three items: the subsidy for the production of controlled cloth (Rs18 crores), the rebate on the sale of handloom cloth (Rs42 crores), and the free distribution of *saris* and *dothies* to landless agricultural labourers and the poor in urban slums (Rs42 crores). In the same year the cooperatives sold handloom cloth worth Rs288 crores. If we assume that 20 per cent of the sales price went to the weavers (namely Rs58 crores), it is clear that the directorate spent twice as much on the promotion of handlooms as weavers in cooperatives earned from handloom weaving! Indeed the budget of the directorate underestimates the promotional support to the handloom sector in Tamil Nadu. It does not reflect the loss of excise on hank-yarn for handlooms, the budgets of various national-level promotional agencies, as well as of other agencies based in the state, such as the Tamil Nadu Handloom Development Corporation.

The Madras Institute for Development Studies (MIDS, 1988: 231) assessed the effectiveness of such policies as follows:

> . . . it must be stated that although the support extended by the government to the industry has been significant in preventing it being wiped out, because of the loopholes and shortfalls in the support structure, it has not been possible to prevent the erosion of the handloom weaver's income and livelihood. Handloom weavers have to look for other occupations to maintain their standard of living above the poverty line . . .

The weavers would thus have benefited far more from direct cash hand-outs of the resources available for *khadi* and handlooms, rather than from supposed benefits and subsidies, much of which gets siphoned off before they reach the weavers.

Other village industries have also been protected and supported, although not as much as *khadi* and handlooms. For example, pottery and textile products are protected by not allowing larger-scale units to take up these activities, including the production of ready-made garments (unless made in export-oriented units). These sub-sectors have also received promotional inputs (raw materials, credit, marketing, and so on) from a plethora of different organizations.

The Khadi and Village Industries Commission (KVIC), established by an Act of Parliament in 1957, is the primary promotional agency for village industries. Thirty state governments have also set up state-level Khadi and Village Industries Boards (KVIBs), which are autonomous of KVIC, but receive grants and loans from the commission. The number of village industries, in addition to *khadi*, supported by the KVIC system has risen from 10 to 96.

According to KVIC's annual reports, in 1992 the KVIC system supported 2320 organizations and 29 813 cooperatives. In 1990–91 the total production under KVIC was Rs286 crores of *khadi* and Rs1994 crores of village-industry products. These industries employed about two million full-time and three million part-time workers. Sales through 13 000 outlets totalled Rs2895 crores. In 1991–2 the government allocated a budget of Rs193 crores to the KVIC, which together with the KVIBs also received finance from banks, state governments, national agencies and some foreign donors such as the United Nations Development Programme (UNDP).

Only the hard facts can be used to evaluate the success or otherwise of these promotional efforts for traditional rural industries. Employment in the handloom sub-sector was almost stagnant between 1977–8 and 1987–8, while employment in the powerloom sub-sector grew at over 13 per cent a year (Papola, 1992: 243). In fact, household manufacturing (under which most village industries fall) is the only part of the RNFS that saw a decline of employment (of −1.2 per cent a year) between 1981 and 1991 (Table 2.1, p. 28).

Protection of these industries has in practice led to the preservation of backward or inefficient technologies, and thus to low productivity and low wages. The average annual earnings of the five million workers supported by the whole KVIC system in 1990–91 were only Rs1771, while the poverty line in 1990–91 was fixed at Rs11 000 for a household of five. Such industries merely provided supplementary income for the workers concerned.

KVIC's record in promoting research and improved technologies has also been poor. While the commission has set up 34 research and extension centres, their impact has been limited. During 1991–2 KVIC disbursed only Rs98 lakhs for 22 research and development (R&D) projects. The Khadi and Village Industries Review Committee (GoI, 1987b) quotes from a study by the Indian Institute of Management, Ahmedabad, that:

> . . . there was lack of clarity in the objectives [of the research institutes], that the progess of research was hampered by poor staff, inadequate number of scientific personnel, delay in release of funds, administrative

overburden, and rigid organizational culture, and above all, that the policy-making body did not provide adequate and timely support to the R&D institutions.

India has clearly paid a high price to protect jobs in the handloom and other traditional sub-sectors.[3] These costs continue even today: the 1995–6 national budget announced an additional Rs1000 crores of bank credit to KVIC (GoI, 1995a: 136). The same amount of investment over the years in education, health, vocational training in new trades, rural infrastructure, or in promoting other rural industries might have given better results.

Indeed, it is depressing that so little has been learnt from past failures. Even after more than 30 years of experience, a policy document on *khadi* and village industries (GoI, 1989b: 16) argued for continuing to reserve certain products and raw materials for them, to grant them fiscal concessions and subsidies, to rely on public-sector and cooperative marketing channels, and to restrict the capacity of larger industries in these product lines, including imposing a cess (tax) on them.

Likewise, the Khadi and Village Industries Review Committee of 1987 highlighted the lack of a marketing approach by the KVIC and the KVIBs, but recommended the establishment of a marketing corporation under KVIC. The functions of the corporation would include not only marketing support, but also managing sales outlets and even common production facilities. Is it likely that such a corporation would perform any differently from the numerous state-managed marketing corporations (see pp. 131–6) or from KVIC's own Directorate of Marketing?

The review committee also recommended, and KVIC has acted on the recommendation, that the commission's activities be limited to villages with a population below 1000, or clusters of small villages with a total of up to 5000 people. This policy will no doubt further limit KVIC's efforts to individual artisan or household enterprises employing mostly family labour, the only part of the rural non-farm sector in which employment is declining.

Technology development, training and technology institutes

Upgrading technology has been a major plank of industrial policy in India. Substantial investments have been made in numerous sub-sectors to upgrade technologies and impart training in their use. These policies have been implemented by an impressive array of institutes for technology development set up by both the union and state governments:

- The two national apex organizations responsible for upgrading technologies are the Indian Council for Agricultural Research (ICAR) and the Council for Scientific and Industrial Research (CSIR).

3. Although far fewer resources have been allocated to village- and small-industry programmes than to industries in the organized sector (Little *et al.*, 1987: 25).

- Under these apex organizations come many sub-sectoral R&D institutes. Examples of those we encountered in the field include the Central Glass and Ceramic Research Institute and the Central Food Technological Research Institute under CSIR; the Central Arid Zone Research Institute and the North Eastern hill agriculture complex under ICAR.
- Other technology institutes are run by departments of the union government. For example, the Office of the Development Commissioner, Handlooms at the Ministry of Textiles manages the Indian Institute of Handloom Technology, the Indian Institute of Handprinted Textile Technology and a chain of weavers' service centres in major centres throughout India.
- State governments have established their own technology units, such as the Rural Technology Institute in Gujarat and training-cum-production centres run by state-level KVIBs.
- Institutes continue to be established. For example, a new technology institute for carpets is being set up at Bhadohi, near Varanasi in Uttar Pradesh, and one for cane and bamboo at Agartala, Tripura.

The mandate for all these bodies is to implement policies for technology development in specific sub-sectors, by upgrading basic production processes, developing new products and process technologies, disseminating these new technologies, and upgrading skills to manage them. They also provide low-cost technological services, such as product- and raw-material testing facilities.

In spite of this impressive array of institutes for technology development, most technologies in the rural non-farm sector are inefficient and backward (see Chapter 3, pp. 72–5). The record on skills and training is equally poor, in spite of the numerous institutes for technology and for training (Box 3.3, p. 76). Such a situation is surely disappointing, granted the substantial investments that have been made in technology and skill development.

It would be unfair to blame this poor state of affairs only on the technology and training institutes themselves. Some causes of retaining inefficient technologies and skills in many RNFS sub-sectors are as follows:

- the deliberate preservation of backward technologies in order to preserve employment, albeit with low levels of skills and productivity and hence low wages (e.g. handlooms and matches); in these cases inefficient technologies have all too often been considered 'appropriate' technologies;
- the policy bias against certain sub-sectors, which has prevented more extensive R&D to upgrade technologies and skills (e.g. powerlooms);
- the protection of domestic producers of machinery against foreign competition (e.g. textile machinery, tool manufacturers, and automotive components);

- the lack of credit for small producers to invest in more capital-intensive technologies or to upgrade their skills (see Chapter 6 for many examples); and
- the dispersed nature of many small producers. Such producers are often difficult to reach for training and have little capital to invest in better technologies.

Other sub-sectors have been largely neglected in terms of technology and training policies. Examples include mining and stone processing, spice processing, wood products, brick kilns and rural transport. In the last case, the prevalence of improvised passenger and goods vehicles, such as the 'Jugadi' in UP, the 'Maruta' in Rajasthan and the 'Peter Buggy' in Punjab, show clearly that there is a need for research and development to design an appropriate rural vehicle. Finally, in some sub-sectors, like repairs and small engineering, entrepreneurs need only general-purpose machinery, tools and skills to respond to the demands of the market.

Adding to these adverse factors, the institutes for technology research and training have often failed, especially in the extension, dissemination and marketing of the processes they have developed. One way to evaluate this would be to see how many of the institutes' developments have been adopted and how many of their trainees have been employed by rural enterprises. Unfortunately such data are not available and we have to make informed judgements based on field interviews (Box 5.4).

Box 5.4: Examples of technology institutes in the field

- The Extension Centre of the Central Leather Research Institute in Kanpur, Uttar Pradesh, is manned by only five scientists. Its role has in practice been limited to linking up with government bodies, such as the KVIB, for providing training to producer groups. Its mandate, however, is much wider and includes disseminating new technologies and providing testing facilities. But the leather industry in Kanpur makes little use of the centre, and rural producers are largely unaware of its existence. A major handicap has been that most initiatives have to be sanctioned from head office in Madras.
- The Central Food Technological Research Institute in Mysore has several regional centres for the development of technologies relevant to food products in their region, to disseminate these technologies and to provide testing facilities. The institute has been fairly successful in developing many new processes, but less successful in generating demand for these from producers. It is largely dependent on government promotional bodies like

the KVIB to generate such demand, and few producers use the testing facilities.

- The Central Institute of Medicinal and Aromatic Plants, Lucknow, has developed a series of technologies for growing and processing herbs and plants, but it has no pro-active programme for disseminating them. Changes are occurring, however, because the institute now has to generate income through fees, and it has already sold distillation-plant technologies.
- In Assam technologies for degumming and decorticating ramie fibre developed by the Indian Agricultural Research Institute and the Jute Technological Research Laboratory have not been widely adopted because they are capital intensive. The Assam Textile Institute has developed a low-cost degumming technology, but this has yet to be used commercially.
- The improved silk-reeling technology developed by the Central Silk Technological Research Institute in Mysore has not been widely adopted, partly because it requires better skills and more investment. Reelers also complain that the improved oven designed by the institute to cook cocoons cannot use popular fuels like paddy husk.
- Potters have faced problems with the new wheel and kilns developed by the KVIC, resulting in a low acceptance rate. The technologies are, moreover, not readily available in the market, but can be obtained only through the KVIBs, thus excluding most potters from access to them.
- The Building Materials and Technology Promotion Council and the Central Building Research Institute have undertaken work on construction materials and brick kilns, on basic building techniques and low-cost housing, but only a few large construction companies have benefited from them.

The poor performance of the technology institutes described in Box 5.4 arises even though the institutes generally have well-qualified personnel in their given field (although this is not always true), and sometimes even have substantial interaction with industry when placed right at the centre of a sub-sectoral cluster. There are several reasons why these bodies have not performed better.

- Although all these institutes are competent in developing supplies of appropriate-technology packages, they are ill-equipped to generate demand for them through effective extension and marketing. They often depend on networking with other government promotional agencies rather than directly on producers. As a result, many technologies developed by these institutes never leave the shelf.

- Because of poor interaction with potential users, new technologies do not address the circumstances of many producers – for example, their shortage of capital. For rural areas in particular, many of the technologies required are not new but existing ones that need descaling and dissemination; the institutes have rarely proved effective at this. Most improved technologies are appropriate only for larger units.
- For many products, including traditional crafts, design inputs to adapt products to modern markets may be as important as upgrading manufacturing processes. The institutes, with their emphasis on in-house technical R&D, have often not been able to provide these.
- Many technologies developed have not incorporated criteria of commercial viability into their design, a fact which deters producer entrepreneurs from taking them up.
- More policy attention, particularly in terms of extension services, has often been given to primary production rather than to processing. Thus many research and extension institutes have concentrated on increasing rice yields but few on improving paddy processing, on promoting sericulture but few on silk reeling.
- Many of the field or extension centres are too small to cover their subsector cluster effectively.
- Finally, many of the institutes have bureaucratic procedures. Above all, they are not accountable in any way to their clients. It is incredible, for example, that the nation-wide network of weavers' service centres is under the administrative control of the distant Development Commissioner (Handlooms) in Delhi. The centres have no accountability to a single weaver, whether small or big, or to any association of weavers in the clusters they serve.

Thus, while these institutes to promote technology development often have specific goals and objectives, they have suffered from a lack of competition and its surrogates (Box 5.1): because they do not depend on the dissemination and sale of their technologies for their survival, these technologies are not subjected to market forces; and the clients for whom they are intended have little ability, or even inclination, to influence the institutes.

To show that such conclusions are more widely held, we cite the Abid Hussain Review Committee on the Council for Scientific and Industrial Research (CSIR, 1986). The committee concluded that while the CSIR had established an impressive infrastructure comprising 39 research laboratories and over 100 extension centres, its performance in commercializing the technologies developed by it had been weak. The report states:

(i) CSIR know-how offered for commercialization by the National Research Development Corporation (NRDC) was often untried, not

> fully backed by detailed pilot plant and engineering studies, and not supported by adequate technical and marketing after-sales service by the NRDC. . . . (ii) it is a matter of concern that the stock of human capital has been allowed to be denuded without being recharged. A distinct lack of training and mobility in the CSIR system has further compounded the problem. . . . (iii) there is a clear need for sharpening of focus, delineation of thrust areas, strengthening of planning capabilities, change in systems of personnel management, change in patterns of funding, and a change in the overall policy environment which leads to an increased demand for the service and talents of the CSIR system.

There are also more positive examples of the success of upgrading technologies that point in the direction of the necessary changes.

Research and development by the National Dairy Development Board (NDDB) in fodder, milk-testing machines, artificial-insemination techniques, and so on, has been spread through NDDB's national network of cooperatives. These technologies have had to be commerically viable since the cooperatives cannot rely on government hand-outs to sustain them.

In Gujarat, institutes like the National Institute of Design and the Central Glass and Ceramic Research Institute have provided valuable technology inputs for modern industrial sub-sectors like plastics and ceramics.

The Pottery Development Centre in Khurja, Uttar Pradesh played a key role in the early development of the ceramic cluster in Khurja. An extension centre of the Central Glass and Ceramics Research Institute was also set up in Khurja in 1982, when the ceramics cluster was already well established. The centre has played an important role in upgrading firing and product technologies, and has begun to sell licences for the use of some of these innovations. Through training, requested by entrepreneurs in Khurja, the centre has also helped units to shift their production to bone-china items.

Box 5.5 provides more detail on the Southern India Textile Research Association (SITRA) in Coimbatore, Tamil Nadu, not because it is the best technology institute we came across, but because the detail allows us to point towards potential solutions.

Finally, there are the examples of more efficient technologies that we cited on pp. 72–5. One feature of these examples was that the investments were largely made by the private sector. Indeed, one alternative to establishing technology-research institutes is to encourage private industry to invest in advanced technologies that can act as industry leaders. The government is already doing this for fruit processing, for example, in which 100 per cent export-oriented units are fully exempted from sales tax and import duties, and these units are entitled to have up to 100 per cent foreign equity. The 1993 National Mineral Policy has also opened the mineral sub-sector to investments by larger corporations. However, such

Box 5.5: The Southern India Textile Research Association (SITRA)

SITRA undertakes technological research, training and consulting in the textile sector, largely for the textile mills, although recently it has given some attention to the powerloom sub-sector as well. It manages various service centres in Tamil Nadu funded by the central Ministry of Textiles, which provide technology and training inputs for powerlooms. The centres inspect and repair looms, test yarn and cloth samples, develop new designs, provide consultation services, and conduct training programmes. According to SITRA's Annual Report for 1991–2, the service centres dealt with at most 70 000 powerlooms (probably far fewer), when there are likely to be well over 400 000 powerlooms in the state. Nevertheless, SITRA has been more responsive to producers' needs, and it is worth considering why this has happened.

In 1991–2 SITRA had 355 members representing 430 textile units; out of 25 persons on the Council of Administration seven elected members outnumbered the four government officials (although a few more members of the council head various organizations in the public sector). Only 40 per cent of SITRA's income came from the government (25 per cent as grants and 15 per cent as sponsored projects), while 36 per cent came from consulting services to various non-governmental clients and 14 per cent from membership dues. Thus both SITRA's board and its sources of income are balanced slightly in favour of its clients rather than of government control and budgets. Moreover, half of its income depends on fees for services, whether for private or public clients, thus making the association more responsive to the needs of its clients.

a strategy will have an impact only at the top end of any sub-sector, especially in those cases where more advanced technologies are readily available abroad, for example for garments and processed foods. In such cases elaborate R&D in India itself may not be needed. Different strategies are clearly required, however, for the large number of tiny producers in the RNFS.

To conclude, our analysis confirms that competiton or its surrogates are indeed critical for the performance of technology-development institutes. The primary reason that so many of the positive examples of upgrading technologies are found in the private sector is that the commerical viability of the private companies concerned depends on successful technological development not just within their own units but also among their suppliers. Competition, however, need not be conceived in terms of a multitude of similar technical institutes competing directly with each other. It is sufficient that these institutes be responsive to market demand in the sub-sectors in which they operate, and above all to their clients, the producer–entrepreneurs in those sub-sectors. The best way of ensuring this is that the income of the institutes be dependent on fees for services as well as on membership dues, and that elected producer–representatives can exercise control over the institutes.

Other promotional policies and their agencies

Infrastructure International experience shows that the provision of sound infrastructure is critical to the development of the rural non-farm sector (Ho, 1986; World Bank, 1983). The provision of basic rural infrastructure, such as roads, water, power and telecommunications, varies significantly, however, across the states covered in this study (see Table 2.16, p. 51). For example, 99 per cent of villages in Punjab are connected with all-weather roads compared to only 15 per cent in Orissa, while 77 per cent of rural households in Punjab have electricity compared to only 11 per cent in Uttar Pradesh.

The inadequacy of basic infrastructure has constrained the growth of many sub-sectors in the RNFS. Of most immediate concern to many producers is the lack of regular supplies of electricity and water. In Andhra Pradesh as many as 84 per cent of rural enterprises run without power (GoI, 1991d). In most states power supplies are erratic, even on government-promoted industrial estates, so enterprises have been prevented from upgrading to technologies which depend on a reliable source of power. Shortages of water are constraining for activities such as processing food, tanning leather, dyeing textiles and producing chemicals, particularly in dynamic clusters of these industries. Likewise, emerging sub-sectors, such as fruit processing, floriculture and phytochemicals cannot take off because the existing transport infrastructure is inadequate.

The most recent and dramatic change in basic infrastructure has been the rapid spread of telecommunication services throughout many rural areas. This example illustrates that by collaborating with private parties, in this case operators of public call offices (PCOs), significant improvements can be brought about.

Basic infrastructure like roads, water, power and telecommunications is the responsibility of the respective government ministries, departments and corporations. Many producers complained that such agencies are bureaucratic and often behave like regulators, rather than like service providers accountable to their customers. Officers are in fact often designated inspectors, and abuse their position of power to take bribes in return for providing services to which enterprises are supposedly entitled.

Much of the fault lies with the heavy subsidies and weak cost recovery for providing infrastructure, in spite of the heavy demand. Supplies have to be rationed, allowing agencies to exact economic rents in allocating scarce resources. The situation is likely to change, however, as more states open the provision of infrastructure to the private sector. Clearly issues of cost recovery, better service delivery and public–private collaboration will be fundamental to any solutions.

State governments also provide specific infrastructure for industrial or service units, such as worksheds, industrial estates and common production facilities. These are often operated by government corporations set up to provide industrial infrastructure or to assist specific sub-sectors. Here we look at common marketing centres, common production or facility centres and industrial estates.

Substantial capital investment has been made in common marketing centres, which have shops and small worksheds for a wide range of products, especially for tiny units. They can be found in most block-level towns. Special centres have also been built for specific sub-sectors, such as the handicraft *Shilpabaris* in Rajasthan. The shops and worksheds are leased to producers, especially those who have participated in other government programmes such as IRDP, TRYSEM and SEPUP.

Common production or facility centres have been set up in many RNFS sub-sectors to give individual small producers access to capital-intensive production facilities that they could not afford to invest in themselves. Common production centres are used by state-owned corporations for their own production, but individual producers are also allowed to use them, often at nominal charges. Common facility centres are manned by skilled staff, and producers pay service charges for using them.

Unfortunately, with all these centres, more attention has been given to the provision of physical infrastructure than to demand patterns, location and the specific needs of the actual users. Even more important has been the fact that these centres are government-owned and hence are often poorly managed. Thus much of the infrastructure remains underutilized or redundant.

Much the same could be said of the many industrial estates established in backward regions in particular. In common with much international experience, these have rarely been successful. Access to infrastructure like power, roads and telecommunications on the one hand, and to raw materials and product markets on the other, has been limited. Only in those areas where the source of raw material is situated close by have some rural industries developed.

Rather than dwell on such common policy failures, we look at the notable exception of the industrial estates developed for rural manufacturing in Gujarat. The rapid growth of employment in rural manufacturing in Gujarat (see Box 5.6, p. 141) suggests that the rural industrial estates are having a positive impact. Several major differences in policies for these estates probably explain this.

- Most were developed not for the backward regions of the state but in the more agriculturally and industrially developed 'corridor' districts.
- Many of the estates have been constructed for specific sub-sectors (for example plastic products), thus encouraging units in the same sub-sector to cluster and share common facilities.
- Many of them have been developed for dynamic and promising sub-sectors, rather than trying to reverse the decline of traditional sub-sectors such as pottery.
- Facilities have been more reliable. For example, while the industrial estates are still constrained by power cuts, in some areas the power supply is at least regular: it is cut on a specific day each week.
- The state government is now thinking of the possibility of producer associations managing these estates rather than the state Industrial Development Corporation, which is still responsible for their construction. In some cases the private sector is also developing estates, for example for diamond processing in Surat.

Raw material supplies A major constraint on the growth of RNFS enterprises is the procurement of quality raw materials: (1) raw materials that are not produced locally may be scarce; (2) the working capital requirements for purchasing and stocking raw materials are substantial and beyond the reach of many small producers.

Both central and state governments have sought to supply raw materials at reasonable rates to rural producers. This applies in particular to traditional artisanal sub-sectors, where governments have tried to free producers from their dependence on traders and middlemen. Thus government-owned corporations, or sometimes the government departments themselves, have supplied raw materials. The most extensive system is for supplying hank-yarn and other inputs to the handloom sub-sector through the National Handloom Development Corporation and other such corporations. There are also some examples in modern sub-sectors, like the Orissa Small Industry Corporation that supplies raw materials to small industries in the plastic sub-sector.

According to producers, many schemes to supply raw materials are not effective because of erratic supply, indifferent quality and, in some cases, inadequate differentials between the controlled and the open (or black) market prices, if the transaction costs of acquiring raw materials from official channels are taken into account. Indeed, whenever raw material supplies have been subsidized, not only have the corporations sustained heavy losses, but corrupt officials have also taken bribes from the targeted producers, and diverted supplies to unintended beneficiaries.

The promotion of the sericulture and silk sub-sector provides an example of an alternative strategy of state governments that is more market-oriented. Thus the Directorate of Sericulture in Tamil Nadu not only provides quality disease-free layings through its own grainages, but also authorizes (through certification) private grainages to do so. The state government has also established several cocoon markets and two silk exchanges where cocoons and silk are auctioned among private sellers and buyers. However, the state government continues to exercise considerable control over such markets by insisting that all reelers using them must be registered, by forbidding farmers to sell cocoons elsewhere, especially out of state, and by allowing the government-controlled cooperative federation TANSILK to become a major buyer and seller in these markets.

In view of this mixed record of government agencies, most producers in the RNFS continue to use private channels for the supply of their raw materials. The evidence is overwhelming that policies to free small rural producers from their dependence on traders have failed. Not only are private channels more reliable, but traders may also link the supply of raw materials with other services, such as extending credit to meet the working capital needs of small producers. Sometimes this leads to a putting-out system where skilled workers cease to be independent entrepreneurs and become wage earners to traders who supply raw materials and credit, and take back and market the finished products.

Marketing assistance Another major bottleneck for rural producers has been accessing markets beyond thir immediate locality. The central and state governments have again tried to supplant their dependency on traders by establishing marketing channels run by government corporations or agencies. These usually manage a fairly standard package of marketing schemes, including sourcing merchandise from producers and cooperative societies; opening retail outlets; holding exhibitions and *melas*; providing design inputs and promoting brand names; and even running their own production units.

There are numerous such government corporations and agencies. For handlooms and handicrafts there are national ones, such as the National Handloom Development Corporation and the large retail network of KVIC-linked shops. There are also the various national export promotion councils. However, in most sub-sectors it is state governments that have established marketing agencies, primarily of two types: corporations that manage state emporia in different metropolitan cities, such as Pragjyotish (Assam) and Phulkari (Punjab); and the apex cooperative bodies, such as the State Weavers' Cooperative Federation in Rajasthan and the Handloom Weavers' Cooperative Society in Andhra Pradesh, that usually focus on a single sub-sector.

As we can see, the policy instrument used for promoting market linkages has been largely the establishment of government corporations or agencies that manage the marketing function, not the creation of a market-friendly policy environment or the provision of incentives to private entrepreneurs to come forward to provide these linkages. Only the direct exporter, far removed from the point of production in rural areas, has enjoyed fiscal incentives for marketing.

It is difficult to assess scientifically the impact of such government marketing support. One important measure is the market share of a sub-sector's products that are routed through the state-run marketing agencies. Relevant figures for handicrafts are available. Excluding gems and jewellery, the total market size of handicrafts in 1985–6 was Rs2200 crores, of which exports comprised Rs503 crores. The share of the public sector in these exports was only 2 per cent, and in the domestic market only 2.5 per cent (GoI, 1989b: 77).

Since handicrafts are the sector for which government marketing channels have been most extensively developed, such figures are likely to be representative of other sub-sectors. There are some exceptions, for example in the dairy sub-sector, and in the handloom sub-sector in states like Tamil Nadu and Orissa, in which handlooms are highly cooperativized. For instance, in 1991–2 Cooptex, a cooperative federation in Tamil Nadu, marketed about 34 per cent of the total cooperative production of cotton handlooms in the state, and probably about 20 per cent of the production of silk weavers' cooperatives (Study Group on the RNFS, 1993a). Cooptex is therefore an important player in the market. Likewise, some cooperatives, such as the Sambalpuri Bastralaya in Orissa and the Yemmiganur Weavers' Cooperative Society in Andhra Pradesh, run their own chain of retail shops quite successfully. It would appear, however, that, except in a few such cases, the impact of public-marketing agencies has been limited, nor do they control enough market share to influence market variables and prices. In consequence, most of the sub-sectors in the RNFS again remain dependent on private trading channels for marketing their products, which may give a lower price but are more reliable, prompt and flexible.

In this section we have so far looked at the provision of infrastructure, the supply of raw materials and marketing of products as promotional strategies. In almost all cases the central and state governments have undertaken such promotional activities through government-owned corporations or other agencies established especially for this purpose. Since many of these policies have not had the expected impact, analysis of the organizations involved is likely to reveal some of the reasons for these policy failures. We look at three types: state-owned corporations; the apex cooperative societies and federations; and the export promotion councils.

State-owned corporations These bodies, while having a core of commercial activity in the chosen sub-sector, also undertake promotional activities such as supplying scarce raw materials, disbursing credit, and providing training, common production facilities and markets. The corporations thus attempt to merge commercial and developmental functions. Such' state-owned corporations exist in nearly every large sub-sector.[4]

These bodies are manned by three types of personnel: (1) the chief executive, usually deputed from the state government and belonging to the Indian Administrative Service (IAS) or the state equivalent; (2) the sectoral specialists who are technically qualified in the sub-sector; (3) the generalist staff recruited either from other government departments on deputation or directly into the corporation. The emoluments of staff in these corporations are aligned to state-employee grades, and other government personnel policies, such as performance appraisal and promotion, have often been extended to these corporations. There is, therefore, little to distinguish the corporations from the state government in terms of staffing pattern and culture.

The corporations are also financially dependent on and accountable to their parent department in the state government, which gives the latter substantial control over them. The corporations use government systems of planning, budgeting and auditing as well. In effect, although they were conceived as autonomous organizations with their own goals, culture and staff, over the years the distinction between the corporations and their parent departments has blurred, and they have lost their autonomy.

At the strategic level, the corporations have often had to balance multiple goals of commerical viability and promotional activities. In the ultimate analysis it is the parameters against which they are evaluated that determine their performance. Until recently financial performance and commercial viability were not important criteria. For policy-makers the objectives of these bodies were not financial, but rather to provide social benefits, which were quantified by counting the number of producers they covered and the amount of subsidies they distributed (compare Waterbury, 1993). The staff of these corporations have often internalized these attitudes, scoffing at the word profits, and believing their organizations serve a public cause that should not be expected to generate financial returns. In reality, however, visibility (number of production centres, hotels, loans and so on) and budgetary allocations have been the paramount performance criteria.

These four factors – of staffing pattern, reduction in autonomy, multiplicity of goals and non-commercial performance parameters – have in practice led to very poor performance. This is not just in commercial terms (many corporations have sustained large losses), but also in terms of promotional impact, which has often been limited, as we have seen above.

4. In Orissa there are Orissa (state) corporations for mining, forest development, plantation development, cooperative coir, fish seed development, maritime and Chilka area development, agro-industries, handloom development, handicraft development, small industry, tourism development, and so on. A similar plethora of corporations can be found in all the states we studied, with some variation in the chosen sub-sectors depending on the economy of the state.

The corporations have therefore suffered from many of the weaknesses analysed by Israel (see Box 5.1). Because of their multiple goals they have lacked specificity; by not being subjected to commercial performance parameters they have not benefited from competition; their management has been bureaucratized; and their parent departments in the respective governments have often interfered with their functioning.

Because of their poor showing, particularly in commercial terms, state governments facing growing fiscal constraints are questioning the role of many of these corporations. Commercial viability, which was never given primacy before, has become much more critical. Indeed, state governments have started disinvesting productive assets owned by the corporations and closing down some altogether – for example, the Punjab State Textile Corporation. Some food-processing units of HORTICO in Uttar Pradesh have been offered for sale and the Orissa Tourism Development Corporation is leasing out some of its hotels.

Less thought is being given to how to transform the performance of the state-owned corporations. Without changes in their goals, performance parameters, staffing and autonomy, these bodies will continue to face the same problems as in the past. Indeed, the reduced budget allocations will only make their functioning even more difficult.

Apex cooperative societies and federations The cooperative movement was initiated with much fanfare in the late 1950s, but had lost much of its lustre by the 1970s (see Chapter 7). One intervention by the states in this movement for cooperativization was the formation of state-level apex cooperative societies and federations of sectorally-based primary cooperative societies.

The example of the UP Industrial Cooperative Association (UPICA) illustrates the problems of such bodies. UPICA was formed in 1952 to act as an apex organization for all primary industrial cooperative societies in Uttar Pradesh. Although promoted by the state, UPICA is legally a membership organization with primary cooperative societies as its members. Over 80 per cent of its some 2000 members are textile (mainly handloom) bodies. Thus, while UPICA was set up for all non-agricultural societies, over the years it has become the apex association for the handloom sector.

Its main activities are to support handloom cooperatives by procuring raw yarn, obtaining and producing *Janta* cloth, providing working capital loans, and marketing textiles through its network of showrooms (13 retail outlets selling over Rs60 crores worth of handloom products).

We found that there is little distinction betwen UPICA and the UP Handloom Development Corporation. Both have primary cooperative societies as members, and the staff of UPICA view their association as a state-government organization. In practice, too, their staffing pattern, salary structure and other organizational characteristics resemble a state-run corporation. Although there is an elected board of primary cooperative members, the political party in power usually appoints the representatives as well as the chief executive. Thus apex cooperative societies like UPICA are in reality more like state corporations than member-controlled organizations.

The similarities between the state-run corporations and the cooperative federations are further emphasized by their overlapping responsibilities. For example, in the fish sub-sector in Orissa there are the Orissa State Fisheries Cooperative Marketing Federation, Orissa Fish Seed Development Corporation, Orissa Maritime and Chilka Area Development Corporation, and the Central Fishermen Marketing Cooperative Society (Chilka), as well as the Directorate of Fisheries and various Fish Farmers Development Agencies. Not only do the responsibilities of all these organizations overlap, but even their staffing is often on deputation from one body to another.

A primary reason for the poor record of the cooperative federations is that such organizations did not evolve from the need to federate that was felt by primary cooperative societies themselves. Apex organizations established by the states were created on a large scale without considering the reality on the ground. This situation could have improved if the cooperative movement had really taken root and become a vibrant sector so that over time the apex bodies became member-controlled. In most cases this did not happen. There are of course exceptions, like some of the cooperative networks promoted by NDDB, especially in Gujarat, and we look further at these and other primary cooperatives in Chapter 7.

The export promotion councils While also set up by government and staffed by bureaucrats, the export promotion councils[5] have tended to perform better for the following reasons:

- most are operating in dynamic and growing export sub-sectors;
- the councils have significant representation of exporters on their boards;
- they depend on fees for services and/or a cess for their income, in addition to government allocations;
- they do not usually undertake the marketing of products themselves, but provide support services like market information, exhibitions and training;
- some have adopted their own administrative practices, for example paying top managers competitive salaries to attract them from the private sector; and

5. For example for handloom products; cotton textiles; Indian silk; apparel; wool and woollen products; carpets; leather; sports goods; gem and jewellery; and plastics and linoleums. In 1996 even a Powerloom Development and Export Promotion Council was set up with support from the new Union Minister for Textiles, himself a former powerloom owner.

- in the case of apparel, the relevant council also controls the allocation of export quotas, thus giving it a powerful role in the sub-sector.

The representatives of exporters on the boards of these councils are, however, predominantly large producers, and the organizations do not interact directly with the more dispersed small producers typical of the rural non-farm sector; nor have they all, for example the Handloom Export Promotion Council, performed as well (Study Group on the RNFS, 1993a).

Overall assessment of promotional policies and agencies

In this chapter we have reviewed promotional activities focused on traditional rural industries, technologies and skills, infrastructure, raw materials and marketing. While there is no comprehensive framework for promoting the rural non-farm sector as a whole, it is clear that there are many promotional policies that impinge on it. As with the regulatory framework (see Chapter 4), it is also clear that a number of sub-sectors have received considerable promotional inputs – for example mining, food processing and handlooms, which have been given a high degree of regulatory or promotional attention – while other sub-sectors, such as chemical and metal products, repairs and rural construction, have been largely neglected. In particular, most service sub-sectors have been ignored (although retail trade and road transport are included under priority-sector credit programmes).

This attention to specific sub-sectors would appear to follow our own recommendations for a sub-sectoral focus for promotional activities. However, the sub-sectors that have received such attention in the past have often not been chosen after an assessment of their economic and employment potential. This has sometimes led to a severe bias in resource allocations, including towards sub-sectors that have little economic potential, as was clear from the example of Tamil Nadu above (see Box 5.3, p. 119). In general, the extent of policy interest and investment in a sub-sector has depended on its political significance, export potential, regional importance and locational concentration:

(1) Some sub-sectors are politically more significant than others and have received more promotional inputs and budgetary allocations. This usually depends on the numbers employed in the sub-sector and their level of organization. For example, because of their roots in the freedom struggle and the large number of workers they employ, *khadi* and village industries were the earliest to receive special policy attention. As mentioned above, this influence continues even today: in 1995 the budget of the Union Government announced an additional Rs1000 crores of bank credit to KVIC. Other sub-

sectors have not enjoyed such exclusive representation among policy-makers.

(2) Sub-sectors that have good export potential have also received special attention. These include, for example, leather, carpets and textiles, and more recently aquaculture, food processing, processed granite and plastics. Specific export-promotion policies and councils have been formed for these (see note 5 on p. 135).

(3) Some sub-sectors have special significance for the development of a region within a state. Examples include sericulture in the northern districts of Tamil Nadu and southern districts of Andhra Pradesh being promoted under the National Sericulture Project; sheep-rearing and wool processing in western Rajasthan being promoted by the Sheep and Wool Development Board; and pineapple cultivation in the southern hill districts of Assam being promoted by the State Horticulture Department.

(4) Those sub-sectors that are more organized and location-specific have generally been more conspicuous. Examples include leather shoes in Agra, Uttar Pradesh; hand-printing of textiles in Sanganer and Bagru, near Jaipur in Rajasthan; silk reeling and weaving in Sualkuchi, north of Guwahati in Assam; prawn cultivation and processing in coastal Andhra Pradesh; and rice milling in Punjab.

Political considerations in particular may divert attention away from the economic and employment potential of sub-sectors. Likewise, the fact that services and rural construction, for example, are often widely dispersed in many tiny enterprises has given them less visibility, even though they are among the fastest growing sub-sectors in the RNFS.

In addition to these biases in policy and resource allocation, our analysis of promotional activities revealed many other policy and organizational failures, especially in terms of impact. In spite of receiving considerable promotional resources, many traditional sub-sectors have retained backward technologies, low productivity and hence low wages. Employment in these sub-sectors has stagnated and sometimes even declined. The impact of the many technology and training institutes has been limited. Rural infrastructure remains poor. Rural producers continue to rely heavily on traders for their raw materials and for marketing their products, while the many government promotional agencies are insignificant actors (for example in terms of market share) in their respective sub-sectors. There is often little to show for the vast resources deployed.

Even more disheartening is that many of the same mistakes have been repeated over and over again, and few lessons have been learnt from previous failures. Early critiques of the Rural Industries Projects and of strategies to support traditional village industries are still as relevant today. For *khadi* and village industries senior policy-makers continue to recommend the same failed policies, with pleas that they be implemented more effectively, and in all sub-sectors the response to the failure of promotional agencies has been to recommend the creation of new and supposedly more effective ones, even though these new agencies suffer from the same internal weaknesses and external constraints as their predecessors.

In seeking to explain these issues we explore first the shortcomings of promotional strategies and then the weaknesses of promotional agencies. We also look at positive examples that point to possible alternative strategies.

Promotional strategies

There are six broad reasons for the lack of success of many promotional strategies:

Protection rather than development The government has often sought to preserve existing employment, especially in traditional sub-sectors, by protecting those sectors from competition, even at the cost of condemning them to backward technologies with low productivity and hence low wages. This is in line with the dominant perception that the rural non-farm sector is a traditional and backward sector without much potential for economic growth and employment generation. The focus has thus often been on artisans in villages rather than on the more dynamic parts of the RNFS usually found in rural towns and other clusters. Since the RNFS is not perceived as competitive, subsidies abound: for credit, investment, raw materials, training and sales rebates. In contrast to such protectionist strategies, the government has sought less often to develop the economic potential of promising sub-sectors, although there are some notable exceptions (such as sericulture).

Intervention rather than facilitation In many cases the state itself has become a party directly involved in a sub-sector, while it has less often facilitated the growth of the sub-sector, for instance by creating a supportive environment for private initiative. For example, governments have run chains of hotels rather than develop new tourist destinations in which private parties can invest. Thus state intervention has been carried out through a plethora of agencies especially created for this purpose, and the shortcomings of promotional strategies have often arisen from the weaknesses of these agencies, which we analyse below.

Inadequate or inappropriate focus In many cases promotional strategies have not been focused. As a result, resources have not been allocated to carefully selected sub-sectors, but have been spread over broad categories such as small-scale and village industries. This has led to rigid schemes that cannot be adapted to local environments and conditions. Such projects have often provided one specific input, such as worksheds or credit, without any consideration as to whether these inputs address the critical needs of the intended clients. Even when promotion has been focused on specific sub-sectors, resources have not been targeted at locations or at enterprises that show particular promise, but at all (small) units, including many that have little potential for growth.

Inadequate attention to links between the primary sector and the RNFS Since agriculture acts as a major source of inputs and of demand for the RNFS, growth in agricultural output and productivity is critical for the growth of the RNFS, yet little attention has been paid to the links between agriculture and the RNFS. There are some successful cases, such as sugarcane and oilseeds, of promoting the primary resource base which has also led to significant processing in the non-farm sector. However, in many other cases, such as rice, fruits, spices and floriculture, more support has been given to primary production rather than processing. There are other primary sectors, apart from agriculture, that provide inputs for the RNFS: animal husbandry, fisheries, forestry, and mining and quarrying, yet some of these have received only limited attention, and more often in regulating their ownership and use rather than promoting them as sources of RNFS inputs.

Inadequate attention to infrastructure Government promotion has failed to provide basic infrastructure, such as connecting roads, water and a regular supply of electricity. Much infrastructure, for example industrial estates and common production facilities, has been built. The failure of many of these shows, however, that constructing physical infrastructure is not sufficient. It also has to be well managed, maintained and financed to provide reliable services to rural producers. Moreover, industrial estates located in areas without ready access to raw materials, skilled labour, transport or markets cannot succeed.

Inadequate attention to social development A well-educated and healthy workforce is crucial for the dynamic growth of the non-farm sector (Chapter 2), yet educational and health indicators for the rural workforce remain very poor, even for the most basic needs such as literacy (Drèze and Sen, 1995). The possibility of skill building of any kind is therefore severely limited. Yet the plethora of concessions, incentives, subsidies and rebates to scheduled castes and tribes and other groups continues. This may be good politics, but it does little to promote dynamic sub-sectors. If these resources had been invested in primary education, vocational training and basic health care, the scope for RNFS employment would have improved.

Some successes The record of promotional strategies is not entirely negative, however. Government interventions that have had a narrow focus on productivity improvements through upgrading technologies, for example of oilseed and paddy processing, have sometimes proved more successful. In some cases, changes to regulatory and promotional policies have led to an upsurge of private enterprises, for example the public call offices (PCOs) throughout India, or the growth of diamond processing (see p. 112, note 6).

The government has also provided support for some emerging sub-sectors with export potential. This applies, for example, to fruit processing in Punjab, prawn farming and processing in Andhra Pradesh, gem processing in Rajasthan and Gujarat, and textile products in many states. Such sub-sectors have enjoyed tax rebates or waivers, special export promotion councils and export processing zones. There have also been programmes and specialized agencies to assist with training, marketing and other promotional inputs.

While government promotion has helped in the development of these sub-sectors, it is important to understand the policies that have been adopted. Tax waivers or rebates are indirect policy measures that change relative prices to which private producers then respond. The export promotion councils have producers as their members and are thus sensitive to the actual needs of at least the larger exporters. In many of these cases producers have also received a complete package of assistance, including raw material supply, technical advice and assured markets. Above all, in each case there has been substantial participation by private industry in the promotional strategies, and many of these emerging sub-sectors are being driven by private initiatives.

In one state, Gujarat, we came across a broader (rather than isolated) positive example of promoting the rural non-farm sector, although the state has not articulated its policies in terms of promoting the RNFS as such. Some details of these activities are given in Box 5.6. This should be set beside even more outstanding examples of promotion in India, for example the Green Revolution, to show that successful promotion is indeed a realistic possibility.

Promotional agencies

It is clear from our analysis that the primary vehicle for promotion has been the many promotional agencies established by the central and state governments. Economic theory provides valid reasons why promotional agencies have usually been set up by the state. In the early stages of a sub-sector's development private entrepreneurs may not have the capacity or knowledge to make investments in R&D or training facilities. Apart from the heavy investments required, these facilities have externalities, whereby the benefits can be enjoyed even by those producers who do not share in the costs. This is true both of technological breakthroughs and of training and skill development for workers, who can always shift to other manufacturers.

Box 5.6: Gujarat: a (relative) success story in the RNFS

Gujarat is going through a significant transformation of its rural economy. RNFS employment has been growing at 3.5 per cent a year (Census, see GoI, 1987a and 1992b). But unlike in other states, this growth has been fuelled by the rapid expansion (at 5.7 per cent a year) of rural employment in non-household manufacturing, which has far outweighed the decline of household manufacturing. Some reasons for this growth of the RNFS have been:

- Promotion initially focused on the regions of the state with greater economic potential. Investments have been more productive than they would have been in the backward regions.
- Promotion focused on the most important sub-sectors: most of the manufacturing sub-sectors with a high share or high growth rate of employment in the state have received considerable policy attention.
- Promotion focused on modern manufacturing, for example of plastic and ceramic products, that has good demand potential.
- Promotion of rural industrial estates, often for specific sub-sectors, but again in the more developed areas, rather than the backward regions of the state.
- The more recent promotion of backward regions has in turn focused on developing infrastructure (ports and roads in Saurashtra) or primary activities (mining in Kutch).
- A positive and supportive government attitude towards industrialization and the private sector. For example, the Diamond and Gem Development Corporation is developing the Surat Diamond Park with government support.
- A large supply of entrepreneurial talent.
- An excellent array of agencies for consultation, research and development.

Some of the challenges Gujarat still needs to address are:

- the regional imbalances in development (even though these were partly created by the initial focus on the more developed regions);
- the rapid urbanization that has accompanied economic growth;
- the lack of adequate physical infrastructure, e.g. power;
- the poorly educated rural labour force; and
- the environmental costs of economic growth.

Thus individual entrepreneurs are reluctant to invest in such facilities and it is necessary for the state to step in.

However, because of the nature of the developing state in India, state control of promotional agencies has meant that the agencies have had to work in an institutional environment that conflicts with the purposes for which they were established. They have enjoyed little autonomy, relied heavily on the central and state governments for their finances, and been evaluated by non-commercial performance parameters. Since they have not been dependent on service fees for their survival, they have often allocated funds to projects and developments for which producers felt no need.

Second, most of these agencies have a multiplicity of goals that are difficult to translate into specific and concrete objectives and methods, except as fairly rigid programmes and schemes. Institutes that were set up to provide technological inputs for specific sub-sectors have enjoyed the highest specificity (see Box 5.1, p. 116) and have thus been relatively more successful. Agencies such as the KVIBs, whose mandate covers rural industries as a whole, have proved less effective because they do not have sufficient in-depth knowledge about any one sub-sector, and therefore do not focus their efforts.

In particular, combining regulatory and promotional functions has proved dysfunctional in agencies such as the government departments and directorates. Since the promotional role requires greater creativity and effort, whenever such agencies also have regulatory functions to perform, it proves easier for them to concentrate on the latter. This is not hard to understand. The functionaries of these agencies can exercise greater power in regulating and releasing (or withholding) funds. There are few incentives to perform the promotional role, particularly because there is no system that recognizes and rewards good work in this area. One clear lesson for the establishment of new promotional agencies is that the promotional and regulatory functions should not be combined in a single entity. Promotion requires a different organizational culture and different attitudes among those performing that role.

The crux of many of these problems lies in the fact that the promotional agencies are neither responding to commercial demand signals from producers, nor are they accountable to producers or their representatives. This can be understood again in terms of the principal–agent relationship (see Box 4.1, p. 86). In the current institutional framework for promotion, the state (and not the intended client) is the principal that appoints the promotional agents to act on its behalf. This has arisen from the paternalistic belief of the government and bureaucracy that the state knows better than citizens or producers themselves what is good for them, and therefore that the state is a more effective principal.

The situation could be remedied by establishing a direct relationship between producers and promotional officials, in which the former as the ultimate users of the services are the principals and the latter their agents. This could be achieved in two ways: by making the promotional agents depend for their income on service fees and so on demand from producers, and by giving producer representatives a significant role in the management of the agencies. Such representatives would have a deeper knowledge and understanding of their promotional wants than has the state, and so enable the promotional agents to serve those needs better. Sometimes the state could be excluded altogether from this relationship, as is clear from successful marketing activities by private actors.

Once again the record is not entirely negative. We have already described some positive features of the South India Textile Research Association (Box 5.5, p. 127) and the export promotion councils, with their reliance on fees for services and the significant influence of their (larger) clients on their boards. There are also examples of agencies that are trying to improve their performance. For example, in Gujarat both GRIMCO and the Gujarat Agro Industries Corporation are trying to focus their promotional efforts more narrowly (on marketing and attracting private investment respectively) and to reduce their direct involvement in production or in supplying inputs.

There are also large private corporations which are promoting, in their own self-interest, the activities of small, rural-based producers. WIMCO has been encouraging agro-forestry among farmers on a commercial basis, to ensure raw material supplies for its match production; Venkateswara Hatcheries has been backing commercial poultry farming in Andhra Pradesh and many other states; the Diamond and Gem Development Corporation has been promotiong diamond cutting in Tamil Nadu, Rajasthan and Gujarat; and Shyam Ahuja trains and employs thousands of weavers on piece-rates in rural Rajasthan and elsewhere in the country. There are many examples in agro-processing, with sugar mills in Uttar Pradesh promoting improved sugarcane cultivation, Nijjar Agro in Punjab developing contract farming for tomatoes suitable for processing, and ITC Agrotech promoting the cultivation of high-yielding varieties of oilseeds in Andhra Pradesh and Rajasthan so that its solvent-extraction plants can run at a higher capacity.

All these efforts have been fairly successful when compared to government or NGO efforts (although they have often fallen short of the business goals of the corporate sector). Such private initiatives have the advantage of a clear focus because of their economic stake in the success of the promotional efforts. They are also open to competition from promotional activities by competing companies. However, such initiatives often skim off the cream in the most profitable parts of the sub-sectors concerned and rarely deal with the poorest producers or farmers.

Conclusions and recommendations

We have seen that many policies and agencies have failed to make a significant impact in promoting the growth of non-farm activities. At the same time there are many examples of successful backing undertaken by the state in India. The Green Revolution is perhaps the most outstanding example. Others we came across during the study include the support of rural manufacturing in Gujarat, of sericulture and silk processing in south India, of prawn farming and processing along the eastern coast, of oilseed farming and processing in Rajasthan, of gem and diamond processing in both the south and west, and of telecommunications throughout the country. We also found many successful promotional activities undertaken by the private sector. Both the failures and achievements point to important features that characterize successful strategies and agencies. These can be summarized as in the following paragraphs.

Scarce promotional resources should be targeted at sub-sectors with potential for future growth in employment, income and output, and should not be wasted on sub-sectors that are likely to remain stagnant or decline (see Chapters 2 and 3). Strategies need to be more focused in terms of sub-sectors, locations and enterprises supported, otherwise promotional policies will continue to evolve into rigid schemes that are unresponsive to the specific conditions and needs of the economic actors involved.

The state should seek to facilitate the growth of promising sub-sectors and need not become a party directly involved in supplying inputs, producing and marketing products. This requires a more positive attitude by the state towards the private sector, and closer collaboration between the public and private arenas. Producer associations are suitable agencies for undertaking private promotional activities, although the organizational performance of many such bodies will need to be strengthened (see Chapter 7). The state will retain the major responsibility for developing appropriate infrastructure, both physical and social, although private parties can also manage some of this. The state will also retain the vital role of developing an enabling environment for the growth of sub-sectors. The rapid growth of diamond processing and even of telecommunications, for example, depended more on establishing a positive policy environment than on undertaking promotional activities directly.

Only with emergent sub-sectors will the state have to become more directly involved. Such engagement will include pilot projects, because entrepreneurs are normally not willing to invest in new activities if their viability has not been proven on the ground. This does not mean, however, that the state has to implement every aspect of a pilot project. Such initiatives require a high degree of sophistication, a thoroughly professional approach and a propensity for inter-agency collaboration. For this, public–private collaboration will again be essential. The state will also have to support effective market mechanisms for emergent sub-sectors, just as it has established cocoon and silk exchanges for the sericulture sub-sector.

Agencies responsible for undertaking promotional activities require the following characteristics:

- They must have a focused strategy of intervention. For this they need to be sub-sector specific in order to have an in-depth understanding of the activities in question. Their interventions should then address the key constraints facing the sub-sector.
- For focus they also need to be cluster or region specific to identify fully with local conditions and constraints in the sub-sector.
- They must be representative. Elected representatives of producers should thus form a majority on their boards or councils.
- They must be autonomous and work independently of the government. They need their own staff and staff policies. Above all they need to be economically viable by generating their own resources to sustain their operations. This will also ensure that the services they supply respond to producers' demand. The agencies will thus have to market their services and become involved in continuous follow-up and interaction with producers.

6 Rural credit policies and agencies[1]

The rural financial sector in India

Rural credit in India has been subject to policy intervention for more than a hundred years, with the Land Improvement Loans Act of 1883, the Agricultural Loans Act of 1884 and the first attempt to establish an agricultural cooperative in 1904. Nevertheless, the All India Rural Credit Survey of 1951–2 found that credit from the formal sector accounted for less than 7 per cent of all loans taken by rural families. The vast bulk of credit (83 per cent) came from moneylenders and landlords, and the rest from family and friends (Naidu, 1986: 185). The survey recommended that the rural branch network of commercial banks be expanded. At that time only the State Bank of India (the nationalized Imperial Bank of India) was under government control, and thus it was given a mandate to establish 400 new branches in rural areas, which was achieved by 1954. Since then policy for the rural financial sector has involved:

- Expanding the agricultural credit cooperative system, comprising three tiers: the Primary Agricultural Cooperative Societies, the District Central Cooperative Banks and the State Apex Cooperative Banks. The Land Development Banks are also part of the cooperative structure.
- Nationalizing the 14 largest commercial banks in 1969, followed by six more in 1981. With nationalization came a massive increase in the number of rural branches of these banks.
- Exercising government control over all banks by specifying interest rates on deposits and advances, liquidity requirements and credit-deposit ratios.
- Introducing the Lead Bank Scheme in 1969, whereby the chosen bank in a district is responsible for drawing up district credit plans.
- Increasing directed lending to selected sectors, especially agriculture and small-scale industry, by establishing the 'priority sector' category with its specified lending targets.

---

1. This chapter draws on several studies in which the authors have been involved: the RNFS investigation itself; 'Financial Services for the Rural Poor and Women in India: Access and Sustainability', sponsored by the World Bank and carried out by Vijay Mahajan and Bharti Gupta Ramola of Price Waterhouse (summarized in Mahajan and Ramola, 1996); and the report of an Indian study group to review rural banking in Indonesia (Fisher, 1995). All the investigations have fed into the process of establishing a new financial and promotional institution (BASIX) for rural livelihoods in India.

- Establishing the Regional Rural Banks (RRBs) in 1975 with a special focus on 'weaker sections' of the rural population, such as small and marginal farmers, agricultural labourers, rural artisans and entrepreneurs.
- Since 1980 linking government programmes for poverty alleviation with bank lending, most notably under the Integrated Rural Development Programme (IRDP), by setting targets for bank lending to specific disadvantaged groups.
- Establishing the National Bank of Agriculture and Rural Development (NABARD) in 1982 as a separate apex body for refinance,[2] promotion and supervision of rural banks.
- All along, maintaining low and often subsidized interest rates for agriculture and other priority-sector lending, for targeted poverty-alleviation lending, and for most small loans.

The dramatic results of these policies should not be underestimated. By March 1992:

- There were 35 254 rural branches, of which 97 per cent had been opened since 1969. In addition, the cooperative sector comprised another 100 000 or so primary agricultural-credit cooperative societies and branches of the District Central Cooperative and Land Development Banks.
- Rural deposits accounted for 15 per cent of the national total, and 23 per cent of the deposits since 1969.
- Outstanding bank credit to rural areas stood at Rs27 500 crores, or 20 per cent of the total credit outstanding nationally.
- The overall credit–deposit ratio (by utilization) for rural areas was 77.0 per cent compared to the national average of 57.7 per cent.

These achievements are also reflected at the micro-level. The All-India Debt and Investment Survey of 1981–2 (RBI, 1989) found that rural households sourced 54.6 per cent of their credit from formal credit agencies, ranging from 23.3 per cent among the poorest to 83.1 among the wealthiest. Sarap (1991: 31, 36, 58) discovered in 1980–81 that 77 per cent of all agricultural families surveyed in a poor district in Orissa were members of primary agricultural cooperatives, and 43 per cent of farm households had taken loans from formal credit agencies. Mahajan and Ramola (1996) reported that even among poor households in a district in Rajasthan over half had at some point taken a loan from a bank (although

2. 'Refinance' is the term used in India for bulk lending at a concessional rate, by 'apex' bodies such as NABARD and SIDBI to primary lending institutions (PLIs) against a portfolio of loans by the latter. It is different from securitization of the PLI loan portfolio in the sense that with refinance the risk remains on the PLI's books.

such loans accounted for only 12 per cent of the total credit used over three years by the households in the survey).

The policies listed above have succeeded in enhancing significantly the outreach of the formal financial system into rural areas. India now has one of the most extensive rural bank networks in the world. Even with a rural population of 622 million (1991 Census), there was one bank branch for every 17 600 rural people, compared to the national average of one branch for every 14 000 people.

However, the expansion of the rural banking system has been achieved through the same strategies and methods that we analysed in the cases of regulation and promotion, characterized by government intervention, control and direction, subsidies and a proliferation of agencies and programmes. Since all the major banks are under government control, the delivery of credit should be seen as the largest promotional activity undertaken by the government in pursuit of rural development. Moreover, this activity has an implementation channel at the grassroots level which exceeds the combined reach of all other government promotional efforts.

To illustrate this analysis we look at the most extensive credit programme, the Integrated Rural Development Programme (IRDP), which was launched jointly by central and state governments in 1980. People below the poverty line are selected and given an income-generating asset of their choice through part loan, part subsidy. This poverty-alleviation programme is of particular importance to the rural non-farm sector because, to encourage diversification, it has a sub-target that 40 per cent of its loans go to activities in 'industry, service and business' (ISB). By 1995 the IRDP had extended Rs22 950 crores to 46.9 million borrowers (GoI, 1995c: 28).

Coupled with the IRDP is the programme called Development of Women and Children in Rural Areas (DWCRA). In this, women are organized into groups around an economic activity, such as rope making, basket weaving or embroidery. They are given part loan, part subsidy to acquire tools or assets individually, and a revolving fund for common production and marketing. There are many other poverty-alleviation programmes which include bank loans, such as the Prime Minister's *Rozgar Yojna*.

The massive direction of credit to the poor which these programmes represent has not come without substantial costs. According to Mahajan and Ramola (1996):

- The design of the IRDP and other programmes, aiming to allow poor men and women to acquire assets from which they can earn a stream of income as self-employed entrepreneurs, is misconceived. More than two-thirds of credit usage by the poor is for consumption, and the formal sector does not lend for this purpose. Moreover, some types of assets may enhance the risks the poor face if the assets do not perform, the poor cannot manage them, or their debt burden is increased. For the poor to become successful entrepreneurs, they need many more inputs besides credit, and programmes like Training of Rural Youth for Self-Employment (TRYSEM) are completely inadequate to meet this need.

- Over half of the borrowers at the time of survey no longer had the asset acquired through the loan. Almost a quarter of these borrowers had never purchased the asset, over half had sold it subsequently (often in times of emergency, such as illness), and for almost a quarter the asset had died (as in the case of cattle) or stopped functioning.
- Capital subsidies of 33 to 50 per cent for the assets acquired under IRDP loans have led to substantial corruption. Over two-thirds of the average transaction costs for obtaining such a loan are due to bribes and overcharging for the asset (which the borrower is often given as loan in kind). Poverty-alleviation loans are also extensively used by local politicians for extending political patronage, as in practice it is they who select beneficiaries. Such political manipulation is naturally accompanied by the assumption on the part of borrowers that the loans will not have to be repaid.
- It is thus not surprising that default rates have been high, with recovery rates in the range of 20 to 30 per cent. Even the level of awareness among borrowers of the terms of poverty-alleviation loans, such as interest rates, repayment terms and amounts outstanding is extremely low. The IRDP and other poverty-alleviation loans have thus created a large pool of wilful or unwitting defaulters who, as a result, cannot in future receive another formal-sector loan.
- Moreover, by taking away the bankers' discretion in selecting borrowers, and the purpose and terms of the loans, the government has completely eroded the rural bankers' autonomy and made them highly cynical about lending to the poor. Rural bankers see IRDP loans as a compulsion at best, and a gross waste at worst. These attitudes are summed up in the Hindi phrase which bankers use as their own long form of IRDP: 'Itna Rupiya Dubona Padega' (we shall have to sink so much money). By causing high default rates and making rural bankers so cynical, poverty-alleviation lending has caused an enormous setback to the possibility of the formal sector ever addressing the credit needs of the poor.

As with promotion generally, numerous agencies have been established to implement such credit policies, with new ones being set up when the existing ones have failed to perform. First came the Primary Agricultural Cooperative Societies and the other tiers of the cooperative structure, then the expansion of rural branches of commercial banks, and then the Regional Rural Banks (RRBs), which the government is now restructuring. At the apex of the rural financial system is the National Bank for Agriculture and Rural Development (NABARD). However, there is also the Small

Industries Development Bank of India (SIDBI) established in 1990 as the apex national agency for the financing, promotion and development of small-scale industries (SSIs). While initially some attempt was made to distinguish the areas of jurisdiction of SIDBI and NABARD, it is now accepted that the two agencies are to an extent both complementary as well as competitive.

There are also many other agencies involved in credit, including the State Finance Corporations, the State Industrial Investment Corporations, the Scheduled Castes Development Finance Corporation, the Women's Development Corporation, and many promotional agencies whose programmes include credit components, such as the Khadi and Village Industries Boards (KVIBs). In this proliferation of credit agencies, the underlying causes of the failure of the existing bodies were rarely considered in the policy solutions recommending new organizational mechanisms.

Thus formal credit, whether extended to farmers, rural producers or the rural poor, is often highly directed, schematized, standardized and subsidized, and is channelled through a plethora of special agencies, programmes or organizational mechanisms. Because central-government control and direction has been particularly strong in the financial sector, there are few significant variations across different states.

The condition of the rural financial sector described above could, potentially, be changed radically by the reforms which the Government of India initiated in 1995. These reforms, which are part of the strategy for restructuring the financial sector as a whole, aim to improve the regulatory environment, restructure and increase the commercial orientation of the nationalized banks, and promote greater private-sector participation. In consequence, all the banks are being subjected to new norms of capital adequacy, income recognition, asset classification and provisioning requirements.

In the short term, these changes have had an adverse impact on rural credit flows. The commercial banks and RRBs have become very conservative under the new regulations and are not willing to load their portfolios with potential non-performing assets. As a result credit flows both to the farm and non-farm sectors have been squeezed. This trend will change, however, within a few years as banks adjust to doing more prudent lending based on sound appraisal rather than disbursing loans in response to top-down targets.

The primary regulatory and planning bodies, the Ministry of Finance and the Reserve Bank of India (RBI), have therefore been principally engaged in trying to solve the problems of the existing rural banks, whose situation is far from healthy (for example, the RRBs are together losing Rs500 crores a year). The RBI has identified 100 of the 196 RRBs for financial restructuring, and NABARD has helped them to draw up 'development action plans'. NABARD has also signed memoranda of understanding with selected state governments and apex cooperative banks to upgrade the performance of the cooperative credit system.

In August 1996 the national government allowed the establishment of new 'local area banks' (LABs) in the private sector, with a minimum capital of Rs5 crores. The operations of each LAB will be confined to three contiguous districts, and so they are likely to serve the rural population as a significant, if not the major, portion of their business. The LABs open up for the first time the prospect of private-sector parties entering the formal rural-credit sector (the informal sector is of course fully private already).

Measures to restructure the RRBs, partially privatize some of the commercial banks and allow private LABs, by themselves, would not suffice, if the interest rates remained controlled. The RBI has, therefore, been proceeding systematically on the most important policy change of deregulating lending rates. Interest-rate ceilings for loans of whatever size from cooperative banks were abolished in 1994 and replaced by a minimum rate of 12 per cent. Ceilings on loans over Rs200 000 by commercial banks and RRBs were lifted in mid-1995. Interest rates on smaller loans by RRBs and LABs were also deregulated in August 1996, but not for smaller loans of commercial banks. However, it is only a matter of time before even this last regulated interest rate falls to the policy of deregulation being followed by RBI.

Rural credit and the non-farm sector

Having looked at the overall rural financial sector, it is time to assess more specifically how the rural non-farm sector has been affected. Much of rural credit has in fact been directed at the agricultural sector, both in the cooperative banking area, which is built up on a base of primary agricultural cooperatives, and among rural branches of the nationalized commercial banks, many of which have appointed specialized agricultural officers. The expansion of the rural branch network by itself may not have had a significant impact on lending for non-agricultural activities.

On the other hand, the priority-sector targets include lending to small-scale industries and small road-transport operators, and 40 per cent of IRDP loans are supposed to go to the ISB sector. Likewise, the KVIBs have provided concessional-term loans and working capital to certified *khadi* and village-industry organizations.

The first formal policy recognition of the credit needs of the rural non-farm sector came with the act establishing NABARD in 1982. Under its automatic refinance facilities NABARD has succeeded in increasing dramatically the availability of refinance for rural, tiny, cottage and village industries from Rs1.4 crores in 1985–6 to Rs328.9 crores in 1993–4 (NABARD, 1994b: 17). However, the non-farm sector accounted for less than 10 per cent of NABARD's total refinancing in each year until March 1993 (excluding refinance for IRDP–ISB loans). It was only in 1995–6 that refinance for the RNFS for the first time reached 15 per cent of the total for that year. NABARD also provides short-term credit limits for production and marketing activities to weavers' cooperatives and some other rural industries (Rs699 crores in 1993–4: NABARD, 1995: 11).

NABARD is handicapped by the fact that it is predominantly a refinance agency, and unless the primary lending bodies (the cooperative, regional rural and commercial banks) take more determined action, there is little NABARD can do to increase credit flows to RNFS producers.[3] NABARD's automatic refinance for the rural non-farm sector also varies across states (see Table 6.5, p. 158). Granted its dependency on the primary lending agencies, NABARD's refinance tends to reinforce the extent to which more credit flows to the more developed states, although Rajasthan, with its more active development bureaucracy, is a striking exception. NABARD is aware of these difficulties and has sought to draw the attention of banks to the RNFS through its District Development Managers posted in nearly 250 districts of the country, and through issuing circulars and guidelines. NABARD also provides refinance for the RNFS on more liberal terms.

In addition to refinancing RNFS loans, NABARD undertakes various promotional activities for the sector, including assistance to train producers, to plan for district rural industrialization, to establish technical cells for RNFS lending in selected banks, and to undertake research. NABARD also has a regulatory role, particularly over the cooperative banks and RRBs. As we saw in the previous chapter, combining both regulatory and promotional functions is difficult and the regulatory culture tends to predominate. NABARD's organizational culture, which is bureaucratic and schematic rather than facilitative and flexible, is not necessarily geared to playing its promotional role effectively.

In 1990, with the advent of SIDBI, a second refinance agency became available for the RNFS. SIDBI disbursed Rs4796 crores for the SSI sector in 1995–6 (SIDBI, 1996: 20). However, data on the extent of refinance and direct finance by SIDBI to rural, as opposed to urban, units are not available, and it was likely to be a small share of its disbursements, since the bank is concerned with all SSIs. The smaller, rural units do not benefit as much from SIDBI's assistance, even though these units represent 42 per cent of all SSIs (GoI, 1992c).

SIDBI undertakes a range of promotional and developmental activities, which include training, marketing support, upgrading technology, and

3. NABARD's dependency on its distribution channels can be seen from variations among states in loans to weavers' societies which it refinanced (NABARD, 1994b: 7). With strong federations of weavers' cooperatives, Tamil Nadu accounted for 49 per cent of the total outstanding in 1992–3, while UP, with a large number of weavers but a weak cooperative structure, accounted for only 3 per cent.

adopting areas for special developmental inputs. It has also used a cluster approach, for example by financing a modernization programme for the brass and bell metal industry at Hajo, near Guwahati in Assam, but again such clusters are mostly urban.

SIDBI is now seeking to rectify its predominant focus on urban SSIs. To this end it has established promotional schemes to reach rural small and micro-enterprises directly, such as the micro-credit scheme for lending to NGOs, self-help groups and individual micro-enterprises. Under this scheme the bank has so far disbursed about Rs6 crores. It also supported the promotion of many rural small and micro-units under its Rural Industries Programme, which was launched in three districts in Andhra Pradesh in 1993. The experiences of this pilot effort were positive, and SIDBI has now extended it to 14 states.

The priorities of the commercial and cooperative banking systems, and until recently of SIDBI and even NABARD, demonstrate that the financial system has still not done full justice to the credit needs of the rural non-farm sector. For example, as of March 1990, the share of bank credit to artisans, village and cottage industries was only 4.5 per cent of the total credit to small-scale enterprises. Even among RRBs, only 8 per cent of their total advances were to village undertakings (NABARD, 1995: 9). While in the last few years formal financial agencies have begun to realize the considerable potential of the RNFS, it will perhaps be many more years before the sector enjoys adequate credit flows. To substantiate such claims, we look more carefully at aggregate data on rural credit to the RNFS in the next section.

Aggregate data on rural credit to the RNFS

Unfortunately, because the rural non-farm sector is not a heading under which most rural banks have categorized their lending in the past, it is often difficult to judge how much credit has been extended to the sector. Nevertheless NABARD, the RBI and the All-India Debt and Investment Survey provide valuable data on credit flows to the RNFS.

According to the Nayak Committee (RBI, 1992), advances outstanding to rural industries were Rs712 crores, which amounted to only 0.7 per cent of the total outstanding, as of March 1990, despite the fact that the rural industrial sector accounted for over half the total industrial units in the country (Papola, 1992: 242).

In terms of credit outstanding for non-farm activities in rural bank branches, in 1992 about Rs3500 was outstanding for each rural main worker (RMW)[4] in the RNFS. This compares favourably with Rs600 per rural main worker in agriculture (or Rs1000 if only cultivators are

4. See Box 2.1 (p. 25) for definition, Table 6.1 for sources.

Table 6.1: Bank credit to the rural non-farm sector (1992)

Category	*Number of accounts (%)*	*Outstanding (%)*	*RMWs in the RNFS (1991) (%)*
Total (absolute numbers)	11.5 million	Rs13 960 crores	39.4 million
Mining and quarrying	0.02	1.7	2.6
Manufacturing	24.0	58.2	32.2
Construction	0.03	0.5	5.9
Housing	1.2	3.3	
Trading	53.2	24.3	18.5
Transport	6.2	6.4	7.0
Other services	15.3	5.6	33.8
Total	100.0	100.0	100.0
Percentage to village industries	15.8	4.1	*12.2
Percentage to SSIs	7.0	14.9	**20.0

Notes: village industries include artisans.
* Percentage of RNFS workers in household manufacturing.
** Percentage of RNFS workers in non-household manufacturing, the majority in small or tiny units (see Table 2.11).
Sources: RBI, 1994: Table 4.3; for 1991 Census data see Table 2.2 (p. 29).

included). Moreover, there were 2.6 million loan accounts for village and small-scale industries, accounting for 19 per cent of all the rural credit outstanding to non-agricultural activities (Table 6.1).

However, various manufacturing surveys show that there are some 15 million rural manufacturing units in India (Table 2.11, p. 45). This suggests that the formal financial sector is extending credit to at most a sixth of all these manufacturing enterprises, and to far fewer service enterprises (see p. 157). Moreover, much of RNFS credit in rural bank branches is outstanding to a few capital-intensive rural factories (Table 6.3, p. 156), and to large traders of agricultural produce based in rural market towns. Thus over 80 per cent of total credit outstanding to the RNFS is for manufacturing and trading, indicating the predominance of these activities (along with agriculture)[5] for rural credit (Table 6.1).

That the formal banking system is failing to extend much credit to the many small and tiny rural non-farm enterprises is supported by data on the usage of credit by rural households. The All-India Debt and Investment Survey (RBI, 1989) suggests that 60 per cent of the cash dues outstanding from rural households are used for agriculture and allied activities. A further 21 per cent, or as much as 80 per cent for the poorest households, goes to consumption purposes, such as household expenses, social func-

5. Over 50 per cent of the total number of loan accounts in rural bank branches, and over 40 per cent of the credit outstanding, is for agriculture; these loans have been excluded from the data given in this section.

Table 6.2: Credit used for rural non-farm business as proportion of total credit usage

Household by assets (Rs 000s) →	*up to 1*	*1–5*	*5–10*	*10–20*	*20–50*	*50–100*	*100–500*	*over 500*	*Total*
Capital expenditure	1.9	5.6	10.0	6.6	7.5	6.6	5.8	13.0	7.2
Current expenditure	3.8	2.5	2.8	2.3	2.2	2.2	1.1	0.3	1.7
Total	5.7	8.1	12.8	8.9	9.7	8.8	6.9	13.3	8.9

Source: All-India Debt and Investment Survey (RBI, 1989: 70).

tions, weddings and illnesses. Only 8.9 per cent, however, are used for non-farm business.

The proportion of credit used for non-farm business peaks with two rural-household groups: those with assets of between Rs5000 and Rs10 000 and those with the most assets (Table 6.2). This confirms some of the conclusions in Chapter 2 that non-farm activities are pursued most by two different groups. The first corresponds roughly to the micro-entrepreneurs such as weavers and potters, and the second to small (and larger) rural-enterprise owners, such as those who operate brick kilns, rice mills and light commercial vehicles.

However, data on credit outstanding from banks or on credit usage by borrowers do not allow us to assess readily whether the credit available to the RNFS is adequate to meet the needs of the sector (which we address below). Nevertheless, comparing the proportions of credit outstanding to various RNFS activities with the proportions of non-farm employment that these activities generate provides at least some insights into the extent to which rural lending supports RNFS employment.

At the aggregate level the allocation of credit by rural bank branches to various industrial categories is not too different from the proportions of RNFS employment generated by these categories (see Table 6.1). Only credit for trading significantly exceeds the proportion of RNFS workers in trading. However, it is not surprising that trading, with its low risks, quick turnover and assured cash flows, should be especially appealing to bankers. The provision of credit to services other than trading and transport seems to fall well short of employment in those services, but about 60 per cent of these jobs are probably in the public sector (see Appendix 2, Table 4).

Among more disaggregated categories within the rural secondary and tertiary sectors, however, the rough match between credit outstanding and employment is no longer maintained (Tables 6.3 and 6.4). Within the secondary sector capital-intensive production understandably receives much more credit than the rural employment it generates. This applies in

Table 6.3: Bank credit for rural activities in the secondary sector and mining (1992)

Category (NIC code in brackets)*	*Outstanding (%)*	*RMWs in secondary activities and mining (1981) (%)*
Total (absolute numbers)	Rs88.8 billion	14.5 million
Chemicals and products (31)	14.1	1.3
Engineering (35–36)	13.0	1.6
Textiles and products (23–26)	9.7	21.6
Metals and products (33–34)	9.3	4.6
Food processing (20–21)	9.1	8.4
Transport equipment (37)	6.8	0.5
Construction	0.8	12.5
Housing loans	5.2	–
Paper and products (28)	3.1	0.9
Mining and quarrying (12, 19)	2.6	3.0
Cement and products	2.1	–
Leather and products (29)	1.8	1.7
Rubber, plastic and products (30)	1.5	0.5
Beverages and tobacco (22)	1.0	8.1
Electricity and water (40–42)	0.9	2.9
Petroleum and coal (10–11)	0.6	2.4
Other* (27, 32, 38, 39)	18.3	29.7
Total	100.0	100.0

* The National Industrial Classification (NIC) codes are given to show how employment percentages were calculated. The credit data do not list wood and products (27), non-metallic mineral products (32), other manufacturing (38) and repairs (39) separately, which presumably come under 'other industries'. In fact, 96 per cent of the loan accounts for the secondary sector are classified under 'other industries', and so we do not give percentages of loan accounts in this table. However, the average credit outstanding per account under 'other industries' is only Rs6138.

Source: see Table 6.1; 1981 Census (GoI, 1987a: Table B12).

Table 6.4: Bank credit for rural services (1992)

Category (NIC Code in brackets)	*Number of accounts (%)*	*Outstanding (%)*	*RMWs in services (%)* *
Total (absolute numbers)	8.6 million	Rs50.8 billion	10.5 million*
Retail trade (65–68)	69.4	51.2	41.1
Transport (71–73)	8.3	17.5	15.6
Wholesale trade (60–64)	1.9	15.8	2.2
Other services (75, 91, 93–99)	11.7	9.9	39.8
Professional services (82–83)*	8.8	5.6	1.3
Total	100.0	100.0	100.0

Note: * The figures exclude the following services which are primarily in the public sector: banking and finance (80–81), public administration (90) and education (92).

Source: see Tables 6.1 and 6.3.

particular to chemicals and engineering, but also to paper, cement, rubber and plastics. Many of these activities have the largest average outstanding balances per account, ranging from just below Rs500 000 for light engineering to almost Rs1 crore for fertilizers. This confirms that much of the RNFS credit outstanding from rural bank branches is for a few large and often peri-urban factories. On the other hand, National Sample Survey data (see Table 2.4, p. 32) suggest that electrical equipment, paper and chemicals are among the fastest growing sub-sectors in terms of rural employment.

In contrast, the proportion of RNFS credit outstanding to textiles and textile products, beverages and tobacco, and construction falls well below the proportion of rural non-farm employment these sub-sectors generate. The majority of jobs in beverages and tobacco are in *bidi*-making, and this activity receives minimal credit from the formal sector. Much employment in construction is in the public sector, for example building roads, but the credit data confirm that rural construction is a neglected sub-sector in terms of public policy (as we have already seen for regulation and promotion). Finally, much employment in textiles and textile products is in traditional activities in the tiny sector (notably handlooms). The same applies to wood products and pottery, which are not even classified separately in the aggregate credit data.

The data on services confirm the heavy predominance of trading in bank lending (Table 6.4). Two-thirds of all credit outstanding to services is for wholesale and especially retail trade. In contrast, services other than trade – transport and professional services – account for 40 per cent of rural employment in the tertiary sector (even after excluding public-sector jobs in administration and education), but receive only a paltry 10 per cent of the credit outstanding to services.

One important conclusion that the aggregate credit data confirm is the gender bias in bank lending. Personal services, tobacco, textile and wood products, pottery, construction, miscellaneous services, and repairs, together account for two-thirds of all female employment in the rural non-farm sector (see Table 2.6 p. 36). However, each one of these sub-sectors accounts for a far smaller proportion of the credit outstanding in rural bank branches than the employment figures might suggest is justified. Among those sub-sectors which have better access to credit, only retail trading is important for women's rural employment. However, larger male retail traders would undoubtedly be taking the lion's share of credit even in this sub-sector. If we add the fact that formal financial agencies do not provide any consumption credit (of particular importance to women), it becomes all too apparent that the formal banking sector is not serving the credit needs of rural women.

Inter-state comparisions suggest that the extent of rural non-farm employment is correlated with the amount of credit outstanding per capita

Table 6.5: Rural bank credit in eight states

State	*RNFS workers as % of rural main workers (1991)*	*Credit outstanding at rural branches per capita (rural) (in Rs, 1992)*	*Credit outstanding to small-scale and village industries at rural branches per capita (rural) (in Rs, 1992)*	*NABARD refinance to RNFS (cumulative up to March 1993) per capita (rural) (in Rs)*
Punjab	25.8	1345	60	7
Tamil Nadu	20.6	660	51	14
Gujarat	19.6	623	75	16
Assam	18.6	513	31	5
Orissa	17.5	282	28	3
AP	17.1	548	38	5
Rajasthan	15.6	324	24	11
UP	14.9	310	37	2
India	17.7	442	43	9

Note: The credit data do not distinguish between agricultural and non-agricultural lending at the state level, and thus we can use figures only for credit outstanding to small-scale and village industries.

Sources: 1991 Census (GoI, 1992b); RBI (1994), computed from source of Table 4.6 (pp. 209–240); NABARD (1994b: Statement 4).

(Table 6.5). This correlation does not of course prove causality. While more credit undoubtedly assists the growth of the rural non-farm sector, the banks are also likely to extend more rural credit in more developed states such as Punjab and Gujarat.

Perspectives from fieldwork

There is an enormous variety of credit needs in the RNFS. This is not only because of the diversity of activities within the sector, ranging from primary industries like mining through manufacturing to tertiary services, but also because of the diversity of enterprises even within individual sub-sectors. For example, in the stone-processing sub-sector, a small artisan carving stone may need a loan of only Rs15 000 while a modern and advanced granite-processing unit may require investments of lakhs, even crores of rupees.

In spite of this diversity, general conclusions on credit for the RNFS do arise from our study. The most obvious point is that the credit needs of the

RNFS are not well serviced by the mainstream financial agencies. Of 129 producers,[6] only a third received a loan from a commercial bank, RRB, state financial corporation, or development agencies such as the KVIBs. Moreover, this is by no means a statistical or representative sample, but one that overestimates the share of formal credit sourced by RNFS enterprises.[7] A survey by the Madras Institute of Development Studies (1985) of cottage units in the match industry in Tamil Nadu found that less than a quarter of cottage units had borrowed from a bank, even though such units are a special target group for KVIB's support for the industry. Only two of the fourteen repair units covered by our study in Andhra Pradesh, and one of the ten restaurants in Tamil Nadu, had taken bank loans. Such figures are likely to be more representative for the RNFS as a whole. Indeed, it was striking how many producers said, in response to fieldworkers' questions about credit, that they had never even approached banks for a loan.

It is thus fair to say that the supply of formal credit falls well short of demand in many sub-sectors, including those which are targeted under priority and directed lending. The shortage of formal credit is particularly acute in failing to meet the working capital needs of many non-farm enterprises. This was almost a universal complaint among those enterprises, both small and large, covered by the study. Even in dynamic clusters like Tiruppur (for hosiery) and Pallipalayam (for powerlooms) in Tamil Nadu, where banks have lent to many enterprises, the growth of these clusters far outstrips the ability of the local banks to address the credit demands of all the producers.

As a result, many producers in all the sub-sectors studied turn to informal or private lending channels for their credit needs (see p. 167). However, the profiles and case-studies show that some sections of the rural non-farm sector have better access to formal credit than others. These include:

- Larger enterprises which can offer collateral, show formal accounts and generally enjoy better cash flows. Many export units would fall into this category. Such larger enterprises can compete for credit under general category advances (non-directed lending).
- Enterprises in modern sub-sectors, such as powerlooms, hosiery, ceramics, cement and plastics. Bankers generally have greater confidence in the potential of such activities. This is confirmed by the aggregate data

6. Many more producers were interviewed during the study (see Appendix 1), but credit data on these 129 producers are given in case-studies or sub-sector profiles produced for the study.
7. The sample is not representive for three reasons: (1) during fieldwork we often sought out producers with greater insights into a sub-sector as a whole, and these tend to manage more successful units; (2) we deliberately included a greater proportion of larger units: a representative sample would comprise predominantly tiny enterprises (see Table 2.11, p. 44); and (3) we sometimes used information from formal financial agencies to select producers for interview.

on credit outstanding to modern manufacturing such as chemicals, engineering, paper, cement, rubber and plastics (see Table 6.3).

- Manufacturing enterprises, which have better access to formal finance than services. Forty per cent of such businesses covered in our study profiles had received some form of bank finance, compared to 24 per cent of service enterprises (or only 14 per cent if we exclude the transport businesses, half of which had received bank finance under priority-sector lending).
- Enterprises which fall under categories which are specifically targeted by the formal financial sector, the most important of which is that of small-scale industries, although most lending to this sector is to urban and peri-urban units. Other activities form part of the priority sector, such as transport and many village industries. Some sub-sectors, such as sericulture and fisheries, benefit from wider promotional programmes which usually include credit components.

Priority and directed lending through the formal banking system has without a doubt increased credit flows to those activities and groups which are targeted. Such lending has, however, also meant that many enterprises, especially small and tiny units, which do not fall under any scheme for directed lending, are often excluded from formal credit channels. Many producers we interviewed said that they had been refused bank loans on the grounds that their businesses did not fall under any scheme. Enterprises in sub-sectors like bricks, construction and many services which are not regarded as part of the priority sector have been particularly affected. Village artisans, such as potters, have been turned away by bankers as well, on the grounds that credit for such activities was the responsibility of the KVIBs.

The problem is also acute for new and emerging sub-sectors, such as floriculture, the processing of herbs and spices, and rural tourism. Gem-cutting in Tamil Nadu is a good example of the influence of directed lending. This expanding sub-sector had to rely almost entirely on private traders until the District Rural Development Agency persuaded the commercial banks to include targets for gem-cutting under the IRDP.

Apart from the need to meet their priority and directed lending targets, bankers have few incentives to lend to small borrowers: they have little confidence in their businesses, the transaction costs of such lending are much higher than for larger loans, and the interest rates on small loans are lower under the current regulatory regime. Mahajan and Ramola (1996) found that only 7 per cent of borrowers below the poverty line surveyed in Uttar Pradesh had been able to obtain a commercial bank loan which was not tied to some poverty-alleviation scheme. In effect, the bankers use the highly schematized nature of lending to small and tiny borrowers as an excuse to exclude large numbers of such borrowers, especially the poor and women.

It is important to recognize that these attitudes have been encouraged by priority, directed and schematic lending, which suggest to bankers that the targeted borrowers can survive only with subsidies and cannot run viable businesses. The high transaction costs of small loans mean that bankers prefer to make up losses incurred on priority-sector lending with profits earned on larger loans.

A further drawback of schematized lending was that loan amounts were determined according to standard 'unit costs' drawn up by NABARD for each state, even though states often span a wide variety of agro-climatic zones with different cost structures. Moreover, since standard unit costs were in many cases not updated for two to three years, the amounts were invariably too small, and those producers who obtained a loan under a particular scheme found they had to borrow from other sources to make up the shortfall. It is only recently that unit costs are being calculated for each district and updated at least once a year. More generally, however, such inflexibility remains a problem for the special needs of rural people, which are characterized by informality, seasonality and a diversity of livelihoods.

Finally, directed and other lending has become highly politicized. The selection of IRDP borrowers by local politicians is a well-known phenomenon, and justifies the claim that the programme is often little more than a system of distributing political patronage. Cooperative banks are particularly prone to political manipulation, with managing bodies often appointed by state governments, and local élites, such as large farmers, often receiving the greatest share of the credit available (and being responsible for the bulk of bad debt).

But even the nationalized commercial banks are closely intertwined with government structures. For each administrative block there is a Bankers' Committee, chaired by the Block Development Officer, to plan and monitor government sponsored poverty-alleviation programmes. At the district level there is a Consultative Committee, chaired by the District Collector, and on which officers of all the government departments are represented in addition to banks and other agencies. At the state level there is also a Bankers' Committee, and the chair and managing directors, as well as the board of directors, of each nationalized bank are appointed by the central government.

Political pressures on the rural banking system are thus extensive, and the banks have had to indulge in much imprudent lending as a result. In addition, many borrowers regard directed loans as grants from the government, reinforced by a series of government-mandated loan waivers, most notably in 1989 when the central government, under its Agricultural and Rural Debt Relief Scheme, waived all loans by commercial banks to borrowers owing below Rs10 000. With both imprudent lending and wilful defaults, the prevailing culture of default is one of the most serious problems facing the rural banking system in India.

This culture of default also affects RNFS producers directly. Banks have become reluctant to lend to numerous activities because they have experienced high default rates. *Khandsari*, silk, pottery, leather, diamonds and hotels were just some of the examples we came across in the course of the study. Fortunately the Reserve Bank of India and NABARD are beginning to take remedial action. For example, NABARD refused to extend refinance facilities to cooperative banks in Karnataka in 1994, and later in Orissa in 1995, when the state governments concerned announced waivers on interest and loans. Politicians themselves, however, will have to change their attitudes towards the credit system before the culture of default can be tackled directly.

In the light of this analysis, it is not surprising that while credit policies have succeeded in reducing the physical distance between bankers and potential borrowers, the effective distance still remains as bankers consider loans to small rural producers as a tedious social obligation rather than a business opportunity. Those producers who succeed in obtaining loans from the formal sector thus find it a time-consuming, expensive and often harassing exercise, all generating high transaction costs.

Mahajan and Ramola (1996: 215) found that the transaction costs for the poor of acquiring a loan are indeed substantial, ranging from '17 to 22 per cent of the loan amount for commercial bank loans'. These costs include 'out-of-pocket costs, payments to middlemen, and the price difference of assets received as loan in kind versus their cash price in the market. . . . If, in addition, the wage loss due to time spent in getting the loan is accounted for, the transaction costs are even higher.' On average it took six months in a Rajasthan district from the selection of the borrower under a government scheme to the actual disbursement of the loan, and 62 per cent of borrowers said they had paid money to middlemen and officials to get their loan processed.

The transaction costs are even higher for smaller loans, suggesting that the millions of tiny RNFS units suffer in particular from the poor quality of banking services available. Transaction costs are also higher for women: 24 per cent of the loan amount (in Rajasthan), compared to 14 per cent for men. Women receive fewer and smaller loans and face longer processing times (8.4 months). It is thus not surprising that a third of all borrowers surveyed in Rajasthan (and half of the women borrowers) considered their experience of dealing with banks as bad or very bad.

Granted such high transaction costs, it is perhaps surprising that borrowers still pursue such loans. Indeed, during our study we came across many examples of borrowers who had not approached formal financial agencies for loans because of the expected hassles and transaction costs. However, if the interest rates on loans to the poor are adjusted for the transaction costs involved, the effective interest rates range from around 22 to 33 per cent (higher for women by 4 to 5 percentage points). But these rates are still at least 3 or 4 percentage points lower than the lowest rates to which those surveyed had access in the informal sector. Moreover, in the case of IRDP loans, a 33 per cent capital subsidy for general borrowers reduces the effective interest rate to between 0 and 7 per cent, and a 50 per cent subsidy for borrowers from scheduled castes and tribes makes the effective interest rate negative. The significant financial incentives for obtaining such loans are apparent.

A closer look at the banks

Not only are the transaction costs to borrowers important in assessing rural credit for the RNFS, but also the costs to the banks themselves, not least of all because so much of their rural lending is mandated by the central government.

Priority and directed lending in fact accounts for most of the business of rural branches. Mahajan and Ramola (1996) show that in such a branch of a commercial bank, IRDP and other sponsored loans accounted for two-thirds of the loan accounts and half of the total loan amount advanced. Many of the other loans would fall under the priority-sector, and small loans in total accounted for 97 per cent of loan accounts and 74 per cent of the loan amount advanced. The branch's average annual administrative cost for small loans was just over 5 per cent of the average loan outstanding. This was much higher than for larger loans, even though under the current regulatory framework smaller loans attract a lower interest rate.

The most critical aspect, however, has been the weak recovery of loans. Due to poor record-keeping at branch level, the already low rates given in Table 6.6 are likely to overestimate recoveries. Mahajan and Ramola (1996) found that for a statistical sample of loans the actual recovery rate was 21 per cent. Only 30 per cent of the sample accounts were regular. As a result, rural branches would have to derecognize at least 50 per cent of their total term-loan interest income to be in line with prudent norms of

Table 6.6: Recovery of loans by different rural financial agencies (%)

Agency	*1982–3*	*1987–8*	*1989–90*	*1991–2*
Primary agricultural cooperatives	60	62	51	NA
Land Development Banks	52	54	28	49
Regional Rural Banks	52	49	34	40
Nationalized commercial banks	55	57	49	57

Source: NABARD (1994a: 23). Note: NA = not available

income recognition. If subsidies from regional, zonal and head offices are also taken into account, it is clear that all the branches are incurring losses. The position of the Regional Rural Bank surveyed in Rajasthan is even worse!

In terms of internal practices and attitudes, including towards customers, it is striking that these are very similar across the numerous different types of formal rural banks. The expansion of rural banking has happened on account of central-government directions, not because the banks were pursuing market opportunities in a competitive environment. Indeed, competition between banks has been stifled, initially by coordinated district credit plans, in which each bank in the district was given specific targets for directed lending, and later by the Service Area Approach, whereby bank branches were effectively given monopoly rights in their area of operation. However, the changes made in the Service Area Approach since 1994 have diluted the scope for such monopolies considerably.

Thus it is not surprising that few attempts have been made to differentiate products, services and delivery mechanisms to match the specific needs of diverse groups within the rural non-farm sector. In fact products and procedures in rural branches are similar to those in urban areas, and the majority of rural loans are extended under schemes of the government or NABARD which specify unit costs and the terms of the loan in substantial detail. The perception of rural bankers is that they have almost no control at all over their systems and practices, which are determined by the government, the RBI, NABARD and their own head offices.

Bankers also spend much of their time on deposit mobilization, recovery follow-up and housekeeping, the last being entirely manual and requiring innumerable *ad hoc* reports. These, and meeting targets for loan disbursals, are also the main criteria on which the performance of bankers is measured. Far less time is spent on loan appraisal and interaction with customers, and no recognition is given for innovation in reaching out to rural producers. The incentive structure thus strongly reinforces the aversion to risk already endemic among most bank staff.

This is partly because most personnel policies are determined centrally for all public-sector banks. The Banking Services Recruitment Board selects personnel for all the banks, and individual banks have no say on those chosen on their behalf. Personnel policies are often limited by centralized agreements with the powerful officers and staff unions. Salary grades and scales are fixed and increments awarded on the number of years of service.

And so the commercial banks and other financial agencies in the formal sector suffer from many of the weaknesses we ascribed to promotional agencies in the previous chapter (see Box 5.1, p. 116). The banks have little autonomy, they are not subject to competition and their staff are evaluated according to non-commercial parameters. Even the specificity of their goals has been diluted by using them as channels for distributing subsidized resources regardless of whether this is compatible with their commercial objectives. Such conclusions further justify our claim that the delivery of credit through the formal financial sector should be seen as the largest promotional activity undertaken by the Indian government in pursuit of rural development.

How do these internal practices and attitudes of rural banks affect lending to the rural non-farm sector? The identification of the RNFS as a new category for directed lending is not just confusing to bankers because it overlaps with existing ones, especially SSIs and *khadi* and village industries. It is damaging for the prospects of the sector because, as a result, bankers do not look at the RNFS as a potentially profitable market segment. Bankers regard such lending as another burden beyond their commercial purview, and it is targets and policy guidelines that exercise most influence in determining the structure of lending. An additional incentive to bankers is provided by NABARD through its refinancing (up to 100 per cent of some RNFS loans), which assists the banks' cash flow. However, the pressures of meeting targets for deposits and lending, and of loan recoveries and extensive housekeeping, restrict the extent to which bankers are willing to lend small and administratively burdensome sums to rural non-farm producers outside of schematic lending.

Lending to the RNFS by commercial banks is therefore usually assigned to their priority-sector divisions, which tend to see such loans purely in terms of reclaiming refinance. There are few banks which have specialized staff for the RNFS. NABARD has assisted selected Regional Rural and District Cooperative Banks in establishing special technical monitoring and evaluation (TME) cells for RNFS lending, and the State Cooperative Bank in Tamil Nadu, for example, has officials at its head office who deal exclusively with RNFS work. However, the TME cells tend not to be sustained once NABARD withdraws its financial support.

Bankers' attitudes under general category (non-directed) advances are different. The bank manager considers the viability of a given project, the potential of the entrepreneur and his capability to manage a certain amount of finance. In addition, the bank manager considers general-credit policy guidelines, such as giving priority to exports. The interaction between the potential borrower and the bank manager is direct, and knowledge about the past performance of the entrepreneur, personal rapport and other behavioural aspects influence the process. Priority-sector lending, when not linked to schematic loans, but provided to SSI units, may follow a similar pattern. Such loans are, however, applicable only to the upper end of RNFS units, particularly those in modern export-oriented sub-sectors.

Many of the promotional agencies which we reviewed in the previous chapter also have credit components in their promotional programmes as part of a multiple-input approach to promotion. The foremost among these are the KVIBs, which provide artisans with concessional credit, until recently at 4 per cent. Most states also channel credit to handloom and handicraft workers through their promotional corporations. Over the years many of these organizations have become essentially agencies for distributing cheap credit.

However, as with the banks, the transaction costs of obtaining such loans, including bribes to staff of the agencies, are high in proportion to the loan amount. For the agencies themselves the a priori non-viability of some tiny units, the lack of follow-up after loan disbursement, the diversion of production lending to consumption needs, and above all the absence of a culture of repayment have badly affected loan recoveries. Because the promotional agencies have generally had multiple goals and activities, and easy access to budgetary allocations, they have not given enough attention to managing their credit programmes in an efficient and viable manner.

In some cases we found that the State Finance Corporations (SFCs) have been somewhat better than other financial agencies in extending loans to the RNFS (although their recovery rates have also been poor). They have often been more liberal than commercial banks in promoting new activities. The SFCs, moreover, have access to substantial refinance from SIDBI: nearly 20 per cent of the total in 1995–6 (SIDBI, 1996: 27). NABARD, on the other hand, disburses most of its refinance through the cooperative and Regional Rural Banks.

There are some examples of the formal banks devising their own systems, procedures and practices which might be more appropriate to particular groups of rural borrowers, although few of these initiatives have been particularly successful. There are two of relevance to the rural non-farm sector:

(1) The Rural Development and Self-Employment Training Institute (RUDSETI), set up by Syndicate and Canara Banks, has arranged for bank finance for over ten thousand or 63 per cent of its trainees (up to March 1994). Most of them received loans under various existing programmes like SEEUY and SEPUP for which banks have targets in any case. At least the trainees are in a better position to use their loans well and repayment rates have been higher than for other sponsored credit. The intensive inputs provided by RUDSETI have proved expensive, however, constituting 10 to 15 per cent of total loans advanced in a year to the institute's trainees.
(2) Master policy agreements between the District Rural Development Agency and General Insurance Company (and its subsidiaries) cover a large number of borrowers (up to, say, 6000) at one time for assets such as cattle and pump sets. Initially restricted to IRDP borrowers, banks are beginning to utilize the scheme for other loans as well. The agreements have succeeded in insuring many assets which would

otherwise not have been insured, and at a substantially reduced cost for the insurance company. Few of the borrowers are aware of the scheme, however, and so do not fully realize its potential benefits.

Informal-sector credit

In spite of the massive expansion of the rural branch network since 1969, it is clear that many producers in the rural non-farm sector still rely on their own funds or on the informal financial sector to meet their credit needs. The All-India Debt and Investment Survey in 1981–2 (RBI, 1989) found that 45.4 per cent of credit to rural households still came from informal sources. Reliance on this sector is particularly prevalent among poor producers, with formal financial agencies providing only 23.3 per cent of the credit used by the poorest households.

Informal channels include moneylenders, traders, commission agents, chit-funds and private financial agencies, as well as friends and relatives. Among the 58 producers in our case-studies who had used informal channels, 40 per cent had received credit from moneylenders, traders, suppliers and private financial companies, while 76 per cent had used their own funds, by drawing on their savings or by selling assets, or received funds or loans from family or friends. Poor households are particularly dependent on moneylenders and traders for their credit, and obtain less than a fifth of their credit from family and friends (Mahajan and Ramola, 1996).

Interest rates in the informal sector vary widely (Table 6.7). Sarap (1991: 31) found that interest rates charged by the informal lenders vary from very nominal rates to 120 per cent or more, depending on the personal relationship, nature of collateral offered, and the urgency of loan for the borrowers. It is difficult to see how such high interest rates reflect perfectly

Table 6.7: Informal-sector loans for poor households in a district in Rajasthan

Source	*As % of total informal-credit sources*	*Annual interest rate (%)*
Shopkeeper	33.7	67
Milkman	5.2	39
Moneylender/landlord	36.7	31
Friends/relatives	16.5	14
Labour/farm/owner contract	7.5	92
Private financier	0.5	26

Note: The labour, farm or owner contract is an advance payment made by a farmer or owner of a business enterprise (such as carpet-weaving) at the beginning of the season to retain the services of the borrower.
Source: Majahan and Ramola (1996).

competitive credit markets, and traditionally it has been assumed that moneylenders, traders and commission agents use their monopoly powers to raise interest rates and exploit their borrowers. In the Indian context it would indeed be foolish to ignore power relations between influential local economic actors and the poor, relations which are often reinforced by the different communities and castes to which the different groups belong.

Sarap (1991) argues strongly that terms and conditions of loans vary with the bargaining power of the borrowers. The poor in particular may be forced into taking loans interlinked with the supply of inputs, the purchase of outputs at a price agreed in advance, or the provision of labour by the borrower. Effective interest rates on such interlinked credit transactions tend to be higher, and the interlinkages give the lender considerable control over the borrower. In the case of the rural non-farm sector, small producers may be reduced in effect to wage labourers in a putting-out system whereby the trader provides the raw materials and credit and takes back the finished product.

The traditional policy prescription in this situation has been to provide cheap credit from formal banks, and an important objective of expanding the rural banking system, and also of the country's legislative measures has been to get rid of exploitative moneylenders and other informal-credit channels. While access to formal credit has indeed improved, the evidence we have cited suggests clearly that the informal channels are still very important, especially to smaller and poorer borrowers.

Part of the problem is that policy-makers have assumed that only the interest rate is of importance. Borrowers continue to use informal channels for other reasons, however. They do so, firstly because the private-credit channels and loans from them are easily accessible to a tiny producer. In contrast, there are many barriers to accessibility, such as social, cultural and economic differences, that characterize large, formal banks or promotional agencies. Second, credit has to be provided when it is needed; the short term is very important. A weaver needs yarn against an order he has received and has to produce in a month. Silk reelers, or those running agro-processing enterprises, need credit during the peak season. None of them can wait for the long time required by the banks or promotional agencies to process their applications. In contrast, the transaction costs that a borrower has to incur in time, effort and money to secure a loan from informal channels are often negligible. Finally, credit interlinked with, for example, the supply of raw materials or the purchase of the final products may provide an extremely valuable service to a small producer who does not have the ability to access wider markets.

Recent theoretical perspectives on rural credit markets have shed more light on the strengths of informal-credit channels by building up an institutional framework focusing on concepts such as transaction costs, imperfect information and interlinked markets. These perspectives also provide valuable insights into the success or failure of specific policy interventions. Hoff and Stiglitz (1990: 235–8) provide an excellent overview of the issues involved:

> *Traditional Views and Puzzles.* Rural credit markets do not seem to work like classical competitive markets are supposed to work. Interest rates charged by moneylenders may exceed 75 per cent per year, and in some periods credit is unavailable at any price. The high observed interest rates were attributed by many to the monopoly power of the village moneylender. The policy response arising from this explanation of high interest rates was clear – it was to provide cheap institutional credit as an alternative to the moneylender.
>
> But the past forty years of experience of government intervention in rural credit markets suggests that the creation of institutional alternatives has failed to drive the traditional moneylender out of the market and, whatever competition it has provided, interest rates charged by traditional moneylenders remain high. . . . In addition, high default rates have prevented the institutions from being self-financing: recurrent and often large injections of government funds have been required. And despite these subsidies, many of these credit programs have had little success in reaching farmers without collateral or with below-average income.
>
> This apparent failure of policy intervention did not come as a surprise to those who did not believe in the monopoly power explanation of high interest rates, but believed instead that credit markets worked as classical competitive markets should. In this view, observed high interest rates were a reflection of perfect credit markets that took into account the risks of default. . . . The policy conclusion of this line of argument is not to intervene in rural credit markets, at least not on efficiency grounds.
>
> But neither the traditional monopoly nor the perfect markets view can explain other features of rural credit markets which are at least as important and equally puzzling as high interest rates:
>
> - The formal and informal sectors coexist, despite the fact that formal interest rates are substantially below those charged in the informal sector.
> - Interest rates may not equilibrate credit supply and demand: there may be credit rationing . . .
> - Credit markets are segmented. Interest rates of lenders in different areas vary by more than plausibly can be accounted for by differences in the likelihood of default . . .
> - There is a limited number of commercial lenders in the informal sector, despite the high rates charged.
> - In the informal sector interlinkages between credit transactions and transactions in other markets are common.

- Formal lenders tend to specialize in areas where farmers have land titles.

Neither the monopoly view nor the perfect markets view can account for these features taken as a whole. An alternative approach is required – one that is better able to help us understand the workings of rural credit markets, and thus help us design appropriate policy interventions.

The Imperfect Information Paradigm. In the past decade there have been major advances in our theoretical understanding of the workings of credit markets. These advances have evolved from a paradigm that emphasizes the problems of imperfect information and imperfect enforcement. . . . The new views of rural credit markets are based on the following three observations:

(1) Borrowers differ in the likelihood that they will default, and it is costly to determine the extent of that risk for each borrower. This is conventionally known as the *screening* problem.
(2) It is costly to ensure that borrowers take those actions which make repayment most likely. This is the *incentives* problem.
(3) It is difficult to compel repayment. This is the *enforcement* problem.

The new view holds that it is the markets' responses to these three problems, singly or in combination, that explain many of the observed features of rural credit markets, and that they must therefore inform the policy perspective for designing specific interventions.

Private lenders overcome these problems through the characteristics and measures that are commonly associated with informal credit channels. Moneylenders and traders have a closer and repeated interaction with producers through which a certain trust develops, even in an unequal relationship; this helps to reduce the screening problem. Interlinking credit with supplies of raw material and the purchase of final products is a mechanism used to reduce the incentive problem, and thus reduces the risk to the lender significantly. For loan recovery, local private channels have strong follow-up systems, so reducing the enforcement problem.

In a detailed study of formal and informal credit in the Philippines, Floro and Yotopoulos (1991) have shown that the higher interest rates charged by private traders and moneylenders are determined not so much by monopolistic powers as by the service they provide and the risk involved in providing it. This new perspective does not exclude the possibility of monopoly powers enjoyed by the lender. It may point to 'a monopolistically competitive structure with interest-rate spreads between different segments of the rural credit markets'.

This suggests that the moneylenders' power is unlikely to be broken by the entry of institutional credit, unless the new institutions themselves find substitutes for the direct mechanisms used by moneylenders to overcome the problems of screening, incentives, and enforcement. (Hoff and Stiglitz, 1990: 238)

In their study of alternative financial agencies Hulme and Mosley (1996: 75) come to the same conclusion: 'the right approach to the rural moneylender . . . is neither to seek to wipe him out nor to romanticise him, but rather to seek out alternative methods of risk management to his as a means of competing with him'.

The current formal-credit agencies in India have failed so far to address the problems revealed by the imperfect information paradigm. In many cases, particularly within schematic lending, a loan is a one-off event. In addition, bank managers are posted to rural branches for only short periods. In consequence, no relationship of trust can develop between borrower and lender. Because the formal agencies do not address the primary needs of the borrowers, many loans are diverted, particularly from productive purposes to consumption. Finally, the formal banks have weak enforcement machinery, especially in a political climate which has encouraged default through the prospect of loan waivers.

The issue is, therefore, how formal credit agencies can learn from the new insights into informal-credit channels and address the problems of screening, incentives and enforcement. Hulme and Mosley (1996: 74–5) discovered that alternative financial agencies which are properly designed (see next section) can compete with moneylenders. By interviewing the latter they found that some of them stopped lending in face of the new competition; some (in Indonesia) became commission agents for the new banks; but most reduced the element of monopoly profit in their interest rates and broadened their loan portfolio: 'Across the entire range of samples the consensus was that the volume of lending *from traditional sources* had expanded since the advent of competition even though its price had gone down'.

At the same time, the formal and informal sectors should not be seen only in terms of competition. Ghate (1992: 17) argues that:

> . . . formal finance is better suited to the needs of large and medium-scale industry, organized trade and commerce, and well-to-do urban households. But it is less successful in serving the needs of the large unorganized sector in developing countries, small and micro-entrepreneurs, small traders and small and poor borrowers generally. . . . Policy should proceed on a recognition of this complementarity and facilitate informal finance in its own areas of comparative advantage. This will increase the flow and reduce the cost of credit to borrowers hitherto neglected by the formal sector . . .

Regarding the formal and informal sectors as complementary is particularly important because, in spite of the current weaknesses of the former in India, the informal-credit sector provides only a very partial solution. Moneylenders tend to lend for consumption and contingencies while traders provide working capital. Very few informal channels provide credit for capital investment, crucial for the long-term development of the rural non-farm sector. Many rural producers who cannot get formal loans have to rely instead on their own resources, or on funds from family and friends, for their investment capital, particularly to start a new enterprise.

Lessons from alternative and innovative financial agencies

In India Hoff and Stiglitz were writing when there were few examples of successful alternatives to the informal-credit channels and the failed public-sector banks. In recent years, however, evidence on such alternatives has been growing, including in India. These alternative agencies have taken transaction costs and the problems of screening, incentives and enforcement seriously. They are not only financially sustainable but also reach many rural producers, including the poor. Good examples in India include the Gujarat Rural Housing Finance Corporation, the SEWA Bank and the many self-help groups being promoted by non-governmental organizations (NGOs), as well as the growth of non-banking financial companies.

The Gujarat Rural Housing Finance Corporation (GRUH), a private housing finance company, has placed special emphasis on adapting its systems to its potential market and on reducing its borrowers' transaction costs. Borrowers are assessed before they fill out an application, much of the paper work is done by post, and the size and periodicity of the instalments and other terms of the loan are based on the size and flow of the borrower's income. To overcome the screening, incentive and enforcement problems GRUH has, for example:

- targeted milk and sugar cooperatives which provide records of their members' income;
- provided technical verification of houses built by contractors which are then eligible for finance from GRUH; and
- adopted a policy that borrowers first have to use their own contribution in laying the foundations of the house, which is verified by on-site visits.

Overall GRUH has addressed the social need for housing by pursuing a market opportunity represented by the untapped demand for rural housing finance, and has been unencumbered by target groups laid down by government regulation.

The Shri Mahila Sewa Sahakari (SEWA) Bank is a cooperative bank for poor, self-employed women workers. The bank reaches out to its thousands of customers through a team of mobile workers who visit specified collection areas regularly. Transaction costs for borrowers vary from 1 to over 8 per cent of the loan amount, depending on their location. SEWA Bank's performance both in terms of access and sustainability has been creditable. The bank has also shown that the poor can be good savers and borrowers despite the chronically deficit nature of their pattern of income.

SEWA and many other NGOs, such as the Cooperative Development Foundation, MYRADA and PRADAN, are also promoting self-help groups (SHGs), particularly of poor rural women, as a means of providing financial services to a segment of the rural population usually ignored by the formal financial sector. The members of each group themselves decide on their lending policies and conditions. Because they know each other and their local context, and are bound by a host of social linkages, their appraisal of loan requests is usually good and their repayment rates high.

In 1992 NABARD promoted a pilot project for linking SHGs with banks:

> . . . for meeting the credit needs of the poor by combining the flexibility, sensitivity and responsiveness of the informal-credit system with the strength of technical and administrative capabilities of the formal-credit institutions. (NABARD, 1995: 15)

By March 1995, over 2000 SHGs, most assisted by NGOs, had been linked with banks, and these groups had received bank loans totalling Rs24.5 million. The repayment rates are reported by NABARD to be 95 per cent and above.

The rapid growth of non-banking financial companies (NBFCs), the majority of them private limited companies, has been even more significant, although they do not focus on the poor. NBFCs are a kind of bridge between the formal and the informal sectors. Most of them are small, localized and enjoy relatively low costs. In rural areas they have primarily mobilized deposits, although they are also becoming an important source of finance in the RNFS, especially for light commercial vehicles. They have extended loans and leased equipment in selected clusters of modern sub-sectors, such as powerlooms, granite processing and textile products, and in the construction, repair and small-engineering sub-sectors. With fierce competition among NBFCs, interest rates are competitive, ranging from around 12 to 24 per cent, and procedures are simple and involve little delay. NBFCs are tapping, in an efficient manner, a profitable market segment that is underserviced by the formal and informal sectors. NBFCs need tighter regulation, however, to improve their financial stability and weed out dishonest companies.

Outside India In spite of these examples, a number of countries are ahead of India in developing innovative rural financial agencies. Hulme and Mosley (1996) provide case-studies from Indonesia, Bangladesh, Sri Lanka, Kenya, Malawi and Bolivia. They conclude that certain characteristics are needed if such financial agencies are to be financially viable and to address issues of poverty:

- the provision of savings and insurance facilities, and also emergency consumption loans, in addition to production loans;
- strong incentives for borrowers to repay;
- mobile-banking facilities whereby bank staff go to the customers rather than customers coming to the bank;
- market-determined interest rates allowing sufficient spreads, including higher interest rates on smaller loans to compensate for the higher transaction costs to the banks;
- intensive loan collection;
- good staff, who are well trained and motivated, often through competitive salaries, performance-related pay and good promotion prospects. Incentives for staff which link their remuneration to the profitability of their branch are particularly important; and
- decentralization of decision-making down to branches or zonal offices.

The focus of Hulme and Mosley's study was on the role of these financial agencies in tackling poverty. In almost all the case-studies they found that the incomes of borrowers had increased significantly more than among the control groups of non-borrowers. However, the authors warn against over-optimism. While the alternative financial agencies had helped with poverty reduction, poorer borrowers, being risk-averse and having fewer opportunities, were disinclined to invest income from a successful project either in new technology or in hiring labour from outside the family:

> . . . it was unusual for credit to trigger a continuous increase in technical sophistication, output or employment: it was much commoner for each of these variables to reach a plateau after one or two loans and then remain in a steady state. (Hulme and Mosley, 1996: 103–4)

To get beyond this point, the entrepreneurs need other inputs such as training, new technologies, and above all growing markets.

In Indonesia The transformation of the rural financial sector that has taken place in Indonesia is of particular interest to India. The countries are similar in terms of their population density, the importance of agriculture to their rural populations and the great regional divergence in their economic development. Indonesia, however, embarked upon significant financial reforms almost a decade before India, and has taken the route of lending to individuals rather than to groups (as in Bangladesh), and of transforming the existing public-sector banks in addition to developing new financial agencies.

The results have been dramatic. Almost a third of all Indonesia's households receive loans from five profitable financial agencies or networks: Bank Rakyat Indonesia (BRI), the network of Badan Kredit Kecamatan (sub-district credit bodies or BKKs), two other networks of rural banks and one private rural bank. Of the five only the BKKs still receive subsidized government resources.

BRI has the most to offer when making comparisons because it is comparable to India's commercial banks. Its unit system, predominantly serving the rural population, has 3357 *Unit Desas* (units at the sub-district level) and 524 village posts. In 1994 outstanding loans totalled about US$1 billion, and the long-term loss ratio was below 3 per cent, the average loan size between US$750 and $1000, and the cumulative total of borrowers since 1983 was two million. In 1986, 15.1 per cent of borrowers were below the poverty line compared to 16.4 per cent in the total rural population, indicating that BRI also reaches the poor.

In providing these services to the rural population, the unit system generated US$33.8 million in profits for the bank in 1991, about two-thirds of the total profits generated by all BRI's financial services. The unit system for rural banking was thus by far the most profitable activity. As Robinson (1992) puts it, the experience of BRI demonstrates that financial institutions can profitably provide large numbers of lower-income people with financial services, and can do so sustainably.

The more than 500 BKKs indicate that it is also possible to operate small rural banks profitably, and with greater outreach to the poor and especially women, as BKK customers are generally smaller and poorer than those of BRI. In 1993, 31 per cent of their borrowers were below the poverty line. However, the network had over US$23 million outstanding in about 500 000 loan accounts and was generating significant profits.

The rural financial sector in Indonesia demonstrates many of the characteristics of successful financial agencies that Hulme and Mosley deduce from their study. Several other factors have also proved critical, not least a positive environment, including economic growth, a stable political context (especially without any loan waivers) and a more enabling regulatory framework. All the banks have adopted simple and swift procedures for sanctioning loans and provide strong incentives for repayment, including the offer of subsequent and often larger loans to borrowers who maintain a good repayment record. The majority of loans are for working capital, especially in trading.

This record is all the more striking granted that BRI's *Unit Desas*, which were originally established for a government agricultural-credit programme, formed a typical loss-making system for subsidized credit. When the programme was wound up in 1983, BRI had to transform its network of *Unit Desas* into a profitable rural-banking system. Within two years of introducing new loan and savings products, BRI's units broke even, and have been profitable ever since. The bank's new savings instruments have in fact been so successful that since 1989 BRI has been able to fund all its loans at *Unit Desas* from deposits collected.

Financial reforms provided an enabling environment for this swift and radical transformation, especially in allowing large interest-rate spreads which enabled the *Unit Desas* to earn substantial profits. Moreover, banks in Indonesia face no fixed-interest rates, no stipulated credit-deposit ratios or liquidity requirements, reserve requirements of only 2 per cent, and almost no priority-sector targeting.

However, BRI also had to undertake important organizational reforms and develop a new culture, including professionalism, accountability, innovation, strategic thinking and respect for customers. These internal reforms involved completely reorganizing management and staff at all levels, putting a comprehensive system of employee incentives in place, and introducing new mechanisms which allowed village units to be treated as independent profit centres. Organizational changes were as important as reforms of the financial system.

The transformation of the rural financial system did not require the removal of all subsidized lending. Some such loans, for agriculture, co-operatives and small businesses, have been maintained for political reasons. This suggests that adopting the full package of reforms dictated by economic theory is not necessary for the transformation of the rural financial system. What is essential, however, is that rural banks be allowed to generate substantial profits from unrestricted financial intermediation between savers and borrowers. As the source of funds for such intermediation is savings, its scope need not be restricted, while subsidized lending programmes will continue to be limited by the scarcity of budgetary funds.

Conclusions and recommendations

Credit policy in India has, until recently, been characterized by four primary strategies to enhance the availability of credit in rural areas:

- spreading the bank branch network to rural areas;
- low (subsidized) interest rates;
- directed lending to particular activities (priority-sector targets); and
- sponsored lending (with government subsidies on principal) for selected groups, such as the rural poor.

Credit policy has succeeded in greatly expanding the number of bank branches in rural areas, and millions of rural households have received loans from the commercial, cooperative and regional rural banks.

This expansion and outreach has been accompanied by many features which maintain distance between formal lenders and borrowers, in spite of their physical proximity, and which undermine the financial sustainability of the rural financial sector. Formal-sector banks have been driven by government regulation, direction and targets and bankers have lost discretion over their lending policies. The results have been harmful to the health of banks and other financial agencies, as well as to the long-term interests of the borrowers. Rural lending has become standardized across all formal financial agencies, with no innovation or adaptation to the special needs of the local population. The formal sector is thus failing to address the primary needs of rural borrowers for credit, in particular working capital for rural enterprises and consumption credit for poor households engaged in subsistence occupations.

Linking lending to poverty-alleviation programmes with their large subsidies has also brought problems in its wake. Lending has become politicized, with local politicians using poverty lending for extending patronage, and governments declaring loan waivers to buy votes. Subsidies, and hence the need to seek official approval, have led to extensive corruption. As a result transaction costs to borrowers have risen to as much as a quarter of the loan amount. Since subsidies are rarely available to a household a second time, subsidized loans are seen by borrowers as one-off handouts, rather than as an entry point into the formal-credit system. Repayment rates are woefully low, since borrowers have no incentive to build a good credit history, as they know that formal financial agencies will not lend to them a second time in the absence of government subsidies. Lending for poverty alleviation has created a vast mass of wilful and unwitting defaulters (some 30 million defaulter households due to the IRDP alone) who are not eligible for further loans from the formal sector.

The financial implications for the banks have long been concealed by poor or creative accounting, but with new norms of income recognition and asset provisioning, commercial banks and the RRBs have posted record losses. Collectively the RRBs lost Rs500 crores in 1994–5, and if the rural branches of the commercial banks were treated as separate profit centres to which all costs were ascribed, most of them would be making losses. The cooperative banking system is also in poor health. Equally damaging has been the effect on the bankers themselves, who have become cynical about lending to small rural producers and the poor. High default rates suggest to bankers that such borrowers are not creditworthy, and without the obligation to lend, most bankers would stop making credit available to them.

These features of the rural financial sector have had a severe impact on the RNFS, which is not well served by the formal financial sector. For example, we estimate that at most a sixth of rural manufacturing enterprises have access to bank finance. Some larger modern manufacturing units and large traders have received the bulk of rural credit. Mining, traditional manufacturing, construction, most services and the majority of the smallest enterprises have received very little, yet it is these sub-sectors or units that employ the vast majority of RNFS workers. Women have fared worse than men, receiving fewer and smaller loans and facing higher transaction costs. In fact, apart from retail trading, the sub-sectors that employ three-quarters of rural women in the RNFS have little access to formal credit.

Clearly bureaucratic and schematic lending cannot serve the genuine needs of rural producers. Activities and enterprises in the RNFS are far too diverse to be captured by a few standardized categories and costings. Numerous small producers who do not fall into an existing category are excluded by bankers. So are many producers in emerging sub-sectors which have not yet been identified as official targets. Many RNFS enterprises, especially those involved in seasonal business, need timely credit. Almost all complained about the lack of working capital available from the formal banks.

As a result many rural producers are forced to rely on the informal-credit sector, on moneylenders for credit for consumption and contingencies, on traders for working capital, and on relatives and friends for investment capital. The advantages to the borrowers, for example of accessibility and lower transaction costs, and the advantages private lenders enjoy over the formal banking system, such as better screening and enforcement, will ensure that private-credit channels remain important. However, the informal sector by itself cannot provide adequate resources for the dynamic growth of the rural non-farm sector. Formal- and informal-credit channels are both complementary and competitive. Rather than trying to displace private channels, which has been the (unsuccessful) thrust of credit policies so far, the formal banking system should collaborate with private lenders, as well as learn from some of their practices.

Set against this gloomy scenario is the vision presented by alternative development-finance agencies. This vision draws on international experiences, but is already being explored and realized in India as well. Such agencies often perform the role of intermediation between rural savers and borrowers, thus freeing them from reliance on external funds. They demonstrate that there are profitable market opportunities for rural lending which have not been exploited by formal-credit channels, whether it is dynamic manufacturing clusters, rural housing or the mass of the rural poor, who are regarded not as beneficiaries but as customers.

To exploit these opportunities such agencies adapt their products to their markets, go out to their customers in order to reduce the latter's transaction costs, and establish mechanisms to overcome the problems of screening, incentives and enforcement. Many such agencies enjoy low costs and have professional and motivated staff, who are given strong incentives to perform. But to be financially sustainable they charge market interest rates on loans, which cover their cost of funds, overheads and reserves for bad debt, and still allow them to earn profits.

While most of the examples we have given are individual cases, the rural credit sector in Indonesia demonstrates that a whole sector can be transformed, ranging from a large commercial bank like BRI to small independent rural banks like the BKKs. The example of BRI is particularly exciting because India has many commercial banks which could potentially emulate its performance. Above all, BRI demonstrates that there is an alternative to closing down unprofitable rural branches. They can be transformed into branches which not only provide financial services which address the needs of the rural population, including the poor, but also do so profitably and without receiving subsidies.

Such transformation in India, however, requires that the regulatory framework for the rural financial sector be overhauled, together with a broader vision of transforming the banks as organizations, by changing products, procedures and incentives for bank staff. A policy is needed for restoring credit discipline and ensuring loan recoveries through changes in the legal framework for rural credit (including a ban on political loan waivers). However, two of the most important changes required – increasing interest-rate spreads by freeing up lending rates for all banks, especially on small loans, and allowing the entry of new private-sector banks – have now been effected by the Reserve Bank of India, as recently as August 1996. The benefits of these far-reaching changes will take at least three to five years to take effect, but they are clearly dramatic steps in the right direction.

7 The organization and representation of producers

Representation and the right to association

In the last three chapters we looked at regulation, promotion and credit and the various agencies responsible for their implementation. In the Indian context these bodies have been almost exclusively in the public sector, and the impression can thus arise that only state actions are important for the rural non-farm sector. The primary stakeholders in the RNFS are, however, the millions of entrepreneurs, producers and workers who derive their livelihoods from the sector. In this chapter we look at the extent to which they are represented in policy-making and implementation, and the extent to which they are organized.

In a country which is proud of its democratic traditions, one might expect to find mechanisms which ensured both broad-based participation by the primary stakeholders in the processes of formulating, implementing and monitoring policies that affect the RNFS, and their control or at least influence over agencies meant to assist them. The logic for such representation and participation is simple: the lack of them leads to bad policies and practice (as we have seen in previous chapters), and leads to the alienation of producers and workers from regulatory and promotional agencies; representation and participation on the other hand, as well as a genuine partnership between public and private actors, could lead to tremendous gains in the efficiency and dynamism of RNFS sub-sectors.

Representatives of entrepreneurs and their associations, usually the chambers of commerce and industry and the small-scale industry (SSI) associations, are in fact often nominated to become members of various consultative committees. For example, central or state governments may consult producers before passing or amending legislation, fixing tax rates or input prices. Sometimes such consultation is undertaken by establishing a committee on which there are both official and non-official members. Some mechanisms for periodic consultation and monitoring, as in the advisory committees of various agencies, are in place. Moreover, it is common practice to have representatives of entrepreneurs or their associations on the governing structures of various councils, boards and corporations, such as the export promotion councils and the apex cooperative federations.

Entrepreneurs are often consulted on proposed legislation or promotional initiatives, however, only when these are in the advanced stages of formulation by bureaucrats. Most positions on advisory, consultative or governing bodies are nominated, often based on political affiliation or social status, and so the individuals who tend to get appointed do not always represent producers more widely. A cosy relationship has often developed between government officials and representatives from mainstream organizations, such as the chambers of commerce and industry and the SSI associations. The officials impose many regulations, but also grant many concessions, while the associations lobby to maintain and enhance those concessions, often to the extent that these groups have become co-opted into the prevailing institutional framework. Those who are not organized, particularly the smallest producers, are usually neglected; it is only larger entrepreneurs who are appointed to 'represent' producers.

There are, moreover, many examples where representation is simply non-existent. For example, in Chapter 5 we noted that the nation-wide network of weavers' service centres is under the 'administrative control' of the distant Development Commissioner (Handlooms) in Delhi. The centres have no accountability to a single weaver, whether small or big, or to any association of weavers in the clusters they serve. Similarly, the All-India Motor Transport Congress (1992) complains bitterly that the Transport Development Council (TDC):

> . . . is the so-called supreme policy-making body for roads and road transport. . . . Ironically . . . the TDC does not formally involve, at any stage, the people for whose development it is supposed to be concerned. Much worse, not only the details of deliberations but even the decisions taken in the TDC meetings are kept 'confidential'.

This is not uncommon. On many important committees that have gone into questions of regulation, policy development, planning, credit and so on, representatives of the affected groups have had hardly any involvement at all.

In reality there are therefore no effective mechanisms in the rural non-farm sector, or indeed any other sector, to ensure representation of producers, workers and consumers in policy-making processes and public agencies. In spite of India's democratic traditions, in most sub-sectors policies are formulated and implemented with little or no discussion with those for whom these policies are supposedly designed. Policy-making is considered the prerogative of the bureaucrat, with directions coming from the political party which is in power. Those affected by the policies can merely lobby from outside the decision-making process. This is possible only if those affected are sufficiently organized as a lobbying force, drawing on the power of vote-banks and/or money. As a result it is the majority of small and less-organized producers that are excluded most from decision-making, even about issues that affect them directly.

Organizing producers and workers can thus enhance their representation and participation by enabling them to act as countervailing forces in the political, economic and social arenas of the RNFS. In the Indian context the freedom of association is also a fundamental democratic value. Associations, cooperatives and other groups are a vital component of democracy, fostering systems of local self-governance and avoiding the concentration of economic power (Baviskar and Attwood, 1995: 3-5; Shah, 1995: 257; Ostrom *et al.*, 1988). Indeed:

> [a] multiplicity of primary units may. . .be a necessary condition of the social learning that is relevant to political development. It was in this sense that de Tocqueville[1] characterized local institutions as the primary schools of democracy (Oakerson, 1988: 149).

The Indian state has often violated that freedom of association, particularly (in terms of the RNFS) by interfering in and controlling cooperative societies, which we review below. Taken as a whole, however, the right to associate is strong in India, and in the course of our study we came across numerous groups of RNFS entrepreneurs, traders, producers and workers: industry associations, cooperative societies, trade unions and many informal associations. While overall those who derive their livelihoods from the rural non-farm sector are not well organized, it is remarkable how many such groups exist. If we also include caste-based associations or *panchayats*, informal guilds, self-help groups, nascent consumer groups, as well as non-governmental organizations (NGOs) which provide support to or advocate the cause of producers, the number is significant. Yet many of these groups are not very strong or active, even though in most situations those working in the RNFS would benefit from being better organized.

Below we look at trade unions, industry associations, cooperative societies and NGOs in greater detail. Consumer associations on the other hand are the least developed form of representational organization in India. There are judicial bodies for addressing grievances of consumers, most notably the new consumer courts established at the district, state and national levels. Few associations are formed by consumers themselves, however, and most of them are set up by urban rather than rural consumers. For example, the Consumer Education and Research Centre in Ahmedabad and Common Cause in New Delhi promote consumer awareness and take offenders to court. The most successful consumer groups have been the environmental lobbyists, who have had some impact, although often limited, in restraining pollution and other environmental damage caused by specific RNFS activities, such as tanning leather and processing minerals and plastics.

It should be clear that all these different types of associations do not form a common front on behalf of the rural non-farm sector. The interests of

1. Alexis de Tocqueville, *Democracy in America*, first published in 1835.

workers, entrepreneurs and traders often conflict as each is extracting surplus from the same activity, and the interests of consumers may diverge from those of all types of producers. These associations tend to compete with each other for official patronage and concessions, and this competition is an important feature of the political economy of the sector.

In the following sections we look in greater detail at trade unions, small-scale industry associations, other industry organizations, cooperative societies and NGOs. We then introduce some important theoretical writing on collective action, as well as on power and ideology, to better understand why some groups are formed and sustained, while others are not. Introducing power relations, which affect adversely the weakest producers and workers in particular, is important for a comprehensive understanding of the rural non-farm sector, because it raises issues of ideology and exploitation to which we have not given prominence in previous chapters.

Trade unions

Trade unions, while common in the formal industrial sector in India, are less common in the RNFS. They have usually been formed to protect workers' interests in those sub-sectors where manufacturing activity is clustered in a geographical location, or is based on a factory mode of production. For example, we came across unions among workers in the tea, *bidi*, match and garment sub-sectors. There are also some unions among transport and hotel employees, but even in these sub-sectors many workers are not unionized. In Tiruppur, a town dominated by a dynamic knitwear industry, over a third of the workforce is not unionized even though six unions operate in the town. Moreover, most labour in other sub-sectors, such as textiles, brick kilns, construction, repairs and retail trade, is unorganized. This is in spite of the fact that laws to protect workers are widely flouted in the RNFS, as we saw in Chapter 4. Even the unions that do exist are usually not very powerful; for example, unions of workers in the match industry in Sivakasi in Tamil Nadu have failed to abolish child labour in the industry.

There are a few exceptions. Workers in the carpet industry around Jaipur were able to raise their wages by taking strike action. The Self-Employed Women's Association (SEWA) is a trade union representing self-employed women in Ahmedabad in Gujarat, although its members are of course urban. However, the most well-organized and active trade unions in rural areas are found in the *bidi* sub-sector. Because of the sheer size of the workforce in this sub-sector in states like Andhra Pradesh, Karnataka, Maharashtra and Uttar Pradesh, political parties have taken an active interest in workers' organizations. As a result the central and state governments have introduced various policies and programmes, including welfare programmes, specially targeted at *bidi* workers, just as they have done in the handloom sub-sector. Weavers have been organized into cooperatives, while in the *bidi* sub-sector political parties have given support to the trade unions. Indeed, in the *bidi* sub-sector tripartite meetings among manufacturers, workers and government representatives (from the state departments of labour) are held regularly. It appears that because of the high profile given to labour in this sub-sector and the existence of the powerful unions, some of the worst malpractices, even the extensive use of child labour, have been reduced, although wages remain very low and working conditions poor.

Small-scale industry associations[2]

There are many associations for industries in India, notably the chambers of commerce and industry, some of which date back to pre-independence days. These form a system with chambers or their federations at the district, state and national levels. At the national level they are federated into the Federation of Indian Chambers of Commerce and Industry (FICCI) and the (rival) Associated Chambers of Commerce and Industry (ASSOCHAM). There are also national bodies like the Confederation of Indian Industries (CII) and the All-India Manufacturers' Organization (AIMO).

Local chambers of commerce of traders (*vyapar mandals*) exist in almost all small towns. These associations are significant because traders control the markets in many RNFS sub-sectors, and often the credit flows as well. The organizations tend to address such issues as sales tax, *octroi* and municipal regulations. In addition, they often take a lead in organizing or financing local festival celebrations and charitable activities.

All these associations for commerce and industry address the needs of traders or of larger industries. Small-scale industries (SSIs) have therefore established their own associations, which date back to the 1950s. For example, the Tamil Nadu Small and Tiny Industries Association (TANSTIA) and the Andhra Pradesh Small-Scale Industries Association were formed in 1956. Many SSI associations received strong support from the relevant state governments. The formation of TANSTIA, for instance, was motivated by R.Venkataraman, then minister of industries of Tamil Nadu, and later to become president of India.

Some state-level associations are federated at the regional level, and all belong to the national Federation of Associations of Small Industries of India (FASSI), which was set up in 1959 with the encouragement of the central government. Below the state-level associations are either district-level branches under the control of the former, or more autonomous bodies,

2. This section and the one that follows draw heavily on Mathew *et al.* (1995) and Sanket (1995), two studies of industry associations commissioned by the SDC as a follow-up to the wider RNFS study.

either at the district level or below. So there are now five tiers forming the SSI structure at the national, regional, state, district and lower levels.

The associations at all the different levels have been largely engaged in lobbying activities, and in providing information to their members about government regulations and promotional activities. This narrow focus is less the fault of the associations themselves than of the environment that their member enterprises have faced. In Chapter 4 we analysed this highly complex regulatory environment. Many regulations have affected individual enterprises directly, for example in controlling vital raw materials like steel and coal. In Chapter 5 we showed how the state has often taken upon itself almost sole responsibility for promotional activities to the exclusion of most private actors. In Chapter 6 we described how small-scale industries have been made a special target group for priority lending. In each of these cases government and other public officials have been able to exercise extensive control over enterprises, often indulging in pervasive rent-seeking. In such an environment it is not surprising that the primary role of associations of small-scale industries has been to lobby against excessive harassment of its members on the part of officials, and for ever more concessions and other benefits to be doled out by a paternalistic bureaucracy.

Government agencies in their turn have used the associations as distribution channels for some of these benefits, for example of controlled raw materials to individual enterprises. The associations were not only established with the support of the central or state governments, but over time a close relationship between the governments and associations has often developed. As we saw above, leaders of these organizations are regularly appointed as industry representatives on various committees, councils and governing bodies in the public sector, and the same leaders have been able to exercise considerable power by controlling access to government concessions and hand-outs.

Some SSI associations have been particularly effective. CODISSIA, the small-scale industry association in Coimbatore District, Tamil Nadu, is the largest district SSI association with 3600 members. It is well-known for its dynamism in providing many services to its members, including purchasing raw materials, testing products and materials, and organizing industrial trade fairs. The state-level association in Tamil Nadu (TANSTIA) is also developing a wide range of services for its members with the support of the Friedrich Naumann Foundation. However, others would more readily fit the description of the Kerala and Andhra Pradesh small-scale industry associations given by Mathew *et al.* (1995: 33): 'the KSSIA and the APSSIA show tendencies of disintegration mainly because of lack of innovative activities and disillusionment by a significant section of the members'.

The SSI associations nevertheless form a powerful lobbying force on behalf of their members. However, although 42 per cent of all SSIs are rural (GoI, 1992c), most associations cater more for urban SSIs, and have not been very effective in representing the interests of tiny units. In fact, the majority of enterprises in the rural non-farm sector are not well served by the system of SSI associations and their federations.

The economic environment is also changing rapidly. Liberalization is not only opening up the SSI sector to competition from larger and foreign industries (particularly with the reduction of items reserved for production by SSIs), but also removing many of the concessions and benefits to which SSI units have become so accustomed. Some SSI associations, therefore, with their focus on lobbying and liaising with government, are becoming increasingly irrelevant. It is interesting that in this new environment, rival organizations are beginning to emerge, such as the Small Industries Development Council (SIDC) in Kerala formed in 1988, and the Andhra Pradesh Federation of Small-Scale Industries established in 1992. SIDC has been successful not only in enrolling many members but is also unusual in articulating the cause of tiny rather than small units (see Box 7.1, p. 189).

Other industry associations

Beyond the SSI associations there are numerous less formal industry organizations. Most of these are specific to a particular sub-sector, and represent entrepreneurs at the district, regional or state levels. We came across such associations in almost every sub-sector. Some of them are active primarily in the dominant cluster in the area, such as Kancheepuram (silk) and Tiruppur (knitwear) in Tamil Nadu and Surat (diamonds) in Gujarat. In addition to associations for specific sub-sectors, many industrial estates also have an association of units to liaise with the relevant government corporation managing the estate, and the various public agencies providing services like electricity.

Like the SSI associations, the principal function of these associations is to influence government policies and officials in favour of their members. Many of them also provide information, especially on government policies, through seminars, exhibitions, publications or simply informal exchange among members. Some arbitrate disputes among members or between members and, say, public agencies; some negotiate common wages for all member enterprises (e.g. for powerloom workers); some agree common rates among members to prevent undercutting each other (e.g. among repair units in a given locality) or to create and enforce a local cartel (e.g. transport unions).

However, only a few provide other services, like professional financial services, training, research and development, supplying raw materials, testing products and marketing, and even then some industry associations provide them only through public channels, for example procuring raw materials from the relevant state corporation, selling products to state-marketing agencies, and assisting in the implementation of government schemes such as the Prime Minister's *Rozgar Yojna*.

Our findings confirm those of a study on the 'Structure and Promotion of Small-Scale Industries in India' conducted by the National Council of Applied Economic Research and the Friedrich Naumann Foundation (1993: 21). This study concluded:

> A few [industry associations] are strongly involved in industrial counselling, training, information, marketing and export promotion. However, the role of most associations is limited to liaising with the government for removal of their grievances, and provision of additional facilities, subsidies and concessions. Overall, the development work has taken the back seat.

In fact, many of the associations we came across are informal, without their own staff and offices. Often they are run by one or a few of the more prominent entrepreneurs in the area who are not elected by members. If there are elections, the same entrepreneurs are often re-elected over and over again, partly because they have the necessary political contacts for effective lobbying. Many associations therefore do not have professional managers and cannot provide professional services. Most also have limited funding which restricts further their ability to diversify the services they provide to their members. Indeed, in many cases it would be fair to say that the associations contribute little to their respective sub-sectors beyond promoting the particular interests of the few entrepreneurs who have set them up. They cannot be regarded as representative of a wider set of enterprises.

This analysis is in line with international experience. A study undertaken by Durham University Business School (DUBS, 1994) covered 133 'small business membership organizations' in three South Asian countries, including India, and four African countries. The researchers found that many of the organizations were weak, with few members, poor leadership and inefficient management and administration. For example, a third of the bodies surveyed had no full-time staff, democratic practices for selecting leaders were often not effective and finance was usually limited. Above all, for most the primary activities were advocacy and the provision of information and advice. Far fewer offered services like supplying inputs and credit, providing insurance, conducting training, and (in Ghana) even collecting taxes from their members on behalf of the government.

The same could be said of small business associations in those industrial countries where membership of such groups is voluntary (DUBS, 1994: 4–7). For example, in Britain most associations of small businesses also focus on advocacy, advice, information and networking. It is only in countries such as Germany where small firms must legally be members of a chamber of commerce (or similar body) that such associations regularly provide services such as training, management education, consultancy and export promotion. Such a compulsory system would, however, clearly be impractical and inappropriate for India.

Such comparisons should not conceal the potential of industry associations to contribute constructively to economic development in India, as in other developing countries (IDS, 1996). In particular, the process of economic reforms currently underway in the country has brought about major changes in the environment for industry associations. As we have seen, the primary cause for the existence of many associations, whether for SSIs or particular sub-sectors, has been the high degree of state control over the economy, in terms of both regulation and promotion. So the primary role of the associations has, in the past, been lobbying and liaising with governments and other public agencies. With the reduction of industrial regulation and of state involvement in promotional activities, this role of the associations is diminishing.

The new environment provides opportunities as well as threats for the associations. The main opportunity is to shift the focus of their activities to provide more direct business support and services to their members. These might include, for example, the provision of information about international trends in the industry and its markets, assistance with introducing better quality control and product testing, and so on. Most of these services would seek to gear members to the upcoming competition, whether from larger domestic enterprises or international competitors. It is the new competition which is also the greatest threat to the current organizations. If their members cannot compete, and the associations themselves cannot transform their traditional role of interacting with government by adding more substantial business development services, they will become increasingly irrelevant.

This challenge is not easy, but evidence of the transition is becoming widespread. For example, more and more associations are taking over the management of industrial estates or developing new ones themselves. There are also many examples of dynamic bodies, some old, some new, which point to the potential that industry associations have in promoting economic development, including in the rural non-farm sector (see Box 7.1). Most of these examples come from two states covered by our study and the subsequent studies of industry associations (see note 2 on p. 184): Gujarat and Tamil Nadu. These are the two states in which industry associations appear most active and dynamic, partly because they are the most industrially developed among those we covered.

Even the most successful associations, however, have failed to address issues of gender. Almost all bodies have only male entrepreneurs as their members. 'Even when women become members. . .they tend to become either marginalized or are driven to indifference. The culture of patriarchy is deep among most industry associations, even among apex-level associa-

Box 7.1: Some active industry associations

The Tiruppur Exporters' Association in Tamil Nadu not only provides the standard advocacy and information services to its members in the knitwear industry. It has also built an industrial estate and plans to invest in further infrastructure such as a spinning plant, an effluent-treatment plant, housing for workers and a water company. Likewise various diamond associations are working closely with the Diamond and Gem Development Corporation (a non-profit company) to establish the Surat Diamond Park in Gujarat. In both these cases the associations are working closely with public sector bodies, the respective Export Promotion Councils for Apparel and for Gems and Jewellery.

The South India Hosiery Manufacturers Association (SIHMA), also based in Tiruppur, has 1250 members and since its establishment in 1956 has led the industry through several successful campaigns. These have been not only for concessions, such as excise exemption on garments and the supply of yarn from the National Textile Corporation mills, but also for important business services, such as a common brand name provided through the National Small Industries Corporation and support from the Bureau of Indian Standards in upgrading quality in the industry. The association's president, a leading entrepreneur and influential politician, has been democratically elected each year for 20 years running!

The Gujarat State Plastic Manufacturers Association provides the usual advocacy and information services. It has also worked with the All-India Plastic Manufacturers Association to set up a plastic research and promotional body in Bombay called the Plastindia Foundation. The state association collaborates with the Central Institute for Plastic Engineering and Technology as well, and has co-sponsored workshops and larger events, such as a major exhibition in New Delhi directed at an international audience.

The Small Industries Product Promotion Organization (SIPPO) Ltd in Madurai, Tamil Nadu, was set up as a company by successful small-scale entrepreneurs (with some public funding and support). It provides services to its members like testing the quality of products, training, upgrading technology and other technical services. It also markets products through a network of agents, showrooms and outlets, and through government agencies, and undertakes market research and promotion.

The Small Industries Development Council (SIDC), which broke away from the Kerala State Small Industries Association in 1988, has been able to attract 1800 members, primarily from the tiny sector. SIDC not only lobbies on behalf of its members, but also helps members in disputes with customers, for example over late payments from larger firms, runs a mutual fund to meet small credit needs of its members, and has adopted a code of conduct on the price and quality of products and services offered by its members.

tions such as FICCI, ASSOCHAM and CII' (Sanket, 1995: 47). Our study on the RNFS and the two additional studies on industry associations (see note 2), which together covered ten states, failed to uncover more than a handful of associations for women. These included the Association of Lady Entrepreneurs of Andhra Pradesh (ALEAP); the Kerala State Women's Industries Association in Cochin; and the Federation of Indian Women Entrepreneurs in New Delhi. There is also an Association of Women Entrepreneurs in Karnataka (AWAKE) and a women's wing of the National Alliance of Young Entrepreneurs. Mathew *et al.* (1995: 3) conclude that 'even the very limited industry association activity among women is exclusively élitist and urban-centred', with most members operating modern small-scale industries. Thus the millions of women who are self-employed in micro-businesses are almost entirely unrepresented in any industry associations. SEWA, the trade union of self-employed women, is a notable exception.

The failure to cater for tiny units is not specific to female producers, however. Our examples (see Box 7.1) have shown clearly that it is the more dynamic sub-sectors, usually using more modern modes of production, which have stronger industry associations. There are several reasons for this. These sub-sectors are dependent on modern technologies, production processes and products, for which they need to keep in constant touch with the latest trends, both in technologies and markets. The sub-sectors are driven by growing demand, including from abroad, while at the same time also facing intense competition. These sub-sectors must therefore be dynamic to survive, and industry associations play a vital role in providing services that individual enterprises cannot by themselves afford.

In many cases the enterprises involved are clustered, which makes the common provision of services through an association easier. In particular, 'industrial districts' which bring together many small enterprises, not just in 'Third Italy' but also in many developing countries, have been able to compete successfully in national and international markets (IDS, 1992; Holmstrom, 1994; Pedersen *et al.*, 1994; Humphrey and Schmitz, 1995). Industry associations have played an important role in the success of these industrial districts by providing common services to their members.

In addition, these dynamic sub-sectors attract the larger entrepreneurs who have greater economic power, are often better educated, and have a wider understanding of the sub-sector in which they operate. They have greater know-how and management skills to deal with more complex businesses. All of these qualities also prove valuable for their industry associations.

In contrast, smaller producer-workers in the RNFS are often widely dispersed, have limited business skills and only a limited perspective of the broader context of their sub-sector. As with the SSI associations, most of the bodies we came across do not cater for the tiny rural units in their respective sub-sectors. SIDC in Kerala is a notable exception (see Box 7.1). There are also local groups of smaller entrepreneurs, especially in rural towns, for example among silk reelers and twisters, cottage match units, repair units, retail traders and restaurant owners, although the role of these associations is mostly limited. In addition, there are many caste *panchayats* which bring together artisans in traditional sub-sectors, such as leather and pottery (as most artisanal activities are undertaken by specific castes), but these groups are not focused exclusively or even primarily on economic issues, and usually perform more social functions. So the most common form of association for producer-workers who are self-employed or manage only very small units is in fact the cooperative society, which we review next.

Cooperative societies

The cooperative is an important, and probably the most common, form of producer organization in the rural non-farm sector. The Indian Cooperative Societies Act was enacted in 1904, and the initial focus of the cooperative movement was on agricultural societies (Baviskar and Attwood, 1995: 7). Many primary agricultural cooperative societies have therefore been established as part of the cooperative credit system (see previous chapter), as well as for supplying inputs, and processing and marketing outputs. In the 1960s various states promoted cooperatives for many non-farm activities, mainly traditional *khadi* and village industries. Cooperative societies were set up for artisans in wood, leather, pottery and stone, and above all for handloom weavers; others were promoted in the dairy sub-sector, particularly by the National Dairy Development Board (NDDB). NDDB has promoted the 'Anand pattern' of cooperatives, with primary cooperatives which collect milk federated into unions at the district level which process the milk, and these unions themselves joining state-level federations. More recently, NDDB has also been promoting such cooperatives in the fruit and vegetables, oilseeds and tree-growing sub-sectors. The process of promoting cooperatives continues still.

In 1989 there were about 116 000 primary credit cooperative societies with some 108 million members, of whom 85 per cent were in the agricultural sector. There were also 178 000 non-credit cooperative societies with some 29 million members. The majority of these were members of consumer cooperative stores (24%), milk (24%), marketing (16%), industrial (8%) and weaver (6%) cooperative societies (GoI, 1992d: 153–9). The majority of primary cooperatives are federated up to state-level organizations, mainly the apex cooperative banks and the apex cooperative federations in various sub-sectors. And so the cooperative system in India is extensive, and is the best known form of association for producer-workers.

Certain states are particularly prominent in the movement. For example, around 20 per cent of the total populations of Maharashtra, Karnataka and Tamil Nadu are members of various credit societies, and about 10 per cent of the populations in the same states are members of various non-credit societies. Among the eight states we studied, Tamil Nadu stands out, with almost six million members of agricultural credit societies, over a million members of non-agricultural credit societies, 1.7 million members of primary milk societies, and almost 400 000 members of primary weavers' societies (GoI, 1992d; Baviskar and Attwood, 1995: 142–54).

However, with the exception of those in Gujarat and Maharashtra, and to some extent in Kerala, most cooperatives have failed to develop a significant role in their respective local economies or sub-sectors. In 1988–9 the non-agricultural credit societies on average had only some Rs300 of share capital, Rs600 of deposits and Rs1000 of loans per member. Many non-credit societies were small (with 160 members on average) and had only Rs500 of share capital and Rs2300 of working capital per member (GoI, 1992d).

In fact many of the cooperative societies promoted for artisanal activities have become dormant or died, and many cooperatives, both credit and non-credit, are sustained purely by subsidies or subsidized inputs provided through their district or state-level federations. Indeed, access to subsidized inputs, services or other privileges is often the chief motive for members to join cooperatives. There are in fact numerous false cooperatives which have been established by master-weavers, for example, to gain access to the special benefits granted to weaver cooperatives. As a result, the aggregate figures on the number of cooperatives and of their members greatly exaggerate the importance of cooperatives in the rural non-farm sector.

There are several different causes for the widespread failure of the cooperative sector. Some concern structural factors such as the ease of organizing different types of non-farm producers, or the governance of the cooperative societies. Others concern the socio-political context in which the cooperatives operate.

Cooperative societies are more appropriate to some sub-sectors than others. For example, many producer-workers in traditional non-farm activities, such as pottery, may be widely dispersed, with one or a few of them residing in each village. Under such conditions it is difficult to promote a cooperative which could be monitored and controlled effectively by its members. Moreover, much of the raw material (clay) is available locally, and because pottery is fragile, most is also sold locally. Thus two of the primary functions of many cooperatives, supplying raw materials and marketing products, are not really applicable in this sub-sector. Seeking to promote cooperatives among such producer-workers may therefore have been misconceived, even had it not led to political interference as well. Such cooperatives could never have achieved significance for their members, or within their sub-sectors or local economies.

Other sub-sectors, on the other hand, may be more suitable for this type of organization. For example, both sugarcane and milk are perishable and bulky and so need to be processed swiftly and locally. At the same time, processing facilities require large investments which need a guaranteed and regular supply of raw materials. Cooperatives of the primary producers which also own the processing facilities are a good solution for these problems, and the sugar cooperatives in Maharashtra and the dairy cooperatives in Gujarat have been particularly successful. Maharashtra produces about a third of India's output of industrial white sugar, and almost all comes from the cooperative sector. The more than 100 cooperative sugar factories in the state have more than half a million farmers as members (Baviskar and Attwood, 1995). The development of dairy processing, and more recently of oilseed processing, has also relied extensively on cooperatives. Thus there are many examples of successful cooperatives which have achieved salience, providing many services and benefits to their members, both economic and social, and even transforming their local economies or their sub-sectors (Shah, 1995).

Most of these examples, however, are found in western India, and regional social and political factors have proved critical in determining the success or failure of many cooperatives. Baviskar and Attwood (1995) argue that the political economy in western India is far more favourable for cooperatives than in the rest of the country; they substantiate this argument by reviewing the different class and caste structures in various regions, the different colonial legacies, and so on. For example, in rural Maharashtra the 'middle peasants' (the Marathas) predominate, which avoids the more extreme polarization of inter-caste and inter-class rivalries. Moreover, through their numbers the Marathas dominate state politics, thereby ensuring that the state government does not interfere unduly with the cooperatives. In Gujarat the Patidars have performed this role, although their rivals, the Kshatriyas, are taking over as the dominant group. This transition has not, however, caused too much disruption for the cooperatives, and the two groups have been able to balance their interests. In contrast, in other states there are many different and competing castes and classes. At worst feudal dynamics and the absence of the rule of law can be devastating for the functioning of cooperatives (Shah, 1995: 131–42; 195–6).

Shah (1995: 31), however, warns against taking such arguments too far:

It is common knowledge that during the 1950s and 60s, Tamil Nadu, Karnataka and Andhra Pradesh had vibrant and growing rural cooperative movements which were stifled in their infancy by a mindlessly repressive macro-policy environment. Alternatively, one would find numerous examples of failures in central and north Gujarat. . . .

Moreover, as we have seen, Tamil Nadu, like Gujarat, has many strong industry and other associations, if not cooperatives.

In his path-breaking book on cooperatives, Shah (1995) therefore seeks to go beyond the regional or even local socio-political context, suggesting that two other factors are also important for the success of these organizations. The first is the role of the federal system, of which the primary cooperatives are members, in making demands on the primary cooperatives and providing them with the support, such as resources, markets, technologies and expertise, to meet these demands. At its best, the relationship between the primary cooperatives and their federal system is one of mutuality, equality and partnership. The federal system, however, can all too easily play a detrimental role because it is usually in a monopoly relationship *vis-à-vis* the primary cooperatives. At worst the district or state-level federations exercise extensive control over their primary cooperatives, reducing them to little more than distribution channels for subsidized credit or inputs, and so the latter become 'lifeless appendages' (Shah, 1995: 47) to their federal systems.

The second factor, the governance structure, of both the primary cooperatives and the federal system, is even more important. The cooperatives can perform highly only if they are controlled by their members. Elected leaders or directors must feel responsible and be empowered to ensure the proper functioning of the cooperative, and be able to aggregate and balance the needs and demands of the various members. To this end it is vital that the directors have not only formal but also substantive control, and that the federal system itself is answerable to the primary cooperatives

The reality on the ground, however, is often very different. Most cooperatives and their federations were promoted by government officials, and did not stem from the initiative of producers themselves. Many state governments in turn exercise extensive control over the federations, and even over the primary cooperatives. In Uttar Pradesh many of the managing directors at all levels of the cooperative structure are appointed officials, such as IAS officers for the state-level federations, deputy commissioners or district magistrates for the cooperative processing factories, and state cadre officials as secretaries of the primary cooperatives, ensuring that bureaucratic control is complete (Shah, 1995: 245–6; Baviskar and Attwood, 1995: 114–5). Even in cooperatives where the boards of directors are elected by members, the boards have little substantive control over the operations of their cooperatives. In sum, the cooperative structure functions like any other state-managed agency and is not at all responsive to the needs of its members (see our analysis of apex cooperative federations in Chapter 5, pp. 134–5).

In several states, particularly in the south, government interference has gone even further. Politicians regard the cooperatives as potential vote-banks, power-bases and vehicles for distributing patronage, and thus seek to gain control over them, or prevent their political rivals from doing so. In Andhra Pradesh in 1984 the newly elected Chief Minister suspended the elected boards in all major cooperatives in the state and appointed government administrators in their place (Baviskar and Attwood, 1995: 115). In Tamil Nadu the boards of directors in all cooperatives have been superseded several times in the past two decades, and the organizations are managed by 'special officers' appointed by the party in power.

Such extensive and blatant political manipulation of the associations is permitted under the various state cooperative acts, which give substantial powers to the Registrar of Cooperatives, ostensibly to protect the interests of the organizations' members (see the section on incorporation in Chapter 4, pp. 85–8). Therefore, although in theory cooperatives are organizations of producers, they have often in practice become a mere extension of the state machinery. Under such circumstances, it is hardly surprising that the cooperative sector has failed to develop as a dynamic vehicle for promoting the non-farm sector.

The role of NGOs in catalysing producer associations

Because many rural non-farm producers, especially the smaller and poorer ones, lack any representation or effective organizations, non-governmental organizations (NGOs) have often performed the role of promoting their interests. NGOs can do this because they are often innovative in their approach, and tend to work with poorer people, particularly scheduled castes and tribes, and women, and to work in remote, difficult locations where the reach of the state is weak. Almost all these NGOs believe strongly in organizing the poor, strengthening existing organizations, or more often promoting new cooperatives or societies (the latter registered under the Societies Registration Act of 1858).

There are three main types of such NGOs. First are those in the Gandhian tradition, such as Gandhigram and the Association of Sarva Seva Farms (ASSEFA) in Tamil Nadu, the Saghan Kshetriya Vikas Samiti in Uttar Pradesh and the Tamulpur Anchalik Gramdan Sangh in Assam. These Gandhian NGOs tend to focus on traditional artisan crafts and are often highly dependent on the Khadi and Village Industries Commission and Boards for their marketing and finance.

Second, activist NGOs have concentrated on specific issues within the RNFS like child labour, for example protesting against such labour in the match industry in Tamil Nadu and in the carpet industry in Uttar Pradesh. Many have also played a vital role as outsiders in catalysing poor producers to organize (see further below), although this may involve years of struggle requiring strong leadership from within the groups themselves. The various rural producers' cooperatives promoted by SEWA around Ahmedabad are a well-known example of this.

Other NGOs have been founded more recently, many of them by urban, professionally educated people who wanted to work for rural development. Examples of these are PRADAN working with carcass flayers and leather tanners, handloom weavers and fishermen in Uttar Pradesh; the Social Work and Research Centre in Tilonia, near Ajmer in Rajasthan, working with weavers, leather workers and handicraft artisans; the URMUL Trust in Bikaner, Rajasthan working with wool weavers and wood carvers; and the Vivekananda Kendra in the Karbi Anglong district, Assam, working with weavers and cane and bamboo workers. These NGOs have sought to create or sustain employment among poor producers, and in some cases have done useful work in technology intermediation and the establishment of marketing linkages. Because these NGOs usually use grant funds, however, a lot of the projects tend to neglect commercial considerations.

Moreover, NGO programmes are often small, covering only a few producers in a handful of villages. They often seek to provide basic relief or income rather than tackling the sub-sectors in which their beneficiaries work in any strategic manner. So their reach and impact are limited. In effect, they deal with only a tiny proportion of the poor producers in the rural non-farm sector. Above all, they cannot claim truly to represent such producers. While they often perform an important role in mobilizing poor producers or enhancing their livelihoods, they are rarely directly accountable to those they assist, and are often driven by agendas that the NGO leaders in particular have developed rather than the producers themselves. Nevertheless, granted that most poor producers are not organized, NGOs are often the only agencies that can provide the necessary external push for such producers to come together for collective action.

The logic of collective action

So far we have looked at trade unions, industry associations and cooperatives, as well as NGOs, and have begun to address the reasons why some function well and others do not. There is in fact an important body of literature on the theory of group organization, which was given particular impetus by Mancur Olson's seminal work, *The Logic of Collective Action* (1965). Olson argues that individuals may not have the incentive to organize themselves voluntarily into groups to provide public goods, partly because individual costs of participation may outweigh individual benefits (even though group benefits would outweigh group costs) and partly because groups may suffer from the 'free-rider' problem. An individual member thinks that his participation or the lack of it is not likely to affect the outcome significantly and that he can reap the benefits from others' participation in the group even if he does not participate. But if everyone calculates in the same way the group cannot be sustained, or even formed. The only way out of this pessimistic scenario is to apply 'selective' or excludable benefits or costs to individual members, or even a degree of coercion.

This logic seems compelling. However, the large number of groups of all different kinds that we found within the rural non-farm sector seems to contradict Olson's logic, and there are several qualifications that need to be made.

To begin with, it is important to recognize that Olson applies the above arguments to large (or latent) groups, and not to small ones. In small groups, particularly where they are geographically confined, members:

> . . . are often able to cooperate, since they expect to interact continuously over the long term and will thus be able to monitor each other's behaviour and apply formal or informal sanctions to those who go astray. Other things being equal, long-term face-to-face interaction increases the likelihood of stable cooperation (Baviskar and Attwood, 1995: 8, drawing on Axelrod, 1984).

This is the same logic that applies to the self-help savings and credit groups in overcoming the screening, incentive and enforcement problems we analysed in the previous chapter on credit. Likewise, a common characteristic of many of the existing associations and cooperatives in the RNFS is that they are found in a particular locality, such as an industrial cluster or a group of villages. Even if not confined to one area, many of the more successful groups are at least specific to one sub-sector, so that members share common interests, problems and concerns.

In contrast, many non-farm producers in rural India, especially traditional artisans, are scattered over wide areas and communication among them is limited. The problems may to some extent be overcome through caste associations, where a common caste identity allows a certain degree of trust among members. However, although most such caste associations perform social functions, rarely do they provide economic benefits or services to support members, which are costly to organize and difficult to monitor. In particular, for individual poor producers the opportunity costs of participating in a group, in terms of loss of time, work and earnings, may be very high as a proportion of their total income.

It is not only the size and geographical spread that determines the success or failure of collective action. In some cases the group benefits may be high, and the costs of cooperating comparatively low:

> It is possible for an interest-group organization to emerge voluntarily and be sustained largely voluntarily – that is, without selective benefits or costs – if the net collective benefit is high enough. This runs counter to the spirit of Olson's argument (Wade, 1994: 207).

For example, the cost of basic lobbying by an interest group may not be great and can be covered through small membership fees. In a context where critical raw materials, such as coal, are controlled by the government, the benefits of an industry association securing quotas can be enormous. Similarly, in his analysis of cooperatives, Shah (1995) shows that those bodies which achieve salience or importance in the livelihoods of their members tend to grow stronger. In such cases the benefits are significant, while the costs of membership are often small.

The issue of how such cooperatives and other groups are initiated may still remain. Some groups are formed by strong leaders, who may derive status or power through playing such a role. Here, ironically, the benefits one powerful individual derives from the group may exceed the transaction costs of forming and sustaining the group. This is why, for example, so many of the industry associations we came across in the RNFS are dominated by a few leaders, even though other members of the group may also benefit. In some cases, however, powerful individuals may use a group to gain advantage at the expense of other members. The dummy cooperatives of traditional workers formed by contractors in order to acquire licences for lifting carcasses in central Uttar Pradesh or to harvest salt in the Little Rann of Kutch in Gujarat are good examples.

On the other hand, genuine groups of artisans or tiny enterprises, where they exist, have often been catalysed by outsiders, typically by NGOs, thereby reducing the Olsonian transaction costs of cooperation. Examples are the organization of weavers and leather workers in the Jawaja block of Ajmer district in Rajasthan (Matthai, 1982) or of the carcass flayers in Uttar Pradesh, which PRADAN is mobilizing into cooperatives controlled by the member flayers (PRADAN, 1992).

Thus there are many qualifications of Olson's basic argument about collective action. It need not apply to small and local groups. The benefits derived from collective action may be substantial, and strong leaders or outsiders may reduce the transaction costs to other members of forming a group. These qualifications do not mean that we disagree with Olson. His analysis indicates that it is more likely that small groups with special economic interests will be successful in providing collective benefits for their members. It is less likely that large dispersed groups will be able to do so. While exceptions can always be found, this argument is supported by our broad conclusion that strong associations are more common among more modern and dynamic enterprises, often confined to one sub-sector, which form a cluster. They are less common among poor and dispersed producer-workers, such as many traditional artisans.

A political analysis of the representation and organization of producers

The framework of analysis so far has been restricted largely to cost-benefit considerations. While this is a powerful explanatory framework, it does not seem to provide all the answers, and we need to look beyond it. For example, there is growing recognition of the importance of forms of trust for even basic economic or market transactions to function smoothly (Furlong, 1996). In terms of collective action, behavioural norms of trust, fairness and reciprocity can reduce the costs of cooperation, not least by reducing the need for coercion to bind members to a group, and enhance the benefits derived by the group (Oakerson, 1988; Feeny, 1988). Such behavioural norms may of course need to be developed within a group; strong groups tend, therefore, to grow stronger (Shah, 1995).

The lack of trust, fairness and reciprocity on the other hand can prevent producers from organizing. Power and ideology play a critical role in this. Gaventa (1980) (building on work by Lukes, 1974), developed a theoretical framework of three dimensions of power to study the coal-mining workers in an Appalachian valley in the United States, where he found a remarkable degree of quiescence in the face of all-round exploitation. The three dimensions of power are as follows:

(1) A has power over B to the extent he can get B to do something that B would not do otherwise. The first dimension of power thus revolves around who prevails in decision-making, and who gains and who loses. The underlying assumption is that entry to the arenas of decision-making is open.
(2) A not only prevails on issues raised by B but also decides what issues B may raise or whether B may participate at all. In the second dimension of power, therefore, certain participants and groups may be excluded from the decision-making arena altogether. This may be achieved, for example, through the 'mobilization of bias' in favour of certain issues.
(3) In the third dimension of power the powerful are able to influence and shape the perceptions of the powerless about their own interests. Not only might A exercise power over B by prevailing in the resolution of key issues, or by preventing B from effectively raising those issues, but also by affecting B's conceptions of those issues altogether. This dimension of power is largely exerted through the processes of myth-making, information control and the manipulation of ideology.

This framework is useful for analysing different power relations within the rural non-farm sector (Mahajan, 1991). In the first category fall sub-sectors such as handlooms which are organized, due to years of work among weavers by cooperative activists, NGOs and the government. Because of their numbers and organization, they have given rise to 'handloom politics', with politicians, bureaucrats and the media giving considerable attention to them. Their rivals, the powerlooms and mills are also organized into lobbies, and the different groups compete with each other to influence policies, for example on *Janta* cloth and excise levied on hank-yarn, which bring gains to one group and losses to the others.

In the second category are sub-sectors such as handicrafts, including carpets, gems and jewellery, and leather. In these sub-sectors representative bodies are essentially in the hands of large producer-entrepreneurs and traders, who account for a major part of the turnover, especially in exports. They form a nexus with the politicians and bureaucrats, and the vast number of artisans and workers are not involved in any of the decision-making forums, such as the export promotion councils. Even schemes for the welfare of workers are designed by officials in consultation with the big entrepreneurs. However, the artisans and workers are not unaware of their exclusion and have in small pockets come together to fight for a better share of the value added. An example of this was in the carpet sub-sector around Jaipur, where the producer-workers went on strike until their wages were increased. However, such examples are few.

In the third category are sub-sectors such as *bidi*-making, stone quarrying, and gathering and processing forest produce. These sub-sectors employ a large number of people, but are essentially controlled by a few big operators, such as the *bidi* kings or the mining and forest contractors. In many cases the workers do not even see that they should have a role to play in decisions regarding, for example, their wages or occupational safety. The third dimension of power is operating here, with the workers being resigned to their fate and the contractors and regulatory officials playing the role of *mai-baap* and exploiters simultaneously.

The third dimension of power has often been embodied in the caste system, which has ensured that the vast majority of producer-workers have seen themselves in a socially inferior and subservient role. While the power of caste is gradually declining, other myths have been taking its place. One of these is that the state is a benevolent protector of the interests of the poor against the rich. However, such progressive measures as the Bidi Workers' Welfare Fund are often little more than symbolic. More significantly, under various banners such as economic development, industrial growth and environmental conservation, the state has appropriated control of many natural resources, such as land, forest and water, thereby depriving many traditional producers of their ancient livelihoods. The state has also given itself the right to sanction economic activities and the organization of producers. To take the example of flayers again, they have to obtain a licence from the state for lifting carcasses of fallen cattle, in spite of the fact that they were practising this livelihood long before the existence of the licensing state. Likewise, the state has made it compulsory to register all cooperative societies, and in many cases exercises stifling control over them.

Gaventa's framework is also helpful in explaining why many attempts to organize exploited producers or workers have been catalysed by external activist groups, such as NGOs. The approach taken by a wide cross-section of such groups, irrespective of their ideological standpoint, has two essential components: awareness-building and organizing. Depending on their particular ideology, some groups may call this process by such names as conscientization and mass struggle. The essential first step, however, is to work at the level of the third dimension of power by making the producers or workers aware that their situation is the result of very real forces and not fate or sins in their past lives, that forces of domination and exploitation are at work, and that they are not alone in their predicament. Thus the attempt is to undo the psychological hegemony established by the powerful.

Such a process, if successful, then leads to action at the second dimension of power: producers and workers demand that they be heard and the issues of concern to them be brought into the political agenda. In the final stage the first dimension of power may also be addressed, when the rural producers and workers participate in political processes, as has happened to some extent in the handloom sub-sector (even though many of the benefits from handloom policies may in reality have been captured by master-weavers, traders, bureaucrats and others).

Conclusions and recommendations

In this chapter we have looked at the representation and organization of various types of producers in the rural non-farm sector. As we saw, there is no effective policy framework for the RNFS to ensure the representation of producers, workers and consumers in policy-making processes or in the public agencies which implement policies. Instead, policy-making and application are considered the prerogative of the state and its agents within the bureaucracy.

The state has also played an influential role in the organization of producers and workers, by promoting thousands of cooperatives and, indirectly, by developing such a stifling regulatory and promotional environment that producers were forced to organize to fight harassment or capture concessions and benefits. Moreover, many of the different groups play only limited roles, often confined to lobbying and liaising with government in the case of industry associations and acting as a channel for government promotional activities in the case of cooperatives.

Industry associations are often managed by strong entrepreneurs who are not democratically accountable to members; they have very limited finance and provide no professional services. Some even act against wider interests, for example transport unions which establish local monopolies, and bodies of contractors which exclude non-members from obtaining public contracts. More generally, the interests of associations of entrepreneurs and traders may conflict strongly with the interests of small producers and workers, as they compete to extract surplus from the same activity. Likewise, the governance of cooperative societies is rarely accountable to those organizations' members, and in the worst cases has been usurped entirely by politicians and bureaucrats.

Finally, large numbers of RNFS producers and workers are unorganized. Most of these fall into three categories: (1) those in emerging sub-sectors (see Chapter 2), such as silk reeling and small engineering; (2) small producers and workers who are dispersed, poor or exploited and may have only a limited perspective on their sub-sector; and (3) the many women producers and workers, who often fall into the second category as well. While the right to associate may exist, the ability to do so may be limited by 'the logic of collective action' and by various 'dimensions of power' or, rather, powerlessness.

In spite of these flaws in the organization of producers and workers in the RNFS, there are many examples of successful groups. Industry associations, particularly those of relatively larger producer-entrepreneurs in a dynamic cluster or a dynamic sub-sector, have been able to provide valuable and professional services to their members, in addition to advocacy, and have made significant contributions to the development of their clusters or sub-sectors. Among producer-workers there have been many successful cooperative societies, which have not only provided services to their members but achieved salience in their local domain, sometimes enabling them to transform their local economies and communities. NGOs and other external agents have also been able to mobilize exploited producers and workers into groups to allow them to take collective action to fight for their interests, although examples of this have been less common. In many of these cases, whether of associations, cooperatives or other groups, there have been positive externalities: the benefits have extended well beyond the immediate group membership.

The successful examples also demonstrate the important role that organized producers and workers can play in the development of sub-sectors, providing services that many in India had assumed only the state could offer. Indeed, as the state reduces its control over economic activities, the role of groups of producers and workers will become increasingly important. At best a collaborative partnership between private and public actors will evolve, which has been a hallmark of so many successful initiatives in economic development around the world.

To achieve such a goal, however, changes need to occur both in the external environment that groups of producers and workers face, and in the internal workings of those groups. In the former case, the state needs to accept that associations and other bodies should play a more central role in economic development, including areas such as infrastructure, traditionally reserved for state action. For this the state needs to allocate to such groups more responsibilities and more resources, but without controlling them. It will also require legal changes, as the freedom of association needs greater protection. In particular, an overhaul of cooperative law – to reduce radically the role of the state in their functioning – is essential to release the enormous potential the numerous cooperative societies have to serve many small producers and promote local development and self-governance.

Removing constraints on the association of producers and workers, not least by reducing the involvement of the state, will also enhance the internal workings of such groups, which will become more accountable to their members. Changes in the external environment are not, however, sufficient. Good internal organizational practices, such as accountability, financial transparency, professional management and services, and so on, need to be strengthened in new and existing producer and worker groups.[3] Such intervention is not easy, as it can all too easily result in external control and dependency. It requires a partnership between the groups and the external agents (not necessarily public agents!) which the groups enter into voluntarily in search of enhancing their performance. External agents will also continue to be required to mobilize and organize poor and exploited producers through activities ranging from awareness-building to fighting powerful interest groups.

Enabling strong associations, cooperatives, unions and other groups to develop will provide alternative, more responsive and dynamic channels for promoting sub-sectors within the RNFS. These groups could be further supported by government agencies which have been transformed by strong representation of, and control by, producers and workers in the RNFS. Such a strategy would provide an alternative to the past dominance of the state, but also to the policy (all-too prevalent in times of budget constraints and limited vision) of simply dismantling public structures and agencies.

3. For the role governments can play in creating a supportive environment, see IDS (1996); for the (limited) role of donors in strengthening business associations, see DUBS (1994), Mathew *et al.* (1995), Sanket (1995) and again IDS (1996).

8 The rural non-farm sector in the future

In the introduction we set out the central questions for this book: whether, and how, the rural non-farm sector can contribute to the achievement of full employment in India, and to more equitable economic growth. In the first section of this chapter, we revisit these questions in the light both of our analysis and of the most recent economic developments in the first half of the 1990s. In the second section we set out a strategy for promoting the growth of the rural non-farm sector in the future.

Potential for growth of rural non-farm employment

Economic growth, rural livelihoods and incomes

By 1995–6 the Indian economy had gone through five years of liberalization and structural adjustment. It was also the year that the overall annual economic growth rate rose to a healthy 6.6 per cent, far above the proverbial 'Hindu rate of growth' of 2 to 3 per cent, which had characterized the Indian economy until the mid-1980s. Judged by the growth rate, the economic liberalization policies seem to have borne fruit. As soon as we look at the inter-sectoral distribution of growth, however, some disturbing questions arise: in 1995–6 the growth rate of agricultural output was 0.9 per cent, of industrial output 11.1 per cent and of services 7.3 per cent.

Why is this a problem? Let us look at the per capita income in urban and rural India. The level for all India in 1994–5 at current prices was Rs10 299. This was based on a gross national product (GNP) of Rs931 000 crores (CMIE, 1996). Approximately 40 per cent of the GNP was rural in origin, accounting for Rs372 400 crores. Given that this income went to a projected 668 million people in rural India, the rural per capita income was Rs5575 in 1994–5. In contrast, Rs558 600 crores went to 257 million people in urban areas, which gives an urban per capita income of Rs21 735 in the same year. Thus the urban per capita income was already 3.9 times the rural rate in 1994–5. As we know, at least two-thirds of rural income is accounted for by agriculture (see Chapter 2, p. 41). Thus in the following year, when agricultural output grew by only 0.9 per cent, while industrial output grew by 11.1 per cent, the ratio of urban to rural per capita income would have increased further, approximately to a factor of 4.3. And this is dealing only with the averages!

With another three to five years of such growth, the already severe rural–urban inequalities are sure to grow to unacceptable levels. One of the consequences is likely to be a further significant rise in rural to urban migration, with all the attendant negative consequences for the quality of life of both the urban dwellers and the rural migrants. In addition, there is likely to be a spurt in violent rural unrest of the kind already witnessed in many districts of Bihar and Andhra Pradesh. While these are practical considerations which may motivate policy-makers to reduce urban–rural income differentials, the essential purpose of promoting rural livelihoods is to increase rural incomes so that hundreds of millions of Indians can have at least a basic standard of living.

It should be obvious from the above argument that generating a large number of sustainable rural livelihoods, particularly for the poor, is the single most important challenge facing the Indian economy, and that unless it is addressed, the problem will threaten the fabric of India's polity and society. As we set out at the beginning of the Introduction, the 8th Five-Year Plan document had identified the need to generate approximately 100 million new jobs during the decade 1991 to 2000 to ensure full employment in the Indian economy.

The figure of 100 million jobs was based on the existing number of unemployed people in 1990 and the expected increments to the labour force over the decade (see Chapter 1, note 1). On average, therefore, approximately 10 million new livelihoods needed to be created in each year of the 1990s decade. At the mid-point of the decade, however, the backlog of unemployment has grown, because in no year since 1990 did the economy absorb more than six million additional workers; indeed, in the first few years of the decade additional employment amounted to only three to four million a year. The task before the nation is, therefore, to generate 12 to 13 million livelihoods a year if unemployment is to be removed in a decade. A vast majority of these livelihoods will have to be in rural India.

There are broadly two segments of the rural economy: agriculture and the rural non-farm sector (RNFS). According to the 1991 Census (GoI, 1992b), 82 per cent of rural workers were engaged in agriculture and allied activities, and 18 per cent in the non-farm sector. However, in Chapter 2 (pp. 26–7) we argued that the Census is likely to underestimate employment in the RNFS. According to the NSS of 1987–8 (GoI, 1990), over 23 per cent of rural workers, or over 50 million workers, are employed in the non-farm sector. Thus the current division between agricultural and non-farm workers in rural India is likely to be roughly three-quarters to one-quarter respectively, although many workers are engaged in both sectors.

In agriculture, the largest increment for employment can come from increases in the area under irrigation, and therefore in multiple cropping, as well as from investments in soil and water conservation through watershed development in rainfed areas. Changes in cropping patterns, even in dry areas, have led to major increases in employment. For example, the increase in the acreage under oilseeds, particularly soybean over the last 15 years, has generated a substantial amount of rural employment, and led to increases in agricultural wage rates in those regions where oilseeds are grown in some density.

In other areas cultivation of hybrid seeds has led to spurts in the demand for agricultural labour, especially labour skilled in seed-production techniques. The increased demand for vegetables and fruit has also led to greater agricultural employment. The same is true of the demand for dairy, poultry and meat products. It is not uncommon to see large clusters of commercialized dairy and poultry farms belonging to small and medium farmers, who would not have enough good quality land to make ends meet just out of agricultural income. While agricultural labourers, who earn some of the lowest wages in rural India, have been less able to take up such activities, they have benefited from the increased demand for labour and the consequent increase in wage rates, as well as in the number of days of employment per year.

However, between 1977–8 and 1987–8 agricultural employment grew at only 0.7 per cent a year (NSS, see GoI, 1981 and 1990). Only the number of agricultural labourers has been growing faster, and in some states like Andhra Pradesh half of the rural labour force now comprises agricultural labourers. In contrast, employment in the rural non-farm sector grew much faster, at 5.0 per cent (Papola, 1992: 241). Thus the RNFS can be a major source of new rural livelihoods.

The NSS data shows also that the average wage rates for workers in the RNFS were higher than those of agricultural workers. Among labourers, the wage rates in the non-farm sector were 40 per cent higher for men, and 20 per cent higher for women. Among regular workers, wages in the RNFS were 2.4 times those in the agricultural sector (see Tables 2.8 and 2.9, p. 39).

For all its promise, however, growth in the RNFS is clearly boosted by a thriving agricultural economy. For example, according to the 1991 Census, in Punjab, Haryana and West Bengal over 25 per cent of rural workers were engaged in the non-farm sector,[1] while in Bihar and Madhya Pradesh the equivalent proportion was only just over 10 per cent (Chapter 1, p. 21). In areas with sluggish agricultural growth, the RNFS may act mainly as a safety-net of off-season or lean-season employment, even as a last resort. However, robust agricultural growth supports the RNFS in various ways: by providing the raw material for agro-processing industries, including for small rural units, by generating demand for agricultural inputs and services

1. Kerala is an exception in having 44 per cent of its rural workers engaged in the RNFS, because of its mixed urban–rural demographic pattern.

and by increasing rural incomes, which in turn create demand for RNFS products and services.

The growth of the RNFS of course also supports agriculture, for example through improvements in agricultural markets and internal terms of trade, modern inputs and improved technologies, and incentives for increasing productivity and savings among agricultural households (Ranis and Stewart, 1993: 79–80). Granted that between a quarter and a third of rural income is derived from the non-farm sector, the RNFS itself is an important contributor to rural demand.

In looking at the primary sector for inputs for the RNFS, it is a mistake to focus only on agricultural crop production. Other agricultural produce, such as fruit, vegetables, spices, herbs, other plantation crops and flowers, some of which can even be grown in arid and semi-arid regions, as well as activities allied to agriculture, such as dairying, poultry and fisheries, may all provide the basis for RNFS livelihoods in processing, manufacture, storage, distribution, transport and trade. However, in most cases India has not come close to realizing the potential of these primary products. For example, India ranks only seventh in the world in terms of total fish production, in spite of its vast coastline. The country also has the potential for 1.1 million hectares of aquaculture, but only a few thousand hectares have been developed so far.

Forestry is another source of raw material for the RNFS, for example of timber, *tendu* leaves and bamboo, as well as some 5000 plant species, few of which have been exploited commercially. However, forest cover has fallen below 16 per cent of the total geographical area, and so timber and minor forest produce stocks have declined drastically. Regeneration of forests, therefore, can be good not only for the environment, but can also restore the basis of non-farm livelihoods based on forest produce. Finally, mining and quarrying provide many jobs in rural areas, not just in the primary extraction activity, but also in processing, transportation and trade. In addition, jobs arise in related and supporting industries, such as equipment supply and repair services (see Figure 3.2, p. 82). Taken together, the primary sub-sectors of agriculture, plantations, horticulture, floriculture, animal husbandry, forestry and mining have enormous potential for providing raw materials for the RNFS, and for generating demand for RNFS products and services.

In the secondary sector, most rural employment is in traditional subsectors like cotton textiles, and wood, textile, pottery, food, tobacco and metal products, as well as in repairs and construction. However, manufacturing within the household is the only segment of the RNFS in which employment is declining. Many modern manufacturing activities are, in contrast, beginning to emerge, such as electrical equipment, paper and chemicals, as well as iron and steel, powerlooms and repairs.

However, contrary to popular belief, although in line with experiences in almost all developing countries, the majority of RNFS jobs (some 60 per cent) are found in the tertiary sector. Services that generate substantial rural employment include wholesale and retail trade, transport, hotels and restaurants, business services, educational and health services, public administration and personal services. All of these, apart from transport and business services, also generate extensive female employment (see Table 2.6, p. 36).

Moreover, in the period 1978–88, transport, business and legal services, trading activities and public administration were among the fastest-growing sub-sectors in terms of rural employment (see Tables 2.4 and 2.5, pp. 32–3). Yet policy and financial agencies have by and large neglected, if not remained downright hostile to service enterprises in rural areas. To illustrate this, one need only compare a banker's response to loan proposals for a roadside *dhaba* and for a small-scale manufacturing unit.

Projections for rural employment growth

Anticipating the future is always a risky proposition, yet we have to do it to some extent in order to plan strategic options for the RNFS. Four trends which now appear to be well established and which are likely to continue, although the rates of change may be more open to discussion, are:

- greater economic diversification in rural India;
- more urbanization and rural–urban links;
- deeper liberalization in the economic sphere; and
- increased globalization of the Indian economy.

Our analysis above supports the argument that the rural economy in India is becoming more diversified as employment in manufacturing, including of many modern products, and in services, grows much faster than in agriculture. The 1991 Census also shows that the rate of urbanization was faster in the 1980s than in previous decades. Of particular significance to the RNFS is the growth in the number and population of rural towns, where much rural non-farm employment is concentrated.

The present vicissitudes of liberalization notwithstanding, it is a fair assumption that the process of reducing state control over economic activities will continue, with further reductions in regulation, licensing, and control over inputs, credit and infrastructure. This may have had a short-term adverse impact on some sub-sectors which had become addicted to an overdose of protection, but there are already signs that it is leading to a stimulation in demand for the RNFS as a whole. Indeed, in some sub-sectors there is likely to be a shift in production in favour of the RNFS, since rural enterprises use less capital, infrastructure and energy for the same level of production than urban enterprises. With the growing divergence between rural and urban incomes that we described above, and the potential rise in migration to large urban centres, rural enterprises may also increasingly enjoy lower wages and land or space costs, as well as lower transportation costs for bulky raw materials found in rural areas. Again, rural towns may play a critical role in allowing such shifts to take place.

Finally, in 1990–91 the share of India in world trade was lower than in 1947. This is an astounding fact, and shows what a major opportunity has been missed by India's inward-looking policies of import-substituting industrialization. With liberalization, however, the growth of exports has accelerated, although still not as much as was hoped, and while India's share in the global trade in most RNFS products is small, the RNFS makes a substantial contribution to India's total exports. Textile fabrics and manufactures, leather and leather products, and handicrafts, including gems and jewellery and hand-made carpets, are particularly significant. Indeed, India's current low share of global trade represents an opportunity, and enhancing exports in these and other RNFS products can supplement growing domestic demand.

All the four trends above are based on our subjective assessment of the situation, and there is no guarantee that one or more may persist. Nevertheless, the likelihood is that they will do so.

What could these trends mean for the growth of rural employment? In order to make projections, we put forward three different scenarios, based on different growth rates in rural non-farm employment: 2.8 per cent based on the Census (Table 2.1, p. 28), 5.0 per cent based on the NSS (Papola, 1992: 241), and 8.1 per cent based on our calculations of the growth rate that is necessary to achieve full employment (see Table 1.2, p. 2).[2]

The rural labour force in India has been growing at the annual rate of 2.5 per cent from 1972–3 to 1987–8 (NSS). Assuming that this growth rate has been continuing, 277 million people will be in the rural labour force by the year 2001. What part of this labour force can find productive employment in the rural non-farm sector? We set out the different scenarios in Table 8.1.

- In Scenario 1, RNFS employment grows at the low (Census) rate of 2.8 per cent a year, and we assume that the growth rate of agricultural employment also continues at the same rate as given in the Census for 1981–91.
- In Scenario 2, RNFS employment grows at 5.0 per cent a year, while we maintain the 1981-91 growth rate of cultivators, but reduce that of agricultural labourers to 2.2 per cent, assuming that some of the latter will find employment in the RNFS.

2. Unfortunately, the only reliable data on the composition of rural employment take us back to the 1991 Census and 1987–8 NSS, and granted that we use the employment projections for illustrative purposes only, we continue to focus on the current decade until 2001.

Table 8.1: Projected RNFS employment – three scenarios

Category			*Scenario 1: low RNFS growth*			*Scenario 2: medium RNFS growth*			*Scenario 3: high RNFS growth*		
	1991		*Projected annual growth rate (%)*	*2001*		*Projected annual growth rate (%)*	*2001*		*Projected annual growth rate (%)*	*2001*	
	RMWs (millions)	*Share of RMWs(%)*		*RMWs (millions)*	*Share of RMWs(%)*		*RMWs (millions)*	*Share of RMWs(%)*		*RMWs (millions)*	*Share of RMWs(%)*
Cultivators	104.0	48.2	1.56	121.4	45.2	1.5	120.7	44.1	1.0	114.9	40.4
Agricultural labour	69.5	32.2	2.81	91.7	34.1	2.2	86.4	31.5	1.5	80.7	28.4
Activities allied to agriculture	4.2	2.0	0.21	4.3	1.6	1.0	4.7	1.7	1.5	4.9	1.7
Mining and quarrying	1.0	0.5	2.48	1.3	0.5	4.0	1.5	0.5	5.0	1.6	0.6
Household manufacturing	4.8	2.2	−1.20	4.2	1.6	−1.4	4.1	1.5	−1.8	4.0	1.4
Non-household manufacturing	7.8	3.6	2.62	10.1	3.7	4.0	11.5	4.2	7.5	16.0	5.6
Construction	2.3	1.0	2.34	2.8	1.1	4.0	3.3	1.2	8.0	4.9	1.7
Trade and commerce	7.0	3.3	3.73	10.2	3.8	6.0	12.6	4.6	10.0	18.3	6.4
Transport, storage, communications	2.7	1.2	1.34	3.0	1.1	4.0	3.9	1.4	8.0	5.7	2.0
Other services	12.8	5.9	4.45	19.7	7.3	7.0	25.1	9.2	10.0	33.1	11.7
Total rural main workers (RMWs)	216.1	100.0	2.11	268.8	100.0	2.4	274.0	100.0	2.8	284.1	100.0
Total RNFS workers	38.3	17.7	2.66	51.4	19.1	5.0	62.2	22.7	8.1	83.6	29.4
Additional RMWs				52.8			57.9			68.1	
Additional RNFS workers				13.1			23.9			45.4	
Projected labour force in 2001				276.6			276.6			276.6	
Additional unemployment				7.8			2.6			−7.5	

Note: Because of rounding the growth rates, the rate for the growth of RNFS employment under Scenario 1 comes to 2.7 per cent rather than 2.8 as for the Census (see Table 2.1, p. 28).

- In Scenario 3, RNFS employment grows at 8.1 per cent a year, while the growth rates of cultivators and agricultural labourers are reduced to 1.0 and 2.2 per cent respectively, again assuming that some of them will be able to find employment in the RNFS.

As can be seen from Table 8.1, the different growth rates lead to very different outcomes for rural non-farm employment, ranging from 51 million jobs in 2001, according to the pessimistic scenario, to 83 million jobs according to the optimistic scenario. The other notable feature of the projections is the impact of RNFS growth on overall employment. In the first scenario, the growth is far too low even to absorb the increments to the labour force between 1991 and 2001, leading to additional unemployment of 8 million. In the second scenario, almost all incremental labour is absorbed, although the backlog of unemployment in 1991 (over 7 million) is not. It is only in the third scenario that the growth in employment is adequate to wipe out this backlog as well, providing full rural employment.

It is clearly a major swing from one scenario to another, and at least part of the swing can be influenced by policy. If appropriate policies are made to encourage domestic demand and tap export demand, improve factor productivity, stimulate growth of related and supporting industries, including services, and promote competition along with collaboration in chosen sub-sectors, there are reasons to believe that the optimistic scenario can be realized.

We also need to look beyond the rural non-farm sector to demonstrate that the state is capable of playing an effective promotional role. The so-called Green Revolution, which promoted high-yielding agriculture, is undoubtedly one of the success stories of Indian policy-making and administrative action (however controversial the long-term results may be). To go from a situation where India was importing around 15 per cent of its food-grain requirements in 1964–7, to becoming completely self-sufficient in food, took only a few years of concerted action. The Agriculture Minister at that time, C. Subramaniam, was able to muster the necessary inputs from national and international sources. High-yielding seeds were procured from the International Wheat Research Institute in Mexico, fertilizers were imported and then domestic plants set up, agriculture extension and adaptive research systems were quickly established in the most promising districts of the country. Remunerative procurement prices were announced in advance to motivate farmers.

We think there are lessons to be learnt for the RNFS from the Green Revolution: (1) the urgency of the situation should be felt at the highest level and must be given due political importance; (2) it should be possible to translate broad goals into specific objectives, and also establish agreement on specific methods to reach those objectives (see Box 5.1, p. 116); (3) focusing is important: in the Green Revolution the focus was on a few districts and a single crop which were likely to yield the best results; (4) all supportive inputs were made available, including technology (basic and adaptive research and extension) and materials (fertilizers, pesticides and irrigation); and (5) clear economic incentives were given to the primary productive actors.

In more recent times the various technology missions on telecommunications, oilseeds, drinking water, immunization and literacy, have also tried to take a different approach to state-led goal-setting and action. The lessons from the technology missions show that, apart from the signal that gets sent down the system of the importance of the mission due to the high level of political support, the increase in the specificity of objectives and methods (see Box 5.1) is the key to improved performance. Another lesson is that collaborative action among state agencies, and between them and private agencies, although difficult to achieve, is very much worthwhile.

The remainder of this chapter explores, therefore, appropriate strategies for promoting the rural non-farm sector.

Strategies for the future

The role of government

In the introductory chapter we suggested that there remain significant roles for the central and state governments in India in promoting rural non-farm employment. These roles are very different from the interventionist and controlling ones adopted in the past. Instead the governments need to shift to providing an enabling and more market-friendly environment, reliable infrastructure and focused promotional inputs.

The role of the state in economic development in East and South-east Asia is highly disputed, although even the World Bank (1993) admits that the governments concerned often played an active role in promoting remarkably equitable economic growth. However, the broad model that the World Bank (1993: 11) developed to explain this role provides a balanced view which has much relevance for India also. The Bank argues that the governments ensured that the 'fundamentals' were right: a stable macro-economy; high investment in human capital; effective and secure financial systems; limited price distortions; openness to foreign technology; and policies supporting agricultural development. At the same time the governments undertook 'selective interventions', in encouraging exports and financial services, and providing a variety of other promotional inputs, including enhanced social security. The governments also developed sound public agencies. Competitive discipline was ensured either through competition in domestic and export markets or, where governments intervened in markets, for example by providing promotional inputs, through allocation systems in which private enterprises had to compete with each other for those inputs or other benefits.

In India the central and state governments have performed only some of the above functions well. For example, inflation has often remained (relatively) low, and there have been successful efforts to promote agricultural growth, especially during the Green Revolution. However, the governments have failed on many other counts, for example in building human capital, developing sound financial systems, or limiting price distortions. Moreover, interventions have certainly not been selective, and, granted India's political economy, have often been captured by vested interests.

How then do we conceive of the governments' role for the dynamic growth of the rural non-farm s ctor? We look at the central and state governments in turn.

Role of the central or union government The most important role of the central government specifically targeted at the rural non-farm sector is to signal a high level of national priority, as was done for the food-grain sector in the 1960s. As we have seen, the RNFS has often been treated as a residual category, falling between agriculture and (urban) industrialization, while rural non-farm activities have been equated with traditional village or tiny enterprises. It is therefore not surprising that the RNFS has not received adequate policy attention. This needs to be changed, perhaps through another 'technology mission' which would capture the attention of policy-makers and development workers throughout India. It would also provide an opportunity for some radical changes in approach, not least of all encouraging much more extensive private–public collaboration, which must be a key characteristic of any strategy for the RNFS.

Throughout this book we have also stressed that the rural non-farm sector is extremely diverse, and that it is not possible to recommend specific policies which would apply to the whole sector (such recommendations would also go against the purpose of a sub-sectoral strategy which we develop below). However, the central government may have a role in supporting the establishment of a permanent mechanism for scanning the horizon for emergent sub-sectors (again, see below).

In the broader context of economic development, which is equally important for the development of the RNFS, the central government obviously plays a critical role in providing a healthy macro-economic environment which enables the overall growth of the economy. Part of this involves continuing trade liberalization so that the natural competitive advantage of rural production in specific sub-sectors can evolve, and the RNFS can benefit from better access to technical know-how. A healthy macro-environment would also provide a reasonable balance between rural and urban growth, for example in ensuring fair terms of trade for agriculture. Agricultural development also needs specific inputs, such as public investment in irrigation, as well as investments in research and extension, seeds and fertilizers, and improved marketing, although generally the government should support private initiatives in these areas, not implement them through public agencies. As we saw above, there are many other primary sub-sectors, such as livestock, fisheries, forestry and mining, that require a combination of policy liberalization (as has recently been done for mining and quarrying) and more private investment.

Increasing investment in physical infrastructure, particularly power, roads and water, is also important. Once again, however, policy liberalization and establishing attractive tariffs will ensure that private investments flow into infrastructure development. Thus there should be more emphasis on the role of the government in establishing the right policy environment, rather than setting up infrastructure itself. Continuing public investment in social infrastructure on the other hand, in particular in education and health, will remain vital for providing the human capital necessary for the growth of the RNFS.

Credit policy is again largely in the hands of the central government, through the Reserve Bank of India. Major progress has already been made in reforming the rural financial sector, but much still remains to be done (see Chapter 6), not least introducing strict measures to ban all loan waivers and to enforce repayment norms.

Role of state governments The first role of the state governments is to signal high-level attention to the RNFS by declaring state policies for the sector, as has been done in Rajasthan already. Such policies should adhere to the sub-sectoral approach which we develop below. States may also need to establish appropriate organizational structures, such as the RNFS Directorate in Rajasthan, although the role of such organizations should not be in implementing government programmes, but in bringing together different actors, both private and public, and catalysing new action.

The state governments also have roles in promoting agriculture, other primary sectors and both physical and social infrastructure. These governments also determine much of the regulatory environment, and in each state regulation needs radical reform, which has to some extent already begun. The focus of regulation should be on the key objectives of promoting greater employment and growth in the RNFS. This will require changing incentive structures for the staff of regulatory bodies.

The state governments should also collaborate more closely with the various producer organizations, encouraging them to take over many of the promotional roles undertaken in the past by governments. Such roles include pooling raw material supplies, providing common production facilities, other infrastructure, design, training and marketing assistance.

The need for pragmatic flexibility Promoting a new sector, and with a very different approach, will not be easy, and there will inevitably be some successes and some failures. In a more liberalized, competitive and open environment there is, however, hope that the 'path dependency' that has dominated so many promotional activities in the past will not be as strong.[3] The World Bank (1993: 12) study on the East and South-east Asian economies states that the governments:

> . . . used multiple, shifting policy instruments in pursuit of more immediate economic objectives. Pragmatic flexibility – the capacity and willingness to change policies – is as much a hallmark of the [high performing East Asian economies] as any other single policy instrument.

Preconditions for a dynamic RNFS: agriculture and infrastructure

Above we suggested that agricultural growth is important for the development of the rural non-farm sector, and that both the central and state governments retain important roles in supporting the growth of non-farm employment by continuing to promote agriculture (we also described various opportunities for doing this).

Good rural infrastructure is vital for the development of the RNFS. Ranis and Stewart (1993: 91–2), for example, found that a comprehensive rural electrification programme, a high road density, and the promotion of industrial estates and export processing zones all contributed significantly to the healthy growth of the rural non-farm sector in Taiwan.

The provison of infrastructure will remain an important role for government action, although there is increasing recognition that private parties can construct and manage infrastructure effectively with some government support. Power is particularly crucial for non-farm enterprises. The Economic Census of 1990 (GoI, 1995b) shows that over 80 per cent of all rural units operate without power. While some of these do not need power, partly because they still employ manually driven technologies, a majority of units do require a reliable energy supply. Yet, in almost all states, the situation of rural power supply is dismal, to say the least. The condition of other infrastructure, such as roads, water supply and worksheds is equally bad, even in the most dynamic clusters which produce crores of rupees of exports. The states could generate more rural employment by ensuring steady availability of power to every village and connecting every village with a metalled road, than all the money spent on subsidies and direct inputs for rural enterprises would provide, although an initial focus on rural towns and clusters would be a more effective strategy for promoting non-farm employment. Service infrastructure, such as trade and transport, and recently telecommunications, has been reasonably good, mainly as it is in

---

3. Once institutions (in North's wide definition: see Box 4.1, p. 86) are set on a particular path, their long-run direction is difficult to change (North, 1990: 115).

private hands, and in all of these services rural employment has been expanding fast.

Granted that state governments have rarely proved competent in managing infrastructure, opportunities for privatizing this role should be considered. Wherever possible, producer associations should be asked to form companies, for example to generate power, manage industrial estates and handle effluents.

If the central and state governments have been neglectful in supplying basic physical infrastructure to villages, they have been even worse at providing social infrastructure, particularly related to education and health. As we saw in Chapter 2, educational attainments are higher among non-farm workers than among agricultural workers, and education is an important preparation, even precondition, for rural workers to enter non-farm employment. Moreover, one of the major contributing factors to economic development in East and South-east Asia has been the provision of basic education, beginning with primary education (Drèze and Sen, 1995; World Bank, 1993: 21). But primary education is only the first step, as becoming a productive worker in the rural non-farm sector requires acquisition of skills, for which vocational training is necessary and further education up to secondary level desirable. Yet programmes such as TRYSEM have been inadequate for the huge task of enhancing skill levels in the rural population (see Box 3.3, p. 76). In sum, the RNFS can thrive only if the physical and social infrastructure in rural areas is significantly upgraded.

Sub-sectoral focus

A recurrent theme throughout this book has been the need for focus in promotional strategies. In particular, we have put forward the idea of focusing on particular sub-sectors, and in Chapter 3 we developed a framework, on the basis of work by Michael Porter (1990), for analysing the potential of sub-sectors.

The primary lesson from such analysis is the need to consider the demand potential of sub-sectors. Supply-side interventions (such as raw material supplies, technology development and credit), which have been the main characteristic of promotional activities in the past, are completely wasted if they fly in the face of demand trends. That is why so many resources have been squandered seeking to support declining industries, as we saw in Chapter 5. If sub-sectoral analysis reveals that an activity faces demand constraints, these constraints need to be addressed first. This, however, does not mean establishing retail outlets, a strategy which assumes that demand exists. It may mean undertaking market research, including of export markets, potentially leading to the redesign of products or services to meet current and future demand, and promoting products and services through advertising and other means. Government agencies have rarely been effective at such strategies, and it would be more appropriate to encourage or contract private actors to undertake them.

Even if the demand potential for a particular RNFS sub-sector is good, sub-sectoral analysis needs to identify the missing links or ruling constraints in the other components of Porter's diamond (see Figure 3.1, p. 57), among factor conditions, industry structure and related and supporting industries. These constraints have to be systematically addressed, some through promotional measures and others by modifying regulation. Again, it is our strong recommendation that the government should confine its role to analysis of sub-sectoral constraints, jointly with industry representatives, and then make modifications in regulations. As far as promotion is concerned, the government should play only a catalytic role and encourage initiatives by producers' associations or industry-sponsored organizations.

In the light of past experience, it is important to emphasize that promoting a sub-sector requires more than targeting individual manufacturing units. While many states have identified specific sub-sectors for promotion, in practice this has been translated merely into preferential allotment of land, power, credit and so on to units in those sub-sectors. What is also needed for the sub-sector to thrive is the emergence of related and supporting enterprises, as well as other types of entities such as producer associations and research institutes, which provide a variety of essential inputs for the individual manufacturing or service units. Such supporting industries or services include marketing and market research, raw material and equipment supplies, product design, technical development, training, and packaging. The evidence provided in Figure 3.2 (see p. 82) on stone-processing in Betamcherla, in Kurnool District in AP, shows clearly that such related and supporting industries and services generate more employment than the actual stone-processing units themselves.

As the sophistication of a sub-sector increases, the value added by such supporting activities also rises. For example, while India was at one time exporting raw hides, it shifted over a period of time to chrome-tanned hides, then to semi-finished and finished leather. This was followed by a move into shoe uppers, and then to fully-made shoes using sewing machines. The latest move is into expensive hand-stitched shoes and also leather garments. These successive steps in the chain of value addition would not have been possible but for the emergence of a variety of support activities, some of which came from private enterprises, others from industry associations and still others from research institutes.

One final point of caution needs to be noted: it takes a long time to promote a sub-sector. Just for reference, the first steps for the thriving sericulture sub-sector in Karnataka were taken by Tipu Sultan, who died in 1799. There is an apocryphal story that he smuggled in some silk cocoons from China and introduced sericulture in his kingdom. Two hundred years is a long time for sub-sector development! However, with modern planning it is possible to promote a sub-sector in a reasonable time-span, but in no case should the perspective be less than that of a decade. Policy-makers should not be impatient in this period and should avoid the temptation of the state undertaking all the promotional activities itself.

However, granted the enormous diversity of the rural non-farm sector, it is not possible to promote all sub-sectors. Even within a sub-sectoral strategy there needs to be focus, and below we outline three steps to narrow the objective of promotional activities, first to particular sub-sectors, and then to particular locations and types of unit.[4] These steps are sequential. In particular, the choice of sub-sector comes before the choice of location or unit type.

Choice of sub-sectors Given the diversity within the RNFS, the first choice that needs to be made is which sub-sectors should be selected for policy attention. As stated above, the primary criterion for selection should be demand conditions or prospects. In our sub-sectoral analysis in Chapter 3 we divided sub-sectors into three groups (high-share, high-growth and emergent), and discovered that each faced very different demand conditions.

High-share sub-sectors are those which at present account for a high share of rural employment within the non-farm sector (see Table 2.3, p. 30). These include many traditional manufacturing sub-sectors, such as wood products, cotton textiles, pottery and *bidis*, whose demand prospects are uncertain. They may be excluded by our choice of sub-sectors on the basis of demand conditions.

We recognize, however, that many of these sub-sectors generate substantial employment for women, for the poor and for disadvantaged groups. The role of policy here is to identify higher-value niche markets or more productive segments of the sub-sectors concerned, and seek to shift workers there. Taking textiles as an example, policy would seek to move workers to powerlooms which are far more productive than handlooms, or to high-value products (such as textiles with special designs) that can best be manufactured on handlooms. It is unlikely that such a strategy would be able to absorb all the workers in these sub-sectors, and in the face of declining demand prospects, another policy aim would be to ensure substantial retraining of workers and their redeployment in other sub-sectors. Existing employment should only be protected if this can be done with minimal distortion in terms of subsidies, product reservations or production controls. Some protection will in any case be assured through the low cost of labour.

4. Many of the recommendations for a focused strategy that arose from our study of the RNFS are similar to those emerging from the by-now extensive literature on industrial districts (see IDS, 1992; Holmstrom, 1994; Pedersen *et al.*, 1994; Humphrey and Schmitz, 1995).

Some high-share sub-sectors on the other hand face reasonable demand prospects. These include, for example, construction, repairs, land transport, retail trade, and restaurants and hotels. Each of these sub-sectors also appears in our list of high-growth sub-sectors, which we address next.

High-growth sub-sectors are those which have experienced a high growth rate of rural non-farm employment (see Tables 2.4 and 2.5, pp. 32–3). These include, for example, mining, construction, repairs, transport, retail trade, business services, a number of modern manufacturing sub-sectors, such as powerlooms, electrical, paper and chemical products, as well as a few high-value traditional sub-sectors such as silk textiles, embroidery and wooden furniture.[5] The primary reason for the high growth of employment in these sub-sectors is of course that they also enjoy a high growth rate of demand in domestic and/or export markets. High-growth sub-sectors are thus likely candidates for selection as part of a strategy focused on particular sub-sectors.

The role of policy here is to identify and address constraints on the growth of the sub-sector in order to ensure that the favourable conditions created by growing demand for its products or services are backed by adequate availability of raw material, infrastructural support, training, product and process-upgrading services, credit and marketing and other related services. Such services should not, however, be provided by government agencies. The role of the state is to ensure a supportive regulatory environment and to provide appropriate backing for service enterprises in the private sector.

Emergent sub-sectors are those which at present support relatively little employment, but which have potential for growth in the near future because of unmet demand. Examples might be prawn processing in Andhra Pradesh, floriculture and flower processing in Orissa, gem-cutting in Tamil Nadu, and cement-ware in Gujarat. To identify such emergent sub-sectors, the central and state governments should establish 'horizon-scanning' mechanisms. For example, an appropriate organization (in the private sector) could look at world trade data and identify products which enjoy good demand prospects, but also have a high wage share of value added and comparatively low transportation costs for raw materials and finished products. These sub-sectors could then be studied for India's competitive advantage against existing suppliers, and an individual state's competitive advantage against other states, to select appropriate locations for promotion. The Ministry of Commerce already identifies what it considers potential sub-sectors for 'extreme focus', and these could be analysed for their suitability for rural or rural-town production.

5. The fact that powerlooms, silk textiles, embroidery and wooden furniture are high-growth segments of the high-share sub-sectors of cotton textiles, textile products and wood products, lends support to our argument above for shifting workers to the more dynamic segments of high-share sub-sectors.

Granted that such sub-sectors are only emerging, sub-sectoral analysis is bound to identify a series of constraints. Thus a more extensive package of promotional inputs may have to be provided, including setting up pilot projects. However, such promotion should only be given to sub-sectors that face good potential demand, and should be characterized by strong collaboration between public and private parties, granted that it is the latter that will have to take the primary initiative, with government support.

The above analysis appears to provide a wide selection of sub-sectors. Given the paucity of financial resources as well as the need for quality administrative attention, however, it is critical that states select only a few for focused promotional inputs. For example, in Rajasthan the newly formed Directorate for the Non-Farm Sector has selected three: minor minerals, wool and leather.

Choice of location The second policy choice that has to be made is one of physical location: where to concentrate promotional efforts. It is clear from the analysis in Chapter 5 that promotion of individual units, such as village or small-scale industries, across a wide geographical area is not effective, especially as such a dispersed strategy often entails restricting such activities to single inputs, such as credit. The individual units that receive such a single promotional input do not attract or have access to other complementary inputs, nor do they have much impact on their sub-sector or local economy.

There is, however, an alternative to such dispersed promotional strategies. Sub-sectors in the rural non-farm sector tend to be concentrated in specific regions. For example, in Andhra Pradesh prawn processing takes place in the coastal districts, *bidi*-rolling in the north-west, and stone processing in the south. Within these regions, units tend to be concentrated in specific clusters, often in rural towns. Examples include tile manufacturing in Morbi, Gujarat, appliqué textiles in Pipili, Orissa and stone polishing in Betamcherla, Andhra Pradesh (see Figure 3.2, p. 82).

It is not always understood why units in one sub-sector come up in a particular region or cluster (Humphrey and Schmitz, 1995). In some cases they are close to raw material supplies, especially when such materials are bulky or perishable. Many processing units, for example of sugar, fish and stone, will be close to sugar-cane farms, coastal regions and quarries respectively. In some cases the available labour in a particular area may be attractive to entrepreneurs. In Sivakasi, an arid district in Tamil Nadu, the rural population has few employment opportunities, and match units using manual technologies can hire much cheap labour. In some cases clusters may be close to markets. Pipili in Orissa is on the (tourist) route between Bhubaneshwar and Puri. In other cases the growth of a sub-sector in an area may even have been a matter of chance.

Whatever the reasons for particular clusters to develop, it is clear that their constituent units enjoy many advantages in terms of 'collective efficiency' (Humphrey and Schmitz, 1995: 7–8). Promotional policies for the RNFS must therefore recognize the importance of such clustering and use it as another basis for focusing efforts. Concentrating promotional efforts on clusters has many advantages: (1) since most infrastructural facilities are capital intensive and indivisible, having a large number of users in a geographical concentration reduces per-unit costs and makes for quicker returns on investment; (2) units have better access to related services, such as input and machinery supplies, financial and marketing services, which complement inputs provided through any promotional strategy. In fact the further growth of such supporting services may generate more employment than, say, the primary manufacturing activity in the cluster (see Figure 3.2); and (3) producer associations tend to develop, and these associations can act as partners in any private–public collaboration.

We do not recommend attempts to create new clusters. Any promotional activities are likely to prove more successful if they facilitate the growth of existing ones. This does not mean that promotional efforts should focus only on large dynamic sub-sectors; some existing clusters may only just be emerging.

Potential clusters for promotion should be analysed using Porter's framework, which we described in Chapter 3. Such analysis will not only identify promising clusters, but also the ruling constraints holding back their growth. Strategies to address these constraints should be developed with the existing associations in the clusters, or if there are none, promoting such associations may be the first step. In general, government agencies should not seek to become involved as economic actors in the clusters concerned, but facilitate the growth of the clusters by ensuring a supportive regulatory environment and by collaborating with private agents to provide supporting services. For example, it is more appropriate for government agencies to invest in specialized infrastructure such as a research institute or training centre, which the private enterprises in the cluster cannot afford themselves. Such infrastructure would not only provide services to the existing enterprises but also act as a magnet for attracting new enterprises and private capital. In particular, this form of intervention is better than providing subsidies to firms to locate facilities in a region where they would otherwise prefer not to.

It should be noted that the choice of location, that is clusters, is sequential, and not parallel, to the choice of sub-sectors. Thus only clusters of sub-sectors selected under the first option should be targeted for promotional efforts. We suggest this to ensure that the limited amount of promotional energy available to public agencies should be used for the most promising clusters of the most promising sub-sectors in terms of generating employment.

Choice of unit size and type The third policy option that needs to be exercised is on the size and type of units that are to be given maximum incentives in terms of policy and promotional inputs. The traditional policy approach for the RNFS is to promote cottage-scale units, such as the individual weaver, the potter and the village shoe-maker. This has been the strategy of the Khadi and Village Industries Commission and of the industry, service and business (ISB) loans under the IRDP. The average rural enterprise in any case employs only 2.2 workers (GoI, 1995b). Even the average rural small-scale industry employs only five workers and has an average level of fixed investment of only Rs1.1 lakhs (GoI, 1992c:T50–51). In short, RNFS promotion has been confined to very small manufacturing units.

Our study indicates that the whole debate on what is the correct size of unit to promote misses the point. Those who favour cottage and tiny units do so on the ground that it would maximize employment. First of all this assumption itself is questionable, as Little *et al.* (1987: 305, 313) found in their detailed study of five industries in India (see p. 46 above). They suggest that 'total factor productivity is a better measure of efficiency in the use of factors of production than capital productivity alone', and conclude that the smallest enterprises rarely do well measured against this criterion. In addition, 'many small enterprises, with less than 10 workers, are often not the most labour-intensive and their capital productivity and technical efficiency are very rarely the highest in the whole size range of establishments in the industry'.

Moreover, a sub-sectoral approach makes clear that the insistence on ensuring maximum employment per unit can suffocate the growth of a sub-sector due to the adoption of inefficient technologies. Thus less employment gets generated in the sub-sector as a whole than would have been possible if units appropriate to the economics of the sub-sector had come up. We once again refer to Figure 3.2 on the stone-processing cluster in Betamcherla to illustrate that often more employment is generated in supporting industries and services than in the manufacturing units themselves. As a result, an exclusive focus on the employment in the manufacturing units is misguided.

The general principle should be to establish units of whatever scale or type necessary to capture as much of the value addition as possible within the state or country. Thus, for example, if Andhra Pradesh wishes to ensure that it adds value to all the cocoons that are exported to neighbouring Karnataka, the state needs to establish a network of cocoon markets and promote reeling units. Note that the cocoon markets are not even manufacturing enterprises, but a different type of unit, in this case providing a service which is essential for the growth of the sub-sector. Promoting such supporting services in order to strengthen the fourth determinant of Porter's diamond (the related and supporting industries in Figure 3.1, p. 57) may be as important as promoting any of the manufacturing units. Employment in the reeling units may be limited. However, the overall impetus that these initiatives would give to the sericulture sub-sector would generate a large number of jobs both in the pre- and post-cocoon stages, which are labour intensive.

Reorienting organizations

Our analysis in chapters 4 to 7 clearly showed that many policies, even well-designed ones, are distorted in practice by the organizations or agencies charged with implementing them. Simply suggesting an alternative approach to policy, or even giving specific policy recommendations, is insufficient, unless we also recommend concrete means of tackling the widespread atrophy in the organizations serving the rural non-farm sector. We attempt this below, for each of the four types of organization in turn: regulatory, promotional, credit and producer organizations.

Regulatory agencies Our analysis of the regulatory framework in Chapter 4 showed that there is a plethora of laws and regulations which affect the rural non-farm sector, often adversely. Many of these have failed to achieve their objectives, are widely flouted by RNFS producers, and are used by regulators for economic rent extraction and by powerful interests to further their own ends.

The first stage in reforming regulatory agencies is thus to review all the laws that apply to rural non-farm sector units and examine to what extent these need to be amended or curtailed in scope. The current complexity of many regulations makes it almost impossible for the appropriate agencies to enforce them, and puts the producers at a disadvantage when interacting with regulatory officials. Regulatory policies therefore need to be made more selective and simple, but thereafter implemented tightly. Moreover, a strategy for reform could clearly not be done for the whole of the RNFS at once; it would have to involve an on-going process, sub-sector by sub-sector, state by state.

With liberalization, progress has in fact already been made in reducing the regulatory burden: much licensing of production and control of raw materials has been abolished; many import duties have been reduced. Some states have introduced new industrial policies, and limited the number of inspections regulatory agencies can make; and some neighbouring states have moved towards more uniform rates of sales tax. Significant regulatory reforms have also been introduced in specific sub-sectors, for example in mining. In other sub-sectors, such as transport, more private-sector involvement has been allowed (GoI, 1995a: 135–54).

Our study provided evidence that the lighter regulatory environment has already assisted economic growth and employment generation in specific sub-sectors. For example, small units manufacturing metal, cement or plastic products have emerged since steel, cement and plastic raw materials were decontrolled. Easing the regulatory environment has also allowed the diamond-processing sub-sector to grow rapidly and become one of the most dynamic constituents in the RNFS. This process of liberalization needs to continue, however, as there are still many regulatory constraints on the growth of rural non-farm employment.

Both in reforming the regulatory environment, and in enforcing it, several principles need to be followed:

(1) It should be mandatory for the regulatory agencies to consult producers or representatives of producer organizations in all matters of regulatory policy and enforcement. At present this is done sporadically, for example when a few traders are nominated to a state sales-tax review committee. In most cases, however, there is an astounding lack of representation. For example, in Uttar Pradesh, the rental that farmers have to pay to cold storages for storing fruit and vegetables is decided by the government. The committee to decide the rental charges is chaired by the Agricultural Production Commissioner, a bureaucrat 'representing' the farmers, and the Director, Horticulture, another bureaucrat 'representing' the cold-storage owners! No farmers or cold-storage owners are on the committee, although they obviously lobby behind the scenes, and appeal to the authorities, including through the newspapers.

(2) The central and state governments need to promote greater transparency of the (simplified) regulatory environment and of its enforcement agencies, and increase awareness of regulations among producers. This can be achieved, for example, by publishing the various laws and rules in local languages and by allowing the sale of such booklets and the related forms by private parties. The names of bidders, licencees, suppliers, and so on should be published in newspapers or commercial gazettes, so that those who have been awarded government contracts or licences, and the prices they have paid, are known. Such disclosure of information would stimulate competition in future rounds and also enhance the accountability of government officials.

    Periodic open forums of various regulatory departments, such as those for excise, sales tax, industries and factories, should be held, to which producers are invited to air their grievances and where officials also get a chance to educate the producers. The official media can also be used for this purpose; an example was the popular Doordarshan programme *Janavani*. In order to ensure that lower-level field officials of regulatory bodies do not harass producers, an annual rating of the behaviour of such officials by the producers under their purview should be made part of their appraisal process.

Such feedback could be sought through the post and those officials who get above a minimum number of negative comments from producers should get an adverse entry in their confidential reports. Such a policy would significantly enhance accountability and go well beyond merely limiting the number of inspections.

(3) The central and state governments need to rethink whether there is a role for specific regulatory policies and agencies. For example, if there is a shortage of particular inputs, the governments should simply encourage private entrepreneurs and industries to establish production, rather than insist on licensing and canalizing. Market mechanisms and countervailing forces are also important for the effective implementation of regulations. Thus the state needs to reduce its control, and place greater emphasis on supporting market mechanisms, strengthening and balancing countervailing interests, guaranteeing quality and protecting rights. Unions are already protected by law (although little labour in the RNFS is unionized). The new consumer courts will contribute significantly to enhancing consumer pressures. In addition, producer associations need to be strengthened.

Promotional agencies Our analysis in Chapter 5 showed that many of the promotional agencies in the non-farm sector are moribund, with poorly motivated staff and little sense of their original purpose. We recommend that a social audit of all the agencies be conducted (on the lines done for the Department of Telecommunications in 1994 and for Unit Trust of India in 1995).[6] Some of the important criteria to be addressed in such an audit could be:

- the extent to which the promotional agency is actually used by its potential client group;
- the level of client satisfaction with the services provided by the agency, which could be measured not only through polling clients but also by studying the extent to which clients are willing to cover the costs of the services provided by the agency;
- the degree of financial self-sufficiency of the agency; this need not be 100 per cent, but should be significant, judged according to the sub-sector, area and client profile; and
- the extent of innovation by the agency in terms of technology, procedures and outreach.

Those bodies which are performing well may continue to operate as government agencies, but with a clear strategy for increasing both the

6. With growing demands for accountability, social auditing of organizations, ranging from major corporations to small community-based organizations, is becoming increasingly common. See the journal of the Institute of Social and Ethical Account-Ability in London (1996).

control of producers over the agencies concerned and the share of their budget which they earn by providing services to producers. Agencies which are performing badly, on the other hand, may need to be closed down, be taken over by producer organizations, or become employee-owned companies. The last two options are particularly attractive if producers or employees are willing to assume control of the agencies concerned. Such a strategy would obviously require a high degree of political will and administrative skill on the part of the central and state governments. It will be especially difficult because the staff of most promotional agencies work under quasi- or full-government service rules, which are strong on employee rights and weak on employee accountability.

The above suggestions involve a long-term perspective. In the meantime, all promotional agencies should be made board-managed entities, with increasing representation of producers on the board until they form a clear majority. It is incredible, for example, that the nationwide network of weavers' service centres is under the 'administrative control' of the distant Development Commissioner for Handlooms in Delhi, but has no accountability whatsoever to a single weaver, small or big, or to any association of weavers in the clusters the centres serve. The same lack of accountability is characteristic of most promotional agencies.

All promotional agencies should also be encouraged to earn more of their keep from the producers they are meant to serve, rather than through budgetary support from the government. Such an idea has already been proposed by the Abid Hussain Committee for the agencies under the Council for Scientific and Industrial Research (CSIR), and is being slowly implemented there.

Only in emergent sub-sectors may there be scope to increase the presence of promotional agencies. Such bodies may need to promote pilot projects to establish the economic and technical feasibility of these sub-sectors, because entrepreneurs are normally not in a position to invest in totally new activities if their viability has not already been proved. This does not mean that the government agencies need to implement every aspect of pilot projects. Such initiatives require a high degree of sophistication, a thoroughly professional approach and a propensity for inter-institutional collaboration. Pilot projects run by government agencies are managed too bureaucratically, while those run by technology institutes and NGOs tend to ignore commercial aspects. Private corporations, on the other hand, may not become involved until they see an assured return, so it is best to establish private–public partnerships for such projects, but place them outside the government promotional structure.

Any approach to establishing new promotional agencies or restructuring existing ones must therefore consider the following essential characteristics:

- Promotional agencies must have a focused strategy of intervention. For this they need to be sub-sector specific in order to have an in-depth understanding of the sub-sector. Their interventions should then address the key constraints facing the sub-sector.

- For focus they need also to be cluster or region specific to identify fully with local conditions and constraints in the sub-sector.
- They must be representative. Elected representatives of producers should form a majority on their boards or councils.
- They must be autonomous and work independently of the government. They therefore need their own staff and staff policies. Above all, they need to be economically viable by generating their own resources to sustain their operations. This will also ensure that the services they supply respond to the demand of producers. The agencies will thus have to market their services and become involved in continuous follow-up and interaction with producers.

Credit agencies Our suggestions for financial agencies are made against the backdrop of the wider on-going reforms of the financial sector in India. The thrust of these reforms has largely been at the macro-level: on reducing statutory liquidity ratios, deregulating interest rates and reducing the proportion of priority-sector credit. There have also been measures to improve the capital base of banks, to tighten provisions for bad debts and to improve the transparency of reporting. While we are in agreement with these overall reforms, their short-term impact, as we suggested in Chapter 6, may be to reduce the flow of credit to the rural non-farm sector, because many of the reforms have made bankers even more cautious. Clearly organizational transformation of the banks and other financial agencies is essential. This has already begun to some extent, with attempts by NABARD to turn around RRBs, and with a measure introduced in 1996 to allow private local area banks which can serve up to three contiguous districts. The latter measure may prove particularly helpful for the RNFS; the sector clearly requires specific measures like these.

Virtually every producer we spoke to complained of the difficulty of getting loans from banks, of cumbersome procedures, of inordinate delays and of under-financing, especially for working capital. In view of this, we suggest that NABARD and SIDBI take the initiative to draw the attention of the operating managements of the banks to the RNFS as a potentially growing and profitable business segment. However, we are not in favour of earmarking priority-sector loans for the RNFS, as such directed credit is counter-productive in the long run. Incentives for the bankers should come from viewing the RNFS as a profitable market.

One of the difficulties in improving credit flows and financial services to the rural non-farm sector is the lack of the necessary technical and business skills among bankers at the branch level, which makes them extra-cautious in lending. Unlike in agriculture, where norms are well established, the

RNFS spans many diverse sub-sectors, including emerging ones about which bankers may have no prior knowledge.

To overcome this obstacle, we suggest that selected branches be designated RNFS branches, on the same lines as some branches of the State Bank of India have long been termed 'agricultural development branches', and branches in 85 districts with a high concentration of small-scale industries were recently designated SSI branches (GoI, 1995a: 137). While the SSI branches will continue the traditional strategy of seeking to support all small-scale units in an area, we recommend that the RNFS branches should have a narrower focus by being located in important clusters of RNFS activity. They can then be manned by officers with specialized training in the locally important sub-sectors. In clusters where exports are important, branches should also have staff trained in foreign-exchange transactions. Where such specialized branches are not feasible, there should be an RNFS cell at the lead bank office in the district, which could provide specialized assistance to all the bank branches in the area.

No such strategies, however, will improve credit flows to the RNFS unless the basic way in which bankers relate to borrowers is changed. Under the current system of directed lending mostly tied to government schemes such as the IRDP, bankers at rural branches enjoy very little discretion about whom to lend to. They take this out on the borrowers by treating each one, whether good or bad, as a potential wilful defaulter. The borrowers, for their part, harassed by the procedural bureaucracy, get their own back by being tardy on repayments, if not defaulting altogether. This only confirms the bankers' prejudices, and the vicious cycle goes on.

What needs to be changed here are the assumptions branch bankers make about borrower behaviour. The perspective of bankers can partly be changed by the incentive structure prevailing in the banks. At present bankers' performance is monitored on deposit mobilization, branch housekeeping and meeting targets under schemes like the IRDP. They get no good marks, and are more likely to get into trouble, for making innovative loans, assuming they have any time for these, given their enormous load of book-keeping and return-filing. To take up the innovations necessary for lending to the RNFS, bankers need to be given incentives, for example in the form of direct commissions on RNFS business, or of out-of-turn promotions. Of course, before such suggestions can be implemented, the banks will have to tackle their recalcitrant unions on issues like greater automation and better information systems, so that the branch officers can use their energies more creatively.

We have recommended that promotional activities be focused on specific sub-sectors and clusters. However, financial services must also be provided to the vast number of dispersed cottage units, which requires taking a new approach to lending, granted that lending to many such units directly is uneconomical. There is thus a need to think of intermediary structures or distribution channels for bank credit. Three such channels seem appropriate:

- self-help groups of small RNFS producers engaged in the same activity in a cluster;
- associations of larger RNFS producers in a sub-sectoral cluster; and
- cash credit to traders providing raw material to or buying finished goods from RNFS producers.

Progressive bankers are increasingly accepting self-help (or savings and credit) groups as the right way to serve tiny clients (see Chapter 6, p. 173). NABARD has encouraged banks to give bulk loans to such groups to on-lend to their members (NGOs have often assisted in linking the banks and the groups). The bank loans are refinanced by NABARD, while group guarantees ensure repayments. Those bankers who have experienced working with self-help groups swear by the model, and this represents a change in their assumptions about borrower behaviour, particularly that of tiny borrowers. However, few banks have used associations of larger producers in sub-sectoral clusters to assist in credit delivery, for example in guaranteeing loans taken by their members.

Using traders to extend credit to RNFS producers is likely to be controversial, particularly as there is a widespread image ('subjective model') that traders exploit producers. We maintain that 'middlemen', while powerful, often provide valuable services to the producers, which are of far higher quality than those provided by most government agencies. We therefore recommend that commercial banks extend cash-credit facilities to traders for stocking raw materials and finished goods. If loans are given to a sufficiently large number of traders in a cluster, the competition among them will ensure that producers have access to credit at lower interest rates. The advantage to the banks is that this approach is easy to operate, and more secure, since they can insist on the pledging of stocks as collateral for the loan.

In summary, therefore, the following changes are recommended for banks and other financial agencies:

- Lending to rural producers must change from being target-oriented and obligatory to being commercially viable. For this to be possible, the remaining interest rate ceilings on loans, which apply only to loans below Rs2 lakhs made by commercial banks, must be removed, as these are precisely the loans that are extended to most small RNFS producers. All loan waivers must also be banned, and a repayment culture enforced by tightening loan-recovery legislation and procedures.
- These strategies must be accompanied by a marked improvement in the quality of service provided by the banks, for example in terms of simplifying procedures, reducing the time for sanctioning and disbursing

loans, and providing greater assistance to the rural producer in complying with any formalities. If this is achieved, producers would gladly pay higher interest rates, and repay their loans.

- An improvement in the quality of service can be achieved only through the systematic training of bank personnel, accompanied by a more effective reward-and-punishment system which would provide the correct incentives for improved performance.
- Bank branches located in specific sub-sectoral clusters should be manned by staff who are trained in the basics of the sub-sectors they are serving. The branch managers in such RNFS branches should have adequate powers to sanction loans, which would minimize delays and improve customer service.

Producer organizations In Chapter 7 we found that there is no effective policy framework for the RNFS to ensure the representation of producers, workers and consumers in policy-making processes or in the public agencies which implement policies. To enhance representation and accountability of state agencies, we have already recommended that:

- it should be mandatory to have representatives of producer organizations on all sectoral and sub-sectoral policy-making bodies;
- promotional agencies should be managed by boards on which producers constitute the majority; and
- banks should use producer associations, as well as self-help groups of small producers, as intermediaries for disbursing credit.

In Chapter 7 we also found that many RNFS producers, especially small and dispersed ones, are unorganized. Many of the existing producer organizations were promoted and controlled by state governments, especially the cooperatives, and are therefore moribund. Many associations of entrepreneurs are not accountable to their members, and limit their services to lobbying public agencies. Some may act as cartels, for example transport unions which establish local monopolies.

There were also many examples of successful groups, for example of industry associations and cooperatives which have been able to provide valuable services to their members and have had a significant impact on their clusters, sub-sectors and local economies. NGOs have also been able to mobilize exploited producers and workers into groups to fight for their interests. These successful examples demonstrate the important role that organized producers and workers can play in the development of sub-sectors. Indeed, as the state reduces its control over economic activities, the role of groups of producers and workers will become increasingly important.

To achieve such a goal, however, changes need to occur both in the external environment that groups of producers and workers face, and in the internal workings of those groups. In the former case, the state needs to accept that associations and other groups should play a more central role in economic development, including areas, such as infrastructure, traditionally reserved for state action. For this the state needs to allocate such groups more responsibilities and more resources. There is no reason, for example, why part of the budget that would be saved by reducing financial support for government agencies cannot be diverted to producer organizations, which could then undertake promotional activities for their sub-sectors. Another way to devolve resources to them is by levying a cess along with excise duty, with the cess being earmarked for the development of the sub-sector through producer organizations. There is already a precedent for this in the cess imposed on the *bidi* industry for the *bidi* workers' welfare fund, although the management of the fund is not in the hands of producers, and that will have to be changed.

Any support given to producer organizations, however, must not lead to external control of them. Indeed, legal changes are required, as the freedom of association needs greater protection. In particular, an overhaul of co-operative law – to reduce radically the role of the state in their functioning – is essential to release the enormous potential the numerous cooperative societies have to serve many small producers and promote local development and self-governance. The first step in this direction has already been taken by Andhra Pradesh which has introduced a new law for mutually-aided cooperatives, and it is high time that other states followed this example.

Removing constraints on the association of producers and workers, not least by reducing the involvement of the state, will also enhance the internal workings of such groups, which will become more accountable to their members. Changes in the external environment are, however, insufficient. Good internal organizational practices, such as accountability, financial transparency, professional management and services, and so on, need to be strengthened in new and existing producer and worker groups. Such intervention is not easy, as it can all too easily result in external control and dependency. It requires a partnership between the groups and the external agencies, which the groups enter voluntarily in search of enhancing their performance. External agents will also continue to be required to mobilize and organize poor and exploited producers through activities ranging from awareness-building to fighting powerful interest groups.

Enabling strong associations, cooperatives, unions and other groups to develop will provide alternative, more responsive and dynamic channels for promoting sub-sectors within the RNFS. These groups could be further supported by government agencies which have been transformed by strong representation of, and control by, producers and workers in the RNFS. Such a strategy would provide an alternative to the past dominance of the state, but also to the policy (all-too prevalent in times of budget constraints and limited vision) of simply dismantling public structures and agencies.

Conclusion

Policy-makers and development activists need to recognize the urgent necessity of promoting a large number of sustainable rural livelihoods in India to meet the national goal of 12 to 13 million new jobs (both rural and urban) a year. The rural non-farm sector has the potential to generate between two-fifths and two-thirds of these new jobs, or between 50 and 80 million new rural jobs over a decade. While this figure appears high on the basis of past trends, the experience of China in shifting as many as 100 million agricultural workers to the rural non-farm sector in less than a decade (see Box 1.1, p. 4), shows that it is not an impossible goal. The RNFS can also generate those jobs with lower capital investment, fewer demands on infrastructure and energy, and fewer imports compared to urban industry. It also has the potential to aid the export drive for the country substantially, and even to become the most dynamic part of the Indian economy, rural or urban.

To achieve this promise, however, requires a national resolve, at both the political and the administrative levels. The RNFS also has to be liberated from the yoke of unnecessary petty regulation, and the promotional agencies meant to serve it have to become more purposeful and accountable to their clients. The banks and other financial agencies need to overcome their risk-aversion and improve their understanding and methods of assisting the sector. Producer organizations need to be encouraged and enabled to play a leading role in the growth of the sector. Given the convergence of all these factors, there are reasons to believe that the rural non-farm sector can be the hope sector of twenty-first century India.

Appendix 1: Study methodology

Objectives

The study of the rural non-farm sector (RNFS) in India was conducted in eight states: Tamil Nadu and Andhra Pradesh in the south, Orissa and Assam in the east, Uttar Pradesh and Punjab in the north, and Rajasthan and Gujarat in the west. The objectives of the study were:

- to review the characteristics of the RNFS, and assess the policies and institutions related to the sector at the macro, meso and micro levels;
- to assess the potential of the RNFS to generate sustainable livelihoods for a large number of people;
- to identify factors which help or constrain the growth of the RNFS; and
- to develop a strategy for policy-related and institutional interventions to promote the healthy growth of the RNFS.

During the study it became clear that the rural non-farm sector has the potential to contribute significantly to higher rural incomes, to a broader skill base, to lower capital intensity and to increased exports. However, the primary focus of the study was, and remained, employment, or rather sustainable livelihoods. This was justified in light of the need to generate 100 million new jobs in India in the last decade of the millennium (see Chapter 1). This focus was not, however, confined to an economic perspective. The policy and institutional context strongly influences the growth of employment in the sector, and a purely economic framework would have been inadequate to understand these dynamics.

The focus on policies, and on the organizations or agencies that implement those policies, was all the more important because one further objective, in addition to the four listed above, informed the process of the study throughout:

- to influence the policy process to support an evolving strategy for promoting the growth of the RNFS.

It was this additional objective that distinguished the study from a pure research project. It also had significant consequences for the process adopted for the inquiry, ranging from the conceptual frameworks to the methodologies used.

The methodology of the study

The study fell into two phases, covering four states in each phase. The methodology used was as follows.

The first stage involved preparatory work in each state. This included a survey of existing literature and an analysis of available secondary data from the Census of India for 1981 and 1991 and the National Sample Surveys of 1977–8, 1983 and 1987–8. Using these data, a preliminary list of RNFS activities or sub-sectors that generate a relatively high share of RNFS employment was drawn up for each state (the high-share sub-sectors). Another list included those sub-sectors in which the growth of employment has been relatively fast (the high-growth sub-sectors). The disaggregated data from the 1981 Census (that for 1991 was not available) even provided information about the districts in which employment in these sub-sectors was concentrated, and this fed into a plan for fieldwork in each state. Finally a series of schedules was developed: one for interviewing producers; and two for each category of organization (regulatory, promotional, credit and producer organizations), one for their regional headquarters and one for their field offices. These schedules were designed to provide qualitative insights, not statistical data.

The second stage involved preliminary fieldwork: to interview some producers in potential sub-sectors to be reviewed in the study; and to contact key informants at the various types of organizations to get their insights on important existing and potential RNFS activities. Contacting key informants was particularly important in searching for emerging sub-sectors: those which currently do not provide many jobs, and which may not yet display a high growth rate of employment either. Thus they could not be identified from secondary data sources. On the basis of this preliminary fieldwork, ten sub-sectors were chosen for more extensive fieldwork, three to four in each category: high-share, high-growth and emergent.

In the first four states covered by the study, the preliminary fieldwork culminated in a one-day regional consultation in each state. The purpose of these consultations was to present the study objectives and methodology to various potential users, and to find out what they considered to be relevant research questions for the RNFS. The idea was to ensure that the research did not leave out any key issues of concern to any of the important actors in the RNFS. At each of these consultations, held in four state capitals, between 50 and 100 individuals participated. About half of these were producer-entrepreneurs and representatives of producers, traders or workers. The other half were government officials from regulatory and promotional agencies, bankers, researchers and representatives of non-governmental organizations (NGOs).

In each state extensive fieldwork was then conducted, covering key actors, such as producer-entrepreneurs, workers and traders, and from all four types of organization, both in the field and at their regional head offices. For each of the chosen sub-sectors, personal interviews were conducted with at least ten producers and five major agencies, and schedules filled based on these interviews.

Drawing on the insights gained from the fieldwork in the chosen sub-sectors in the first four states, as well as from secondary data, an Interim Report was drawn up. This report was presented at a workshop attended by representatives of both the co-sponsors of the study, and also by members of the advisory committee to the study. A number of substantial modifications to the study design were agreed at this workshop. These included (1) drawing up reports for each state, which would incorporate profiles for each sub-sector studied, and case-studies of individual producers and of each type of organization; and (2) conducting dissemination workshops in each state at the end of the study instead of regional consultations at the beginning.

The process in the next four states followed a similar pattern: review of existing literature and data; preliminary fieldwork leading to the selection of sub-sectors; and extensive fieldwork in the chosen sub-sectors. Based on this work, state reports for each state (including the first four) were drawn up. These reports included not only chapters following a similar outline to this book, but also ten sub-sector profiles, the case-studies of producers and organizations, and a statistical appendix.

Drawing on all these reports, and on national-level data, inter-state comparisons, theoretical work and international experiences, a National Report was drawn up.

The study ended with a series of dissemination workshops, one in each state, at which the results of the study in that state were presented. There was also a workshop at the national level. Again, between 50 and 100 individuals participated in each of these. They were predominantly officials of the various agencies (regulatory, promotional and credit) as well as representatives of producer associations, research institutes and NGOs.

The study was formally completed at the beginning of 1995. However, converting the study into a book took over a year, during which one of the authors was based at the Institute of Development Studies, Sussex University in Britain, with funding from the Ford Foundation. The book includes not only more careful analysis of the extensive materials gathered or produced during the course of the study, but also much new material that became available to the authors, or was developed by them, since the study was formally ended.

Research for policy change

Dissemination

From the beginning the purpose of the study was not just to conduct research but also to influence the policy process. Dissemination of the results of the study thus formed a critical component of the study design. Formal dissemination workshops were therefore conducted, at which the results could be presented to policy-makers. The design of these workshops itself reflected the analysis of the study. For example, representatives from all the different organizations that influence the RNFS (regulatory, promotional and credit, as well as from producer associations) were invited. At many workshops the participants broke into small groups, each one focusing on a particular sub-sector. Representatives from the different organizations involved with that sub-sector were members of the respective small group. So the workshop design emphasized the need to take a sub-sectoral approach and to involve all interested parties within that sub-sector.

The regional consultations at the beginning of the fieldwork in the first four states followed a similar design, although more producer-entrepreneurs were invited to these. The consultations proved very productive in providing opportunities for producer-entrepreneurs, officials, bankers and researchers to meet and consult together in an informal environment. Thus they strongly demonstrated the value of, and need for, more such opportunities to be created. However, the consultations were less successful in providing concrete inputs for guiding the actual study, and in the second phase they were replaced by dissemination workshops at the end.

Other opportunities for dissemination were also taken whenever they arose: at conferences, workshops, seminars, committee meetings, and other meetings with officials, at both the state and national levels. For example, the results of the study have been presented in India at NABARD and SIDBI, at both the senior and field levels, the Lal Bahadur Shastri National Academy of Administration in Mussoorie, the Indian Agricultural Science Congress (1995), the National Foundation of India and the M.S.Swaminathan Research Foundation, and internationally at the annual conference (1995) of the Development Studies Association of the UK and Ireland, at various universities in Britain, at the World Bank and to a small-enterprise development programme in Pakistan.

However, dissemination of the study extended beyond formal meetings. It also involved building commitment to the rural non-farm sector among important actors, including the sponsors of the study themselves. Originally the Swiss Agency for Development and Cooperation (SDC) had proposed a study to draw up a strategy paper for SDC alone. The consultants persuaded the agency to see the wider significance of a study on the RNFS and therefore to broaden its perspective; SDC could always draw its own strategy paper from the results of the broader investigation.

SDC had funded activities by NABARD to promote the rural non-farm sector, and so NABARD was involved with the study from the start. But initially this was only by helping with arrangements for fieldwork and for the various workshops. The consultants and SDC sought to enhance NABARD's commitment by persuading NABARD to designate liaison officers, and to second one officer, to the study for a short period. They also invited senior representatives to the workshop at which the Interim Report was presented. It was after this workshop that NABARD agreed to become a formal co-sponsor of the study. They thus funded the work in the four states covered during the second phase of the investigation. A further workshop to present the interim results to senior officials of NABARD, including the Chairman and Managing Director, was organized in Bombay. The Chairman agreed to open the final national dissemination workshop. By this stage considerable ownership of the study within NABARD had been built up. Indeed, NABARD presented its own RNFS strategy, drawn partly from the results of the study, to the Finance Minister shortly thereafter, and produced a promotional document, again partly drawing on the study, called *A Policy Package for Rural Industrialization* (NABARD, 1995).

Even before the study NABARD was the only national agency to have a formal mandate to promote the RNFS in India. In each year until March 1993, however, the RNFS portfolio remained less than 10 per cent of NABARD's total portfolio, with agriculture making up more than 90 per cent. The study therefore sought to enhance the importance of the RNFS within NABARD's own portfolio, and to convince NABARD that it was a sector with considerable potential. NABARD was already moving fast in this direction, and in 1995–6 its refinance for the RNFS (excluding IRDP-ISB loans) for the first time reached 15 per cent of the total for that year. The other national financial agency involved was the Small Industries Development Bank of India, whose representatives were invited to all the workshops, and with whom the consultants had a series of additional meetings.

A similar strategy to generate commitment among important actors was pursued in individual states. Most of the dissemination workshops took place at important research institutes which could continue work in the same area beyond the duration of the study itself. Usually the Chief Secretary, the most senior bureaucrat in the state, was invited to open the workshop; in some cases the invitation was accepted, in others not. The most successful case proved to be in Rajasthan, where the Chief Secretary took a personal interest in the sector. He later arranged for senior bureaucrats from all the relevant state departments, assisted by the co-ordinator of the study, to draw up a state policy for the RNFS. As a result, Rajasthan is the first state in India to have not only a state policy for the RNFS, focusing on three sub-sectors (leather, wool and minor minerals), but also a state directorate for the RNFS.

Finally, SDC provided a grant for printing additional copies of each report to distribute on request. The agency also published the executive summary of the National Report as a document, illustrated with many figures and photos, entitled *The Rural Micro- and Small-Enterprise Sector in India* (SDC, 1996). From its headquarters in Switzerland SDC is also distributing copies of the various reports (including on disk) to other donors and development agencies.

The study has therefore been used extensively by the co-sponsors, NABARD and SDC, and by Action Aid, India and the Asian Development Bank in drawing up their respective strategies for promoting livelihoods or micro-enterprises in India. In addition to the presentations mentioned above, copies have gone to multilateral and bilateral donors, to development or micro-finance institutions in Bangladesh, South-east Asia and Latin America, and to numerous NGOs and research institutes in the north.

While the study is now over, it would be wrong to assume that the need for dissemination is also over. The investigation has enhanced awareness of the RNFS significantly among policy-makers in India. However, only one state (Rajasthan) and one national agency (NABARD) have a policy for the RNFS, while the central government has a separate Department of Agro-processing, Rural and Small-scale Industries, under the Ministry of Industry. Opportunities for further dissemination continue to be pursued, including through this book. For example, in 1996 individuals involved in the study presented on the RNFS to government officials and others in Andhra Pradesh and Sikkim, to an NGO meeting in Bangalore, and conducted an ODA-funded study on non-land based activities in Karnataka.

Seeking to influence the policy process not only led to an extensive dissemination strategy, but also had an impact on the study design in many other ways.

Organizational focus

Past experience of policy implementation has shown that well-formulated policies often get distorted by the time they reach the ground. Policies are implemented through organizations. Very often these bodies have their own goals or are asked to implement conflicting policies. In such cases they implement these policies selectively, or even reinterpret them to suit their own needs. Hence, to analyse policies in a live context, it is necessary to look at organizations or agencies that have been given the task of implementation. Only with this understanding can an appropriate strategy for promoting new policies be pursued.

Extensive, not intensive

Policy-makers are influenced by the perceptions and images they hold. In China rural enterprises are considered to have enormous potential for the industrial modernization of the state; in India many policy-makers consider them village industries in a largely traditional and unproductive sector fit only for protection (to preserve jobs) or poverty alleviation. To alter such views an extensive approach to the study was essential. It drew together analysis of secondary data, data collected from the field and information from representatives of the various agencies, into case-studies, sub-sectoral profiles and reports. Throughout, an attempt was made to give the producers' point of view due attention, and not just that of officials and researchers. Thus the entrepreneur case-studies, chosen from the producers' interviews, gave a human touch and an intuitive feel for the field-level reality in the sector. The case-studies of organizations provided insights into the working of agencies in the RNFS and their role in executing policies for the sector. These case-studies were exploratory in nature; they served the purpose of validating the hypothesis regarding distortions that creep in during policy implementation. Finally, for the national report, lessons from other countries were also reviewed, focusing on those countries that have been more successful in promoting the RNFS.

From a research perspective, the very different sources of information, ranging from economic data to producer and organizational case-studies, were not always compatible, and sometimes even contradicted each other. Wherever possible, attempts were made to resolve these differences, but this was not always feasible. Sometimes it was not even desirable, as the different sources provided different perspectives on the same reality. Hence they allowed the study to address, and sometimes even change, the perceptions of a very diverse set of actors within the sector.

Flexibility over a long period

The study lasted formally for three years, and this enabled the consultants to pursue a strategy for influencing the policy process over a sufficiently long period. Flexibility in adapting the study design and even the terms of reference to the evolving situation was equally important. The outline of the methodology given above appears to suggest a carefully planned process. The reality was often very different. New issues, new approaches, new frameworks were constantly evolving. These in turn influenced the study design. Regional consultations were replaced by dissemination workshops; case-studies of producers and organizations were added; state reports were drawn up; new members were co-opted on to the advisory committee and even into the group of consultants conducting the study; a second sponsor for the study was brought on board; a more detailed examination of international experiences was undertaken; and so on. For this the first sponsor (SDC) had to be adequately flexible, as the study not only changed direction but also grew and grew. By the end SDC had provided funding under three contracts, with a fourth coming from NABARD, and the costs of the study had escalated well beyond what anyone had at first imagined.

Study Group on the RNFS

To conduct the study a formal but temporary Study Group was established in April 1992. At its peak the group comprised eight consultants as national or state coordinators, five research associates, and three support staff. One NABARD officer also joined the group for a while, as well as one retired NABARD officer. Being outside the existing organizational structures, the group had the necessary flexibility to explore the RNFS, including its organizational features. But it was designed as a temporary vehicle for conducting the study, providing the necessary formality for influencing the policy process, but not requiring a full and permanent organizational structure. One drawback of such a temporary organization was that its managerial and administrative capabilities were limited.

There were other reasons for establishing this temporary structure. On the one hand there was no existing body ideally suited to conduct such a comprehensive study in a relatively new policy area; on the other hand, at the beginning of the study it was not clear whether a permanent body specializing in the RNFS was appropriate. Even if it were appropriate, it was not clear what type of organization it should be, granted that the study also revealed the widespread atrophy of promotional agencies in rural India. As it turned out, over three years the Study Group was able to develop considerable expertise in the RNFS which has moved on to other organizations. For example, the group provided two members of the now strengthened SDC (Delhi) team for enterprise development; one of these is also an adviser to SIDBI. The study coordinator, along with one state coordinator and three of the research associates, has established a new rural financial institution; the study coordinator is also an adviser on rural credit and the RNFS to the Reserve Bank of India and to NABARD. One of the associate coordinators has joined a policy research institute in Britain and continues to work on issues of development finance both in Britain and India. Another member of the former Study Group is working to strengthen associations of artisans, one has returned to a leading NGO promoting rural non-farm livelihoods and others continue to work in similar areas as consultants. The Study Group itself was formally dissolved on 31 March 1995 with a presentation on that day to SDC in Berne.

Appendix 2: Additional data

Table 1: The extent of secondary RNFS employment among agricultural households (NSS, 1987–8)

	Male (%)	Female (%)	Total (%)
(1) Percentage of persons engaged in the RNFS according to their usual activity (principal and subsidiary):			
(a) persons in agricultural occupation households	5.8	4.8	5.5
(b) persons in agricultural labour households	6.9	7.5	7.3
(2) Percentage of persons classified as not in the labour force who are engaged in the RNFS as a subsidiary gainful activity	13.0	8.7	8.8
(3) Percentage of person-days (by current daily activity) agricultural households allocate to RNFS activities:			
(a) self-employed households in agricultural occupation	8.5	6.4	7.9
(b) agricultural labour households	11.8	11.0	11.5
(4) Percentage of person-days (by current daily activity) agricultural households allocate to RNFS activities:			
(a) households in agricultural production	8.7	7.6	8.3
(b) households in livestock rearing	7.7	7.5	7.6
(c) all households in the agricultural sector	8.8	8.0	8.6

Note: For definitions, see Box 2.1, p. 26.
Source: GoI (1990): (1) Table 62(R); (2) Table 66; (3) Table 48(R); (4) Table 50.

Table 2: Distribution of workers in agricultural households by industrial category (%) (NSS, 1987–8)

Industrial category	*Male %*	*Female %*	*Total %*
Agriculture	95.0	94.2	94.7
Mining and quarrying	0.1	0.1	0.1
Manufacturing (household)	0.9	2.0	1.3
Manufacturing (non-household)	0.3	0.3	0.3
Construction	0.7	1.7	1.0
Trade and commerce	1.0	0.6	0.9
Transport	0.4	0.0	0.3
Business and financial services	0.1	0.0	0.1
Social and personal services	1.3	1.1	1.2
Total	100.0	100.0	100.0

Source: GoI, 1990: Table 59.

Table 3: High employment-share sub-sectors in the RNFS (NSS, 1987–8)

NIC Code	*Description*	*Total rural workers (principal status) per 1000*
50	Construction	35
65	Retail trade in food, beverages and tobacco	26
96	Personal services	18
90	Public administration and defence	16
70	Land transport	13
27	Wood, wood products, furniture and fixtures	12
26	Textile products	11
92	Educational services	11
22	Beverages, tobacco and tobacco products	10
23	Cotton textiles	10
32	Non-metallic mineral products	9
20-21	Food products	8
19	Mining (excluding coal, oil, gas and metal ore)	5
69	Restaurants and hotels	5
97	Repairs	3
67	Retail trade in fuel, utilities and durables	3
93	Medical and health services	3

Source: GoI, 1990: Table 57.

Table 4: Rural main workers in public-sector services (Census 1981)

NIC code	Industrial category	Rural main workers (RMWs)		
		Males	Females	Total
4	Electricity, gas and water	422 706	5 942	428 648
700	Railway transport	434 941	4 562	439 503
707	Pipeline transport	199	5	204
710	Sea transport	13 640	87	13 727
712	Dock, port maintenance, etc.	19 136	293	19 429
72	Air transport	6 388	162	6 550
75	Communications	305 867	8 303	314 170
800	Banking	150 660	5 981	156 641
801	Credit institutions (non-banking)	40 302	1 487	41 789
81	Insurance	13 716	655	14 371
90	Public administration and defence	2 087 519	58 243	2 145 762
91	Sanitary services	57 386	26 140	83 526
92	Education services	2 014 815	395 740	2 410 555
93	Health and medical services	487 043	122 597	609 640
954	Radio and television	2 223	69	2 292
956	Libraries and museums	7 606	457	8 063
	Total public-sector services	6 064 147	630 723	6 694 870
10–99	Total RMWs in RNFS	25 055 761	4 769 293	29 825 054
	Public-sector service employment as share of RNFS employment (%)	24.2	13.2	22.4

Source: GoI, 1987a:Table B12

Table 5: Growth of RNFS employment: Census and NSS compared

Category	Activity	Census 1981–91		NSS 1977–8 to1987–8	
		Annual growth rate (%)	New jobs (millions)	Annual growth rate (%)	New jobs (millions)
IV	Mining and quarrying	2.5	0.2	4.4	0.5
V	Manufacturing	1.0	1.2	3.0	4.4
VI	Construction	2.3	0.4	11.2	5.2
VII	Trade and commerce	3.7	2.2	3.5	2.8
VIII	Transport and communications	1.3	0.3	6.0	1.5
IX	Other services	4.5	4.5	2.6	2.8
IV–IX	Total RNFS	2.8	8.9	–	17.3

Compiled from GoI, 1981, 1987a, 1990 and 1992b.

Table 6: Rural unemployment rates (%) (NSS, 1987–8)

	Usual status	*Current weekly status*	*Current daily status*
Males	2.8	4.2	4.6
Females	3.5	4.4	6.7

Source: GoI, 1990, Statements 40 and 41.

Table 7: Rural (principal-status) workers by industrial category and gender (NSS, 1987–8)

Industrial category	*Males (millions)*	*Share of total (%)*	*Females (millions)*	*Share of total (%)*	*Total (millions)*	*Share of total (%)*
Agriculture	113.7	74.0	57.8	82.6	171.6	76.7
Mining and quarrying	1.1	0.7	0.4	0.5	1.4	0.6
Manufacturing	11.7	7.6	5.3	7.5	17.0	7.6
Electricity, gas and water	0.5	0.3	0.0	0.0	0.5	0.2
Construction	5.7	3.7	2.2	3.2	7.9	3.5
Trade and commerce	8.0	5.2	1.7	2.4	9.7	4.3
Transport and communications	3.2	2.1	0.0	0.1	3.3	1.5
Other services	9.8	6.4	2.6	3.7	12.4	5.6
Total workers (principal)	153.7	100.0	70.0	100.0	223.8	100.0
RNFS workers	40.0	26.0	12.2	17.4	52.2	23.3

Source: GoI, 1990: Statements 22 and 34.

Table 8: Rural main workers (RMWs) by industrial category and gender (Census, 1991)

Code	*Industrial category*	*Males*	*Share of RMWs (%)*	*Females*	*Share of RMWs (%)*
I	Cultivators	85 771 315	51.6	21 797 148	38.9
II	Agricultural labourers	43 187 381	26.0	27 150 959	48.5
III	Activities allied to agriculture	3 744 580	2.3	1 196 418	2.1
IV	Mining	881 084	0.5	158 185	0.3
Va	Manufacturing (household)	3 182 846	1.9	1 627 228	2.9
Vb	Manufacturing (non-household)	6 614 155	4.0	1 289 322	2.3
VI	Construction	2 169 643	1.3	148 754	0.3
VII	Trade and commerce	6 694 437	4.0	606 955	1.1
VIII	Transport	2 701 053	1.6	46 151	0.0
IX	Other services	11 347 114	6.8	1 974 851	3.5
I to IX	Total rural main workers	166 293 608	100.0	55 995 971	100.0
IV to IX	Total RNFS workers	33 590 332	20.2	5 851 446	10.4

Note: Figures exclude Jammu and Kashmir.
Source: GoI, 1992b: Table 4.

Table 9: Child labour in the rural sector (Census 1981)

Industrial category	*Proportion of total male workers below the age of 15 (%)*	*Proportion of total female workers below the age of 15 (%)*	*Proportion of total male workers aged 15 to 19 (%)*	*Proportion of total female workers aged 15 to 19 (%)*
Farm sector	5.5	8.9	11.3	12.6
Non-farm sector	2.3	8.1	7.5	14.4
Mining	1.7	7.5	5.4	13.8
Household manufacturing	4.5	10.3	10.5	15.7
Non-household manufacturing	3.3	11.2	10.8	19.6
Construction	1.9	10.3	8.5	17.6
Trade and commerce	1.9	3.1	7.8	5.6
Transport	0.5	3.7	4.7	11.4
Other services	1.4	4.8	3.9	11.8

Source: GoI, 1987a: Table B3.

Table 10: Rural main workers by education and gender (Census 1981)

Educational level	*Total Farm Sector (I to III)*		Total RNFS (IV to XI)	
	males (%)	*females (%)*	*males (%)*	*females (%)*
Illiterate	63.6	90.6	30.8	69.4
Literate (without level)	11.4	3.7	12.6	6.3
Primary	13.8	4.3	19.9	8.8
Middle	6.8	1.2	13.5	4.5
Matriculation or secondary	3.2	0.3	13.1	5.4
Higher Secondary, intermediate or pre-university course	0.7	0.0	3.8	1.1
Non-technical diploma (non-degree)	0.0	0.0	0.2	0.3
Technical diploma (non-degree)	0.0	0.0	1.3	2.0
Graduate and above	0.3	0.0	4.7	2.2
Total	100.0	100.0	100.0	100.0

Source: GoI, 1987a: Table B4.

Table 11: Rural principal-status workers by education and gender (%) (NSS, 1987–8)

Educational level	*Males*		*Females*		*Total*	
	Agriculture	*RNFS*	*Agriculture*	*RNFS*	*Agriculture*	*RNFS*
Not literate	55.5	34.1	87.4	72.3	66.1	42.6
Literate and up to primary	28.8	33.2	9.9	16.2	22.5	29.4
Middle	9.6	14.4	1.9	4.9	7.1	12.3
Secondary	5.2	13.9	0.6	5.2	3.7	11.9
Graduate and above	0.8	4.5	0.1	0.0	0.6	3.8
Not recorded	–	–	0.1	–	–	–

Source: GoI, 1990: Table 54.1.

Table 12: Summary data from various rural-enterprise surveys

Type of enterprise	*Date of survey and source*	*Number of units*	*Workers per unit*	*Output per unit (Rs)*	*GVA per unit (Rs)*	*GVA per worker (Rs)*
Manufacturing: Rural SSIs	1988 (GoI, 1992c)	245 573	5.0	469 202	–	30 140
Manufacturing: DMEs	1984-5 (GoI, nd:d)	179 202	11.1	112 519	37 111	3 343
Manufacturing: NDEs and OAEs	1984-5 (GoI, 1989a)	14 463 725	1.7	–	3 836	2 286
Trading: NDEs and OAEs	1980 (GoI, nd:b)	3 558 328	1.5	–	2 300	1 533
Hotels and restaurants: DEs, NDEs and OAEs	1983-4 (GoI, nd:c)	543 725	2.3	–	8 105	2 974
Mechanized transport: DEs, NDEs and OAEs	1988-9 (GoI, nd:f)	36 999	3.1	–	33 257	6 533
Services: OAEs	1980 (GoI, nd:a)	1 942 750	–	–	2 988	1 957

Source: see col. 2.

Table 13: Data from surveys of service enterprises

Survey of	*Date of survey (source)*	*No. OAEs*	*No. NDEs*	*No. DEs*	*Total no. of units*	*Employ-ment*	*Employ-ment per unit*
Trade enterprises	1980 (GoI, nd:b)	3 388 963	169 365	–	3 558 328	5 162 707	1.5
Directory trade establishments	1986 (GoI, nd:e)	–	–	24 951	24 951	95 222	3.8
Hotels and restaurants	1983-4 (GoI, nd:c)	433 820	94 530	15 370	543 720	1 256 600	2.3
Mechanized transport	1988-9 (GoI, nd:f)	10 864	23 129	3 006	36 999	115 619	3.1
Services incidental to transport	1989 (GoI, nd:g)	3 742	1 270	206	5 218	11 533	2.2
Service sector OAEs	1980 (GoI, nd:a)	1 942 750	–	–	1 942 750	–	–

Source: see col. 2.

Table 14: Important sub-sectors among small-scale industries (1988)

NIC code	*Description*	*Total employ-ment (%)*	*Fixed investment per unit in Rs000s*	*Employ-ees per Rs lakh invested*	*NVA to fixed investment*	*Share of export to production (%)*
32	Non-metallic mineral products	22.7	207	8	0.8	2.6
20-21	Food products	21.1	139	4	0.9	5.7
27	Wood products	8.8	79	6	1.3	1.9
31	Chemicals and chemical products	8.7	340	4	1.8	3.8
34	Metal products and parts	7.2	134	5	1.3	3.6
97	Repairs	5.3	52	5	0.2	2.7
30	Rubber and plastic products	4.0	280	2	0.8	1.4
26	Textile products	3.8	88	9	1.6	32.9
33	Basic metal industries	3.3	429	3	1.3	2.0
35	Machinery, machine tools and parts	2.9	198	3	0.9	2.6
28	Paper and paper products	2.5	193	3	0.8	1.3
29	Leather and leather products	2.1	61	6	2.5	43.9
	Total or average	92.4	160	4	1.1	5.8

Source: Second All-India Census of Small-scale Industrial Units (GoI, 1992c: T-35 to T-37).

Appendix 3: Overview of the rural non-farm sector in eight states

The data for each state are taken from the 1981 and 1991 Census (GoI, 1987a and 1992b); the NSS for 1977-8 and 1987–8 (GoI, 1981 and 1990), as well as the relevant state-level reports, including for 1983; the Economic Census for 1990 (GoI, 1991d and 1995b); the Directory Manufacturing Establishments Survey and the Unorganized Manufacturing Survey, both of 1984–5 (GoI, nd:d and 1989a); the Second Census of SSIs of 1988 (GoI, 1992c); and Drèze and Sen (1995, Statistical Appendix). Other data and information draw on the individual state reports of the Study Group on the Rural Non-Farm Sector (1993–4).

Andhra Pradesh

The non-farm sector in Andhra Pradesh provides 17.1 per cent of rural employment compared to the national average of 17.7 per cent (1991), and has been growing more slowly since 1981 (at 2.2 per cent a year compared to 2.8 per cent nationally). The rural economy in the state is thus still heavily reliant on the primary sector. However, within agriculture there are disturbing employment trends: the proportion of cultivators has declined significantly while that of agricultural labourers has increased sharply. The latter now make up almost half of the rural labour force (1991). Of the eight states, Andhra Pradesh also has the highest work-participation rates, including among women, and a high incidence of child labour, especially among girls.

One might therefore expect diversification into the NFS as a result of agricultural distress, which is supported by a number of indicators: retail trade, personal and miscellaneous services (which may be acting as residual activities for absorbing excess labour) make up almost a quarter of all RNFS employment (1981), and personal services is the fastest growing sub-sector within RNFS employment (1983–8). The secondary sector in Andhra Pradesh does employ more rural workers than the national average (1991), and the state has a large number of rural enterprises of all sizes for its population. However, over half of rural-manufacturing employment is still within the (declining) household sector, and many of the rural enterprises are small and seasonal, and do not have access to power or even to premises. They are among the smallest, and the least productive, rural enterprises in the eight states.

With poor infrastructure, and poor educational levels, the prospects for the dynamic growth of non-farm employment in Andhra Pradesh are not good. The more prosperous coastal districts are, however, faring better than the interior dry districts, and while most of the growth in rural manufacturing is in traditional activities, a few modern manufacturing sub-sectors are beginning to emerge, such as chemicals, paper and machinery. However, the best future prospects lie with the processing of primary raw materials, and some of the promising emergent sub-sectors include sericulture and silk textiles, prawn rearing and processing, and granite processing.

Assam

Assam is the least urbanized of the eight states and has the lowest work-participation rates. In particular, those for women are far below national averages, although female rates of unemployment are by far the highest in the eight states. The Assamese economy is based predominantly on the primary sector, including plantations, and has a proportion of cultivators in rural employment well above the national average, while the proportion of agricultural labourers is relatively small (1991).

Nevertheless, RNFS employment is quite extensive (18.6 per cent of rural main workers in 1991 compared to 17.7 per cent nationally). The manufacturing sector is very small, and the RNFS depends predominantly on the large tertiary sector (second only to Punjab among the eight states), which in turn depends heavily on the public sector and on less remunerative services. The large employment sectors are retail trade, public administration, education, miscellaneous, personal and medical services, which together make up two-thirds of all RNFS employment (1988). Between 1977–78 and 1987–88 retail trade, and personal and miscellaneous services contributed 29 per cent of new RNFS jobs, and public administration, education and health 19 per cent. On the other hand, land transport grew fast over the same period (at 10.4 per cent a year), contributing 10 per cent of new jobs in the sector. Granted the geography of Assam, transport has considerable potential for further employment growth.

According to the Census most jobs in the small rural-manufacturing sector are outside of the household, although this underestimates the extent of household manufacturing, especially on handlooms, undertaken as a supplementary occupation. Manufacturing is almost entirely confined to traditional products, like cotton textiles, textile, wood and tobacco products. Nevertheless, the manufacturing sector experienced strong annual employment growth at 8 per cent between 1977-8 and 1987–8, and generated 24 per cent of the new jobs in the RNFS.

Assam has very few enterprises of whatever size, and almost 30 per cent of them are in the public sector. Thus the enterprises are relatively large in terms of employment, capital and output; they are also relatively productive. Registered SSIs in the state fare less well, however, with an average capacity utilization of only 19 per cent. This problem is aggravated by the poor supply of power in the state.

Gujarat

Gujarat has experienced a significant transformation of its rural economy. The state stands out in particular because of its highly developed manufacturing sector. In 1991 there were five times as many rural jobs in manufacturing outside the household than in the household sector. The former accounted for over a third of all RNFS jobs (far more than in the other states), and grew at a yearly rate of 5.7 per cent compared to 2.6 per cent nationally (1981–91). Thus the secondary sector in Gujarat provided work to almost as many rural workers as the tertiary sector, which is unusual not only for India but also internationally. Within the relatively small tertiary sector more productive activities like transport are prominent (1991), and none of the residual categories, such as personal and miscellaneous services, have experienced high growth rates in employment (1978–88). Tertiary employment is also less dependent on the public sector (1981).

The strong growth of non-farm employment in 1981–91 (3.5 per cent a year compared to 2.8 per cent nationally) seems not to have depended on agricultural growth: for example, food grain production per capita in Gujarat was well below the national average, but the state averages are lowered by the backward regions in the west of the state. The corridor districts on the other hand are highly developed agriculturally, and enjoy some of the best infrastructure, and it is here that non-farm employment is most prominent.

Because of the growing RNFS the proportion of agricultural labourers in rural employment hardly rose in 1981–91, and Gujarat enjoys low or average rates of unemployment. At the same time many women are entering the labour force, although perhaps most often as casual labourers to replace men who have found more productive employment elsewhere.

In spite of a strong RNFS, Gujarat does not have a large number of rural enterprises for its rural population, although these enterprises tend to be larger, and among the most productive compared to other states. The small number of such enterprises may arise because Gujarat is the most urbanized among the eight states. Many enterprises are located in rural towns, and a large number of workers, while continuing to reside in rural areas, commute or migrate for work.

Orissa

Along with Assam and Rajasthan, Orissa is very much a primary economy: less urbanized, with food-grain production per capita somewhat above the national average, a small non-farm sector, and manufacturing confined predominantly to traditional household activities (such as wood, cotton textiles and pottery). In fact Orissa is the only state among the eight in which employment in household manufacturing is still growing (1981–91). Orissa thus has a large number of tiny enterprises, many of them seasonal, run without power and even premises. The state has few larger enterprises, whether DMEs, SSIs or factories, and these are more capital intensive than the national averages, and less productive. Orissa also has relatively high unemployment rates, very poor infrastructure, low educational levels, and the lowest net state domestic product per capita among the eight states we studied. There may also be signs of distress diversification, with many new jobs being created in retail trade, and those in miscellaneous services also growing fast. On the other hand, and perhaps because the disruptive processes of rural economic change have not proceeded very far, many employment indicators for Orissa are not unduly negative, but close to national averages. This applies to work-participation rates, the proportion of cultivators and agricultural labourers among rural workers, and even unemployment rates, as well as to the growth of RNFS employment overall.

However, non-farm-sector employment is bolstered by a large public sector, which employs over a fifth of RNFS workers, if we include educational and medical services. Education in particular employs a greater proportion of RNFS workers than in any of the other states, and public administration has continued to generate a large number of new jobs (1983–8). With its underdeveloped secondary sector, and with many service jobs in less productive sub-sectors such as retail trade, personal and miscellaneous services, or in the public sector, Orissa has a backward rural economy which is highly dependent on government resources. The most promising avenues for the development of a dynamic non-farm sector are in primary processing, either of agricultural products (including less traditional crops such as flowers and spices), of fish and of minor minerals. The handicraft sector could also be developed further, including within the context of growing rural tourism.

Punjab

Punjab is the most agriculturally advanced of the eight states, and also has the highest share of NFS employment in the rural sector. The RNFS now accounts for over a quarter of all rural employment, even according to the conservative estimates of the (1991) Census, and RNFS employment has been growing faster than the national average (3.2 per cent a year compared to 2.8 per cent). Agricultural development is clearly an important factor in the growth of the RNFS, and good infrastructure (almost all villages are connected by all-weather roads and over three-quarters of rural households have electricity) and reasonable educational facilities have played their part. Educational attainments are in fact particularly good (within the Indian context) for women, although very few women participate in the labour force, as a result of a conservative culture combined with adequate household wealth.

Within the RNFS, services are particularly prominent and account for two-thirds of all RNFS employment (compared to only 59 per cent nationally in 1991). They are also growing fast. And these are services which provide higher-quality employment, for example in transport, and in professional services such as education, health and real estate and legal services, while retail trading and personal services are less prominent. Public administration in the state is also a significant rural employer.

The proportion of rural workers engaged in manufacturing is high as well, although not as high as in the more industrialized states of Gujarat and Tamil Nadu, and the proportion changed little in 1981–91 because of the sharp decline in household manufacturing. It is perhaps surprising that the number of rural enterprises per thousand population in Punjab is well below the national average, although the state has the largest number of rural enterprises registered as SSIs and most of them operate all year round, and enjoy access to power and premises. However, the relatively small number of rural enterprises does not reflect the growth of enterprises in Punjab's many rural towns (which are often classified as urban).

Rajasthan

Rajasthan's economy is still widely dependent on the primary sector. Among the eight states, cultivators in Rajasthan make up the largest proportion of rural main workers, and their number grew fastest in 1981–91. The number of agricultural labourers grew even faster (at 6.1 per cent a year), although in 1991 they still comprised a smaller proportion of rural workers than in the other states. Employment in activities allied to agriculture (particularly animal husbandry) has, however, declined sharply. The rural non-farm sector itself is not highly developed. Among the eight states, Rajasthan has the smallest proportion of workers in the secondary sector (except for Assam), and the smallest in the tertiary sector. It is not surprising, therefore, that in comparison with other states rural enterprises in the state are few in number, small and not very productive.

The non-farm sector has, however, been growing slightly faster than the national average. Unfortunately rural jobs in manufacturing declined in 1981–91, because the number of new jobs in manufacturing outside the household did not compensate for the jobs lost in household manufacturing (although in 1991 over 40 per cent of manufacturing jobs were still in the household sector). The largest number of new jobs were generated in mining, construction and transport, as well as in some traditional manufacturing activities such as pottery, wool and metal work (1983–8). The public sector, including public administration, education and increasingly health, is also a significant employer of rural workers. However, both mining and construction involve extensive casual labour in poor working conditions, and the high growth in these sub-sectors, as well as among agricultural labourers, and in retail trade and miscellaneous services, may point to some distress diversification.

Future prospects for the non-farm sector are not very promising, with limits to the potential growth of the primary sector, high unemployment (among men, less so among women), poor infrastructure, and poor educational levels (with those for women by far the worst among the eight states). Nevertheless, there is some promise, for example with new investments in irrigation, the spread of oilseed production and processing, as well as in activities such as gems and rural tourism.

Tamil Nadu

Over a fifth of rural main workers in Tamil Nadu are employed in the non-farm sector (1991). While the proportion of rural workers in services is close to the national average, the secondary sector is much larger (9.5 compared to 6.8 per cent). The state has a strong manufacturing base employing workers outside the household, while retaining a large household manufacturing sector as well. Many of the activities are traditional (such as cotton textiles, wood and food products), but some modern manufacturing has also been growing fast: the growth of powerlooms and chemicals is generating a large number of new jobs, followed by paper and rubber. The strong manufacturing sector is also reflected in substantial exports from the state, especially of textiles and textile products, and in the large number of rural enterprises, especially of the somewhat larger Directory Manufacturing Enterprises and SSIs. However, the secondary sector has not been growing very fast: in terms of employment it grew only just above the national average (1981–91), and in terms of output well below the national average (1985–9).

Output from the primary sector declined over the same period, which led to the stagnation of employment among cultivators (1981–91) and the growth in the number of agricultural labourers, who now make up almost 45 per cent of the rural workforce (1991). In fact the state shows many signs of agricultural distress: some of the highest rural unemployment rates in India (1987–8), a high degree of casualization of labour (1987–8), and the prominence of less productive services, such as retail trade, personal services, and restaurants and hotels (1981). These pressures are enhanced by a very high population density and high work-participation rates, including among women.

To some extent, therefore, the significance of the RNFS in Tamil Nadu reflects past strengths, as one of the earliest states to industrialize, rather than current dynamism, and the decline of the primary sector is of particular concern; on the other hand the state has good infrastructure (although not as good as in Punjab and Gujarat), enjoys the best educational achievements among the eight states, and can also build further on its manufacturing sector, including for export.

Uttar Pradesh

The RNFS in Uttar Pradesh is more prominent in the west of the state, including in the Green Revolution districts, and in the hills to the north. It is less developed in the central region, and least of all in the east. However, the averages across these regions place UP close to Rajasthan, with very small secondary and tertiary sectors making up the RNFS. Thus, along with Rajasthan, UP has the largest number of rural workers engaged in the primary sector (1991). It also has low work-participation rates, especially among women, and low unemployment rates. A number of indicators, however, point to features of rural distress. While cultivators still make up a large proportion of rural workers, this number declined sharply in 1981–91 while that of agricultural labourers grew significantly. Moreover, almost a quarter of RNFS employment is in retail trade, personal and miscellaneous services (1981), and the two broad industrial categories, trading and other services, witnessed very fast growth rates, accounting for three-quarters of all new jobs in the RNFS (1981–91). Prominent in other services was the public sector: public administration and education employed over 18 per cent of RNFS workers (1981) and added 200 000 new rural jobs between 1983 and 1988.

Within manufacturing employment, household activities are still prominent, although their sharp decline in 1981–91 meant that manufacturing employment overall grew at less than 1 per cent a year. While traditional products like pottery, wool and silk continue to generate many new rural jobs, a few modern products like paper, electrical equipment and metals are beginning to emerge. Wool products, especially carpets, contribute significantly to exports.

With a small non-farm sector, there are few rural enterprises for UP's population size (according to the Economic Census, 1991, although not the NSS, 1985). Unfortunately the state has very poor infrastructure (for example, only 17.5 per cent of rural households had electricity in 1991), and educational levels are also low. Granted the continuing prominence of the primary sector, the processing of various primary products, such as fruit and vegetables, herbs and spices, holds the most promise for continued growth. Some services, for example for rural tourism, also have potential.

Bibliography

Acharya, S. (1990), *The Maharashtra Employment Guarantee Scheme: A Study of Labour Market Intervention*, ILO-ARTEP, Delhi

Adams, R. (1994), 'Non-farm income and inequality in rural Pakistan: a decomposition analysis', *Journal of Development Studies* 31(1): 110–33

Ahmad, G. and F. Chowdhury (eds) (1985), *Diversification of the Rural Economy*, Association of Development Research and Training Institutes of Asia and the Pacific, Kuala Lumpur

Ahmad, Q.K. and F.A. Chowdhury (1987), *Rural Industrialisation in Bangladesh: A Synthesis based on Studies on Rural Industrial Development in selected Upazilas*, Bangladesh Institute of Development Studies, Dhaka

Alexander, P., P. Boomgaard and B. White (eds) (1991), *In the Shadow of Agriculture: Non-farm Activities in the Javanese Economy, Past and Present*, Royal Tropical Institute, Amsterdam

All-India Motor Transport Congress (1992), Editorial in *Motor Transport* for 1992

Anderson. D. and M. Leiserson (1980), 'Rural non-farm employment in developing countries', *Economic Development and Cultural Change* 28(2): 227–48

Axelrod, R. (1984), *The Evolution of Cooperation*, Basic Books, New York

Balisacan, A. (1993), 'Agricultural growth, landlessness, off-farm employment, and rural poverty in the Philippines', *Economic Development and Cultural Change* 41(3): 533–62

Bar-el, Raphael (ed.) (1987), *Rural Industrialization in Israel*, Westview, Boulder and London

Basant, R. (1993) 'Diversification of economic activities in rural Gujarat: key results of a primary survey', in Chadha (1993a)

Basant, R., B.L. Kumar and R. Parthasarthy (eds) (1994), *Non-Agricultural Employment in Rural Gujarat: Patterns and Trends*, Report of an IDBI sponsored project, Gujarat Institute of Development Research, Ahmedabad

Baviskar, B.S. and D.W. Attwood (1995), *Finding the Middle Path: The Political Economy of Cooperation in Rural India*, Westview, Boulder

Bhalla, S. (1994), 'Poverty, workforce development and rural labour markets', *Indian Journal of Labour Economics* 37(4): 609–22

Bhattacharya, S.N. (1986), *Rural Economic Growth in India in Theory and Practice*, Metropolitan, Delhi

Bliss, C. and N. Stern (1982), *Palanpur: The Economy of an Indian Village*, OUP

Breman, J. (1985), *Of Peasants, Migrants and Paupers: Rural Labour Circulation and Capitalist Production in West India,* OUP

—— (1993), *Beyond Patronage and Exploitation: Changing Agrarian Relations in South Gujarat,* OUP

Breman, J. and S. Mundle (eds) (1991), *Rural Transformation in Asia,* OUP

Byrd, W.A. and Q. Lin (eds) (1990), *China's Rural Industry: Structure, Development, and Reform,* OUP, New York for the World Bank

Cawthorne, P. (1995), 'Of networks and markets: The rise and rise of a south Indian town, the example of Tiruppur's cotton knitwear industry', *World Development* 23(1): 43–56

Census (1981 and 1991), see GoI (1987a and 1992b)

Chadha, G.K. (ed.) (1993a), Special Issue on Non-Farm Sector in the Rural Economy of India, *Indian Journal of Labour Economics* 36(3)

—— (1993b), 'Non-farm employment for rural households in India: evidence and prognosis', in Chadha (1993a)

Chambers, Robert (1988), *Poverty in India: Concepts, Research and Reality,* IDS Discussion Paper 241, Institute of Development Studies, Brighton

Chandrasekhar, C.P. (1993), 'Agrarian change and occupational diversification: non-agricultural employment and rural development in west Bengal', *Journal of Peasant Studies* 20(2): 205–70

Chaturvedi, P. and A. Sinha (eds) (1989), *Strategy for Rural Industrialization,* Indian Association for the Advancement of Science, New Delhi

Choe, Yang-Boo and Fu-Chen Lo (eds) (1986), *Rural Industrialization and Non-Farm Activities of Asian Farmers,* Korea Rural Economics Institute, Seoul

Chuta, E. and C. Liedholm (1979), *Rural Nonfarm Employment: A Review of the State of the Art,* Michigan State University Rural Development Paper 4, East Lansing

Chuta, E. and S.V. Sethuraman (eds) (1984), *Rural Small-Scale Industries and Employment in Africa and Asia: A Review of Programmes and Policies,* ILO, Geneva

CMIE (1996), Centre for Monitoring the Indian Economy, *India's Agricultural Sector: A Compendium of Statistics* (July), Bombay

Cooperative Development Foundation (1996), *14th Annual Report: 1995–96,* Hyderabad

CSIR (1986), Council for Scientific and Industrial Research, 'Report on CSIR Review Committee towards New Perspective', Delhi

Datt G. and M. Ravalliqn (1996), *Why have some Indian States done better than others at reducing rural poverty?,* World Bank Research Working Paper 1594, Washington DC

Dev, S. Mahendra (1990), 'Non-agricultural employment in rural India: evidence at a disaggregate level', *EPW* 25(28): 1526–36, July 14

—— (1996), 'Experience of India's (Maharashtra) employment guarantee scheme: lessons for development policy', *Development Policy Review* 14(3): 227–53

Dreze, J., P. Lanjouw and N. Stern (forthcoming), *A Growth of Sorts: Palanpur 1957–1993*, OUP
Drèze, Jan and Amartya Sen (1995), *India: Economic Development and Social Opportunity*, OUP
DUBS (1994), Durham University Business School, Small Business Centre 'The role of small business membership organizations (SBMOs) in small enterprise development', a research study for ODA
Dunham, D. (1991), *Agricultural Growth and Rural Industry: Some Reflections on the Rural Growth Linkages Debate*, Institute of Social Studies Working Paper 114, The Hague
Dupont, V. (1995), *Decentralized Industrialization and Urban Dynamics: The Case of Jetpur in West India*, Sage, New Delhi
Eggertson, T. (1990), *Economic Behaviour and Institutions*, Cambridge University Press
Feeny, D. (1988), 'The demand for and supply of institutional arrangements', in Ostrom, Feeny and Picht (eds)
Fisher, T. (1995) 'Innovative rural financial institutions: Rural banking in Indonesia', Indian Grameen Services, Hyderabad
Floro, S.L. and P.A. Yotopoulos (1991), *Informal Credit Markets and the New Institutional Economics: The Case of Philippine Agriculture*, Westview, Boulder
Friedrich Ebert Stiftung (Malaysian Office) (1990), *Promotion of Small-Scale Industries and Strategies for Rural Industrialisation: The Malaysian Experience*, Kuala Lumpur
Fureng, Dong (1992), *Industrialization and China's Rural Modernization*, St. Martin's Press, New York
Furlong, Dominic (1996), 'The conceptualization of "trust" in economic thought', Discussion paper, Institute of Development Studies, Brighton
Gaventa, John (1980), *Power and Powerlessness: Quiescence and Rebellion in an Appalachian Valley*, University of Illinois Press, Chicago
Ghate, Prabhu (1992), *Informal Finance: Some Findings from Asia*, OUP for the Asian Development Bank, Manila
GoI, Government of India publications, New Delhi (CSO = Central Statistical Organisation and NSSO = National Sample Survey Organization, both at the Ministry of Planning: Department of Statistics)
—— (1978), Planning Commission: Programme Evaluation Organization, *Evaluation Study of Rural Industries Projects*
—— (1981), NSSO, *Report on the Second Quinquennial Survey on Employment and Unemployment, Survey Results – All India, NSS 32nd Round (July 1977–June 1978), No. 298, Parts I and II*
—— (1987a), Ministry of Home Affairs: Registrar General and Census Commissioner, *Census of India 1981, Series 1 India, General Economic Tables Parts III-A(i) and III-B(i)*
—— (1987b), Ministry of Industry: Department of Industrial Development, *Report of the Khadi and Village Industries Review Committee (KAVIRC)*
(1989a), NSSO, 'NSS, 40th Round (July 1984–June 1985), No. 363/2, Part 2 – States, Tables with Notes on Survey of Unorganized Manufacture: Non-Directory Establishments and Own Account Enterprises'

—— (1989b), Ministry of Textiles: Office of the Development Commissioner (Handicrafts), *Report of Task Force on Handicrafts for the VIII Five-Year Plan*
—— (1990), NSSO, *Sarvekshana, Results of the Fourth Quinquennial Survey on Employment and Unemployment (All-India), NSS 43rd Round (July 1987–June 1988)*
—— (1991a), CSO, *Annual Survey of Industries, 1987–88, Summary Results for Factory Sector*
—— (1991b), CSO, *Enterprise Survey, 1988–89, Report on Services Incidental to Transport*
—— (1991c), Planning Commission, 'Report of the Committee on Model Cooperatives Act'
—— (1991d), Press Information Bureau, '1990 Economic Census of Enterprise for all States and Union Territories', press release
—— (1992a), Ministry of Finance: Department of Revenue, *Tax Reforms Committee, Final Report – Part I, Chaired by Professor Raja J. Chelliah*
—— (1992b), Ministry of Home Affairs: Registrar General and Census Commissioner, *Census of India 1991, Series 1 India, Paper 2 of 1992, Final Population Totals: Brief Analysis of Primary Census Abstract*
—— (1992c), Ministry of Industry: Development Commissioner, Small-Scale Industries, *Report on the Second All-India Census of Small-Scale Industrial Units (Registered up to 31st March 1988)*
—— (1992d), CSO, *Statistical Abstract of India 1990*
(1995a), Ministry of Industry: Office of the Economic Adviser, *Handbook of Industrial Policy and Statistics 1995*
—— (1995b), CSO, *Economic Census, 1990, All-India Report*
—— (1995c), Ministry of Rural Development, *Annual Report, 1994–95*
—— (nd:a), CSO, 'Service Sector Survey 1980'
—— (nd:b), CSO, 'Unorganized trade establishment survey (OAEs and NDEs) 1980' (Summary Results, pp. 11–19)
—— (nd:c), CSO, 'Enterprise survey, 1983–4, report on hotels and other lodging places and restaurants, cafes and other eating and drinking places'
—— (nd:d), CSO, 'Directory Manufacturing Establishments Survey, 1984–85, Summary Results'
—— (nd:e), CSO, 'Directory Trade Establishment Survey, 1986'
—— (nd:f), CSO, 'Enterprise Survey, 1988–89, Report on Mechanised Passenger and Goods Transport'
—— (nd:g), CSO, 'Survey of Services incidental to Transport, 1989'
Haggblade, S. and M. Gamser (1991), *A Field Manual for Subsector Practitioners*, GEMINI, Washington DC
Haggblade, S., P. Hazell and J. Brown (1989), 'Farm-nonfarm linkages in rural sub-Saharan Africa', *World Development* 17(8): 1173–1201
Haggblade, S., C. Liedholm and D. Mead (1990), 'The effect of policy and policy reforms on non-agricultural enterprises and employment in developing countries: a review of past experiences', in Stewart, Thomas and de Wilde

Harriss, B. (1987), 'Regional growth linkages from agriculture and resource flows in non-farm economy', *EPW* 22(1, 2): 31–46, January 3–10
Harriss, J. (1989), 'Knowing about rural economic change: problems arising from a comparison of the results of "macro" and "micro" research in Tamil Nadu', in P. Bardhan (ed.), *Conversations between Economists and Anthropologists: Methodological Issues in Measuring Economic Change in Rural India*, OUP
—— (1991), 'Agriculture/non-agriculture linkages and the diversification of rural economic activity: a south Indian case study', in Breman and Mundle
Harriss-White, B. (1996), *A Political Economy of Agricultural Markets in South India: Masters of the Countryside*, Sage, Delhi
Hazell, P. and S. Haggblade (1990), *Rural–Urban Growth Linkages in India*, Policy, Research and External Affairs Working Paper 430, World Bank, Washington DC
Hazell, P. and S. Haggblade (1991), 'Rural–urban growth linkages in India', *Indian Journal of Agricultural Economics* 46(4): 515–29
Hazell, P. and C. Ramasamy (1991), *The Green Revolution Reconsidered: The Impact of High-Yielding Rice Varieties in South India,* Johns Hopkins University Press, Baltimore and London
Ho, S. (1982), 'Economic development and rural industry in South Korea and Taiwan', *World Development* 10(11): 973–90
—— (1986), *Asian Experience in Rural Nonagricultural Development and its Relevance for China*, World Bank Staff Working Paper 757, Washington DC
—— (1994), *Rural China in Transition: Non-agricultural Development in Rural Jiangsu, 1978–1990,* OUP
Hoff, K. and J.E. Stiglitz (1990), 'Introduction: imperfect information and rural credit markets – puzzles and policy perspectives', *World Bank Economic Review* 4(3): 235–50
Holmstrom, M. (1994), *Bangalore as an Industrial District: Flexible specialization in a labour-surplus economy?*, Pondy Papers in Social Sciences 14, French Institute of Pondicherry and School of Development Studies, University of East Anglia, Norwich
Hulme, D. and P. Mosley (1996), *Finance against Poverty*, 2 vols, Routledge, London
Humphrey, J. and H. Schmitz (1995), 'Principles for promoting clusters and networks of SMEs', paper commissioned by the Small and Medium Enterprise Branch of UNIDO, Institute of Development Studies, Brighton
Hymer, S. and S. Resnick (1969), 'A model of an agrarian economy with nonagricultural activities', *American Economic Review* 59(4): 493–506
IDS (1992), Institute of Development Studies, *Flexible Specialisation: A New View on Small Industry?*, *IDS Bulletin* 23(3), Brighton
—— (1996), 'Business associations in developing countries', *IDS Policy Briefing* 6, Brighton
ILO (1994), International Labour Organisation, *The Rural Informal Sector in Asia: Policies and Strategies,* Geneva

Institute of Social and Ethical AccountAbility (1996) *AccountAbility Quarterly* 2, London
Islam, R. (ed.) (1987), *Rural Industrialisation and Employment in Asia,* ILO-ARTEP, Delhi
—— (1991), *Growth of Rural Industries in Post-Reform China: Patterns, Determinants and Consequences,* ILO-ARTEP, Delhi
Israel, Arturo (1989), *Institutional Development: Incentives to Performance*, Johns Hopkins University Press, Baltimore for the World Bank
Jain, L.C. (1986), 'A heritage to keep: the handicrafts industry, 1955–85', *EPW* 21(20): 873–87, May 17
Jaitley, J. (1992), 'Handloom weaver: victim of adjustment', *Economic Times*, April 27
Johnston, B. and P. Kilby (1975), *Agriculture and Structural Transformation: Economic Strategies in Late-Developing Countries,* OUP
Killick, T. (1990), *A Reaction Too Far: Economic Theory and the Role of the State in Developing Countries*, Overseas Development Institute, London
Klennert, K (1986), 'Off-farm employment in marginal farm households: a hidden development of parts of Pakistan's rural poor', *Quarterly Journal of International Agriculture* 25(1): 37–48
Knorringa, (1994), 'Lack of interaction between traders and producers in the Agra footwear cluster', in Pedersen *et al.*
Kohli, D.N., Sheel Satya and Avasti Preeti (1992), *Central Excise Tariff Ready Reckoner 1992–93*, Cencus, New Delhi
Koppel, B., J. Hawkins and W. James (1994), *Development or Deterioration? Work in Rural Asia,* Lynne Rienner, Boulder and London
Krishna Murty, S. (1996), *The Andhra Pradesh General Sales Tax Act, 1957: Origin and Growth up to May 1996; and the Central Sales Tax Act, 1956 with AP Rules, Forms and Notifications*, 9th edition, Lakshmi, Hyderabad
Kumar, A. (1993), 'Rural non-farm employment: a static and dynamic study of inter-state variations', in Chadha (1993a)
Lanjouw, J.O. and P. Lanjouw (1995), *Rural Nonfarm Employment: A Survey*, Policy Research Working Paper 1463, World Bank, Washington DC
Little, I., D. Mazumdar and J. Page (1987), *Small Manufacturing Enterprises: A Comparative Study of India and Other Economies*, OUP, New York for the World Bank
Lukes, Steven (1974), *Power: A Radical View*, Macmillan, London
Mahajan, Vijay (1991), 'The political economy of rural informal-sector livelihoods in India: a preliminary exploration', Paper presented at the XVth World Congress of the International Political Science Association in Buenos Aires, Indian Grameen Services, Hyderabad
Mahajan, Vijay and Bharti G. Ramola (1996), 'Financial services for the rural poor and women in India: access and sustainability', *Journal of International Development* 8(2): 211–24
Malgavkar, P.D. and V.A. Pai Panandiker (1986), *Impediments to Rural Technology*, Oxford & IBH, Delhi

Mathew, P.M., M.K. Sukumaran Nair and P.A. Krusch (1995), 'A situational analysis of small industry associations in India', Institute of Small Enterprises and Development, Cochin and Swiss Development Cooperation, New Delhi

Mathur, A. and P.K. Pani (1993), 'The character of rural industrialization and its employment impact in India: an inter-regional perspective', in Chadha (1993a)

Matthai, Ravi (1982), *The Rural University : An Experiment in Educational Innovation*, Indian Institute of Management, Ahmedabad

Mellor, J. (1976), *The New Economics of Growth: A Strategy for India and the Developing World,* Cornell University Press, Ithaca

Mellor, J. and U. Lele (1973), 'Growth linkages of the new foodgrain technologies', *Indian Journal of Agricultural Economics* 28(1): 35–55

MIDS (1985), Madras Institute of Development Studies, *The Match Industry in Sivakasi, Sattur – Towards Removal of Child Labour*, MIDS, Madras.

—— (1988), *Tamilnadu Economy: Performance and Issues*, Delhi, Oxford & IBH

Mukhopadhyay, S. and C.P. Lim (eds) (1985), *Development and Diversification of Rural Industries in Asia*, Asian and Pacific Development Centre, Kuala Lumpur

NABARD (1992), *Refinance Assistance for Non-Farm Sector Activities*, Bombay

—— (1994a), *Annual Report, 1993–94*, Bombay

—— (1994b), *Statistical Statements, Annual Report, 1993–94*, Bombay

—— (1995), *A Policy Package for Rural Industrialisation*, Bombay

Nabhi's Handbook of Small Scale, Tiny and Cottage Industries (1991)

Naidu, L.K. (1986), *Bank Finance for Rural Development*, Ashish, Delhi

National Council of Applied Economic Research and Friedrich Naumann Stiftung (1993), *Structure and Promotion of Small Scale Industries in India: Lessons for Future Development*, New Delhi

North, D. (1981), *Structure and Change in Economic History*, Norton, New York

—— (1990), *Institutions, Institutional Change and Economic Performance*, Cambridge University Press

NSS (1977–8 and 1987–8), see GoI (1981 and 1990)

Oakerson, Ronald J (1988), 'Reciprocity: a bottom-up view of political development', in Ostrom, Feeny and Picht (eds)

Ody, A.J. (1992), *Rural Enterprise Development in China, 1986–90*, World Bank Discussion Papers, China and Mongolia Department Series, no. 162, Washington DC

Olson, Mancur (1965), *The Logic of Collective Action: Public Goods and the Theory of Groups*, Harvard University Press, Cambridge

Oshima, H.T. (1984), *The Significance of Off-Farm Employment and Incomes in Post-War East Asian Growth*, Asian Development Bank Economic Staff Paper 21, Manila

Ostrom, V., D. Feeny and H. Picht (eds) (1988), *Rethinking Institutional*

Analysis and Development: Issues, Alternatives and Choices, International Center for Economic Growth, San Francisco
Padmanabhan, K. (1988), *Rural Credit: Lessons for Rural Bankers and Policy Makers*, Intermediate Technology, London
Pai Panandiker, V.A. (1993), *Rural Industrialization in Alwar: Action Research Project*, Centre for Policy Research, Delhi (project funded by State Bank of India)
Pai Panandiker, V.A. and A. Sud (1986), *Rural Industrialization*, Oxford & IBH, Delhi
Papola, T.S. (1982), *Rural Industrialisation: Approaches and Potential*, Himalaya, Bombay
Papola, T.S. (1992), 'Rural non-farm employment: an assessment of recent trends', *Indian Journal of Labour Economics* 35(3): 238–45
Patten, R.H. and J.K. Rosengard (1991), *Progress with Profits: The Development of Rural Banking in Indonesia*, International Center for Economic Growth and the Harvard Institute for International Development, Cambridge, Mass.
Pedersen, P., A. Sverrisson and M. van Dijk (eds) (1994), *Flexible Specialization: The Dynamics of Small-Scale Industries in the South*, Intermediate Technology, London
Porter, Michael E. (1990), *The Competitive Advantage of Nations*, Macmillan, London
PRADAN (1988), *Access to Government Wastelands for Afforestation: Legal Provisions In Ten States*, Delhi
PRADAN (1992), *Promoting Rural Livelihoods for the Poor: Carcass Flayers in Uttar Pradesh*, PRADAN, Delhi
Ranis, G. and F. Stewart (1993), 'Rural nonagricultural activities in development: theory and application', *Journal of Development Economics* 40(1): 75–101
Rau, S.K. (1985), *Rural Industrialization: Policy and Programmes in Four Asian Countries*, Asian Productivity Organization, Tokyo
RBI (1989), Reserve Bank of India: Department of Statistical Analysis and Computer Services, *All-India Debt and Investment Survey, 1981–82, Statistical Tables Relating to Cash Borrowings and Repayments of Households during July 1981 to June 1982, and Cash Dues Outstanding as on 30th June 1982*, Bombay
—— (1992), *Report of the Committee to Examine the Adequacy of Institutional Credit to the SSI Sector*, Bombay
—— (1994), *Banking Statistics, Basic Statistical Returns*, vol. 21 (March 1992)
Robinson, M. (1992), 'Rural financial intermediation: lessons from Indonesia, part one. The Bank Rakyat Indonesia: rural banking, 1970–91', *Development Discussion Paper 434*, Harvard Institute for International Development, Cambridge
Saith, A. (1986), *Contrasting Experiences in Rural Industrialization: Are the East Asian Successes Transferable?*, ILO-ARTEP, Delhi
—— (1992), *The Rural Non-Farm Economy: Processes and Policies*, ILO, Geneva

Saith, A. (1993), *Chinese Rural Industrialization: Some Lessons for Reforming and Developing Economies*, ILO-ARTEP, Delhi
Sanket (1995), 'Situational analysis of industry associations, final report', Swiss Development Cooperation, New Delhi
Sarap, K. (1991), *Interlinked Agrarian Markets in Rural India*, Sage, Delhi
SDC (1996), Swiss Development Cooperation, *The Rural Micro- and Small-Enterprise Sector in India, Executive Summary of the National Report*, Delhi
Sen, A. (1994), 'Rural labour markets and poverty', *Indian Journal of Labour Economics* 37(4): 575–607
Shah, Tushaar (1995), *Making Farmers' Cooperatives Work: Design, Governance and Management*, Sage, New Delhi
Shand, R.T. (ed.) (1986), *Off-Farm Employment in the Development of Rural Asia*, 2 vols, National Centre for Development Studies, Australian National University, Canberra
—— (1987), 'Income distribution in a dynamic rural sector: some evidence from Malaysia', *Economic Development and Cultural Change* 36(1): 35–50
SIDBI (1996), Small Industries Development Bank of India, *Annual Report, 1995–6*, Lucknow
Simmons, Colin and Salinder Supri (1994), 'Participation in rural non-farm activity in India: a case study of cultivating households in Jalandhar District, Punjab', *Salford Papers in Economics* 94–4, Department of Economics, University of Salford
Singh, S. (1993), 'Some aspects of rural non-farm sector development in developing countries', in Chadha (1993a)
—— (1996), 'Rural non-farm sector in Rajasthan: Some empirical findings', Institute of Development Studies Working Paper 71, Jaipur
Sinha, A.K. (1988), *Rural Industry and Rural Industrialization*, Painter Publishers, Jaipur
Sinha, S. (1983), *The Experiences of Developing Countries in Rural Industrialization*, Intermediate Technology, London
Srinivasan, T. and P. Bardhan (eds) (1988), *Rural Poverty in South Asia*, OUP
Stewart, F., H. Thomas and T. de Wilde (eds) (1990), *The Other Policy: The Influence of Policies on Technology Choice and Small Enterprise Development*, Intermediate Technology, London
Streeten, Paul (1995), *Thinking about Development*, Cambridge University Press
Study Group on the Rural Non-Farm Sector, Indian Grameen Services, Hyderabad:
'The rural non-farm sector in India: Interim Report' (1992)
'The rural non-farm sector in Tamil Nadu' (1993a)
'The rural non-farm sector in Uttar Pradesh' (1993b)
'The rural non-farm sector in Andhra Pradesh' (1994a)
'The rural non-farm sector in Assam' (1994b)
'The rural non-farm sector in Gujarat' (1994c)
'The rural non-farm sector in Orissa' (1994d)

'The rural non-farm sector in Punjab' (1994e)
'The rural non-farm sector in Rajasthan' (1994f)
'The rural non-farm sector in India: National Report' (1994g)
'The rural non-farm sector in India: lessons from international experiences in the RNFS' (1994h)
Taori, K. and S. Singh (1995), *Rural Industrialization: A Plan for the Future* (2nd ed.), Vikas, Jangpura
Thorat, S. (1993), 'Land ownership structure and non-farm employment of rural households in India', in Chadha (1993a)
Toye, John (1995), 'The new institutional economics and its implications for development theory' in J. Harriss, J. Hunter and C. Lewis (eds), *The New Institutional Economics and Third World Development*, pp. 49–68, Routledge, London
Unni, Jeemol (1991), 'Regional variations in rural non-agricultural employment: an exploratory analysis', *EPW* 26(3): 109–122; 19 January
Uribe-Echevarria, F. (1992), 'Small-scale industrial development: policy and strategic issues', Institute of Social Studies Working Paper 117, The Hague
Vaidyanathan, A. (1986), 'Labour use in rural India: a study of spatial and temporal variations', *EPW (Review of Agriculture)* 21(52): A-130 to A-146, December 27
—— (1994), 'Employment situation: some emerging perspectives', *EPW* 29(50): 3147–56, December 10
Visaria, P. and R. Basant (1994), *Non-Agricultural Employment in India: Trends and Prospects*, Sage, Delhi
von Braun. J. and R. Pandya-Lorch (1992), 'Income sources and diversification strategies of the malnourished rural poor', *Quarterly Journal of International Agriculture* 31(1): 36–54
Vyas, V.S. and G. Mathai (1978), 'Farm and non-farm employment in rural areas: a perspective for planning', *EPW* 13(6,7): 1369–74, February
Vyasulu, Vinod (1992), 'The non-farm sector in the Indian economy: a research programme', mimeo, Institute for Social and Economic Change, Bangalore
Wade, R. (1990), *Governing the Market: Economic Theory and the Role of Government in East Asian Industrialization*, Princeton University Press
—— (1994), *Village Republics: Economic Conditions for Collective Action in South India*, Institute for Contemporary Studies, San Francisco
Walker, T.S. and J.G. Ryan (1990), *Village and Household Economies in India's Semi-arid Tropics*, Johns Hopkins University Press, Baltimore and London
Waterbury, J. (1993), *Exposed to Innumerable Delusions: Public Enterprise and State Power in Egypt, India, Mexico, and Turkey*, Cambridge University Press
World Bank (1978), *Rural Enterprise and Non-Farm Employment*, Washington DC
—— (1983), 'Report on growth and employment in rural Thailand', Washington DC
—— (1993), *The East Asian miracle: Economic growth and public policy: Summary*, Washington DC

Index

*[Note: **bold** is used to indicate reference to a table]*

www.ingramcontent.com/pod-product-compliance
Lightning Source LLC
Chambersburg PA
CBHW071322180926
51611CB00002B/29
9781853394089